What Is Critical Urbanism?

Osu Market, Accra © Photo: Manuel Herz, 2018

What Is Critical Urbanism?

Urban Research as Pedagogy

Kenny Cupers Sophie Oldfield Manuel Herz
Laura Nkula-Wenz Emilio Distretti Myriam Perret

Elements of Urban Pedagogy   6
INTRODUCTION

Pedagogies: **Learning through "Highway Africa,"** by Kenny Cupers and Manuel Herz | **City Collaborations,** by Sophie Oldfield | **The Research Studio,** by Manuel Herz and Myriam Perret | **Critical Cartography,** by Shourideh C. Molavi | **Experimenting with Publics,** by Sophie Oldfield and Anna Selmeczi | **Finding Your Research Voice,** by Laura Nkula-Wenz and Sophie Oldfield | **City as Archive,** by Kenny Cupers and Aylin Tschoepe | **The Urban Everyday,** by Sophie Oldfield and Laura Nkula-Wenz | **Material Investigations,** by Emilio Distretti and Manuel Herz | **Urbanism across Geographies,** by Shourideh C. Molavi

Ways of Knowing the City   20
MAKING TENSIONS PRODUCTIVE, **by Sophie Oldfield and Laura Nkula-Wenz**

Voices: **Dark and Light at Airport City,** by Naomi Samake | **Sewing Threads,** by Diana Vazquez-Martinez | **The Race, an Exhibit,** by Linda Wermuth | **The Ideal Urban Experience,** by Lee Wolf

THE STATE AT HOME, **by James Clacherty**
VIDEO ACTIVISM AS BOTTOM-UP CITY MAKING, **by Jacob Geuder**
ETHIOPIAN INTERSECTIONS OF ROAD DEVELOPMENT, **by Thomas Betschart**
LUBRICATING LOGISTICS, **by Isabella Baranyk**
SLOW VIOLENCE IN PALESTINE, **by Saad Amira**
WORLDING DESIGN, **by Laura Nkula-Wenz**

The Urban beyond North and South   64
LEARNING ACROSS GEOGRAPHIES, **by Laura Nkula-Wenz and Kenny Cupers**

Voices: **Into Our Homes,** by Rosca van Rooyen | **Toxic Connections,** by Aline Suter | **Learning between Basel and Accra,** by Ernest Sewordor | **Addressing Structural Racism,** by the Racial Justice Student Collective

MADJERMANS, **by Lea Nienhoff**
TRANSFRONTERIDAD, **by Evan Natasha Escamilla**
URBANIZATION BEYOND BORDERS, **by Myriam Perret**
POSTCOLONIAL LOGISTICS, **by Giulia Scotto**
WORLDING GOMA, **by Maren Larsen**

The Presence of the Past   108
IMAGINING ALTERNATIVE FUTURES, by Emilio Distretti and Kenny Cupers

    Voices: **Living Modernities,** by Hanna Baumann | **The Value of (a) Brick,**
    by Alexander Crawford | **Routes of Remembrance,** by Carla Cruz

ON THE COLONIALITY OF INFRASTRUCTURE, **by Kenny Cupers**
NOTES ON HERITAGE (RE-)MAKING, **by Emilio Distretti**
(POST-)APARTHEID NATURE, **by Janine Eberle**
A TALE OF THREE TOWERS, **by Manuel Herz**
HINTERLAND TRIALOGUE, **by Ernest Sewordor**

In and between Theory and Practice   150
ENGAGING THE URBAN, **by Sophie Oldfield and Manuel Herz**

    Voices: **Rasta Mobilities in Cape Town,** by Oliva Andereggen | **Running the City,**
    by Florence Siegenthaler | **Figures of Mobility,** by Carla Cruz

NATION-WEAVING, **by Manuel Herz**
MAKING HOMELESSNESS VISIBLE, **by Basil Studer**
TOWNSHIP COSMOPOLITANISM, **by Florence Siegenthaler**
THEORY AND PRACTICE UNDER LOCKDOWN, **by Shourideh C. Molavi**
ROOTED IN THE CITY, **by Sophie Oldfield**

An Ethos of Critical Urbanism   196
CONCLUSION

Elements of Urban Pedagogy

Introduction

How do we engage with a globally interconnected yet radically fragmented and increasingly unequal urban world? What ways of knowing and doing can address global urban challenges and chart more just and sustainable futures from concrete positions?

Urbanists today are provoked by overwhelming amounts of specialized knowledge about the urban, produced in diverse academic disciplines, by varied types of urban institutions, and different groups of people in and beyond the city itself. As students of the urban, we are deeply immersed in the messy and often contradictory realities of urban life. This position begs the question: What knowledge do we produce and engage with, and to what end? What is the "doing" of urban research, and how does it shape our insights, practices, and projects? How, as urbanists, do we learn from the past, from our own modes of practice, from collaborations and confrontations, and from the unabated creativity of urban life?

These questions have inspired *What Is Critical Urbanism?* and the forms of urban research, practice, and pedagogy we share in it. Rooted in a productive intersection of humanities and social science methods, our work offers an approach to urban studies that works in and across disciplines, debates, and cultures of expertise, and across cities north and south, east and west. In this book, we share how we have cultivated and embraced a notion of critique that is open and nimble, grounded and propositional; one that combines thinking and doing, writing and engaging, caring and challenging. It shapes a pedagogy in which we aim to turn our assumptions—the things we think we know—into questions. In doing so, we embrace an intellectual agility that enables us to see things both up close and from afar, to pivot between perspectives and across city spaces. In these practices, we develop an ethos of thinking, doing, and teaching rooted in questions of justice, situated in the contingencies and contradictions that shape our urban worlds. Inhabiting various layers of privilege and access in the academy and the city, our work takes a relational and dialogical approach. The past, for instance, is not a fixed past; its reinterpretation can make a difference to how we see and live in the present, and thus how we imagine and shape the future. Through these conversations, we open up a space between critical scholarship that traditionally veers away from questions of instrumentality and the imperative to intervene. It is in this journey that we learn to practically and politically activate urban research.

The work presented in this book has been developed through the Critical Urbanisms master's program at the University of Basel. Established in 2016 and developed in a long-term partnership with the African Centre for Cities at the University of Cape Town, this program was creatively built as a unique collaboration between two universities with different traditions, set in different urban worlds—Basel and Cape Town. In this program, we have worked in and from both locations, engaging with the productive tensions that emerged and that articulate the urban problems and inspirations to which we respond. The contributions in this volume show our commitment to immersing ourselves in the everyday realities, past and present, of cities, to embed our approach in practices of engaged research and collaboration, and to take seriously the possibilities and limits of the complex urban and institutional terrains in which we move. Forging a specific form of interdisciplinarity, our pedagogy relies on deep commitment to dialogue within and beyond the university. It is closely bound up with "critical doing," unlearning and challenging canons in higher education and knowledge production. In this approach, the city and its varied publics is not simply a focus or an "object" of study and investigation; rather, it shapes our methodology, inspiring and anchoring the optics through which we engage and reflect in and on diverse urban worlds.

Built on this approach, our program aims to open up essential opportunities for students to get to grips with the everyday realities of cities, to experience the ethos and complex practices of engaged research, to try out different methods, and to find a personal niche in the exciting spectrum of urban research and practice. Through firsthand immersions in cities like Basel, Cape

Town, Zurich, Accra, Mexico City, and Manila, students have worked with communities and civic society organizations, and experimented with embodied research methods. Their projects give insight into complex urban and institutional contexts, the critical experiments that undergird engaged scholarship, and the capacity to work with practical real-world questions. In addition to honing qualitative research skills and gaining confidence in their ability as critical thinkers, students also have experienced directly what it takes to do collaborative research in and beyond the academy.

Experimenting with diverse methods and approaches, these elements of the pedagogy provide the opportunity to explore and research city publics, the spaces and places through which people live their daily lives and build the city. Our students are encouraged to inquire into the city as an aesthetic order—an order made up of layered social patterns that define the distribution of senses and experiences among those who inhabit and traverse urban space. In other words, our aim is to investigate the racialized, gendered, classed, and otherwise segmented allocation of the city's images, sounds, smells, tastes, and tactilities, and how these shift and morph. In turn, we ask what conceptions of the "public"—understood both as a collective political subject and as the collectively shared spaces of the city—give shape to these patterns of distribution. In conjunction with immersive learning in the city, our pedagogy thus encourages creative ways of working that engage with the mediated production of urbanity. We know cities not only through our own immediate sensory experience but also through images, records, digital platforms, testimonies, and the senses of others. In paying attention to these mediations and their technological and aesthetic qualities, our pedagogy embraces reflexivity. We share the elements that make up the pedagogy which shapes the curriculum of the masters program.

The body of this book is organized into four sections. The first section, "Ways of Knowing the City," offers pathways to engage with the radically diverse and at times contradictory ways of knowing the city. Here, we engage transversal logics and conflicting rationalities that shape the urban. This approach facilitates concrete ways for urbanists to attend to (and learn from) the political and ethical tensions that arise from research in real-world settings.

The second section, "The Urban beyond North and South," explores how we develop place-based and context-sensitive understandings of the urban while attending to the diverse geographies from which that knowledge may be produced, circulated, and applied. Through practices of collaboration, translation, and perspectival pivoting, we propose ways to research different cityscapes by challenging borders, boundaries, and imposed—racialized, classed, gendered, and sexualized—difference. The third section, "The Presence of the Past," engages with the complex ways in which the past continues to shape the urban present. As historical legacies are never closed, they can be reproduced or remade to imagine alternative urban futures. By engaging with multiple urban visions and political and aesthetic imaginaries, we explore how historical inheritances and colonial refractions shape contemporary urban debates. In the final section, "In and between Theory and Practice," we turn our attention to how diverse modes of urban engagement can develop from and further engender critical inquiry. It is in the space between theory and practice that our own and our partners' positionalities become visible. We thus place an ethics of engagement at the center of critical urbanism. Such an approach includes partnerships that ground urban research in everyday experience and urban struggles. From this base, our work builds on the creative, embodied, multivocational, and multimedia approaches at the forefront of urban studies today. Each section starts with an introduction that explains our approach and the work on which it builds. Each introduction is followed by a collection of vignettes, which share students' coursework to illustrate our pedagogical approach, while the subsequent essays report on completed or ongoing research by master's and doctoral students, as well as faculty members.

The Trans-African Highway at Limuru, 2017 © Photo: Manuel Herz

LEARNING THROUGH "HIGHWAY AFRICA"

With the end of colonization in Africa came unprecedented ambitions of modernization. Key to such modernization was the development of new infrastructure. Ports, dams, highways, and now energy and communications networks would facilitate industrial production, growing commerce, and new forms of consumption—all of which were crucial to build a newly independent continent after centuries of colonial exploitation. For members of the elite, infrastructure development was first and foremost an economic measure, to facilitate the production and movement of goods and materials across Africa. At the same time, political actors saw in some of the projected infrastructure networks opportunities for nation-building, and for forging a new era of Pan-African cooperation and transcontinental development. For a fledgling African middle class, infrastructure conjured imaginaries of upward social mobility, and for entire communities it opened up hopes of movement and prosperity unlike anything experienced before. A gigantic boom in foreign infrastructure investment across Africa today is again reshaping the continent. African governments and financial institutions are working with Chinese, Brazilian, European, and other international actors to finance and build railways, highways, ports, pipelines, and other forms of infrastructure. These are radically transforming life in cities and rural areas alike. But can such infrastructure make Africa rise from the de-development caused by European colonial rule? Can what was once a key tool of colonialism—the railways built by European powers to extract resources—also be used to undo its results and reshape Africa's relationship with the rest of the world?

Undertaken between 2017 and 2020, "Highway Africa" was a multiyear collaborative research and teaching project that explores how infrastructure reshapes politics and everyday life in African cities. The project structured our Basel-based research studio, which entailed fieldwork stays in Accra during 2018 and 2019, and has inspired both student and faculty work throughout this book. **By Kenny Cupers and Manuel Herz**

Community leader Archie Olkers presenting on Ruo Emoh's housing struggle, Cape Town, South Africa, 2018 © Photo: Sophie Oldfield

CITY COLLABORATIONS

What are concrete practices that build a "right to the city"? In the City Research Studio in Cape Town, we work with neighborhood organizations and a shelter rights NGO focused on solving political and technical problems in housing delivery to engage this critical question. Exploring housing issues as policy and as lived realities in the city, we immerse students in the practices, and the hopes and hardships, of housing activism, as well as in the practices that root policy and its contradictions and contingencies. In the concrete lived struggles to build homes and lives, in NGO interventions to support these initiatives, and in the city and state's responses are complex forms of expertise and debate. These dynamics are what the research makes visible, in documenting the ways in which ordinary people, organizations, and movements struggle to make and sustain homes. The course offers students both a space in which to learn and improve their grasp of qualitative research methods, and a project through which to engage in collaborative approaches to research and knowledge production.

Hazeldean community leaders discussing the collaboratively produced book, 2019 © Photo: Shawn Cuff

Student-community research team working in Napier Informal Settlement, Napier, Overberg, South Africa, 2020
© Photo: Sophie Oldfield

Through this pedagogy, research is practiced as a process of experimenting, learning when things don't work, and building conversations and relationships in difficult circumstances. The research partnership is at the heart of this work. In each project, teams of students and community-based researchers from the neighborhood work together to interview residents and to conduct research on ways families find, build, and secure homes, and, in doing so, encounter the state and its settlement policies. Projects are full of learning: finding confidence in interviewing, figuring out and enjoying writing from interviews to build arguments that embrace the nuances of experience and the complexities of context. At the end of each project, we publish the research in forms that are resonant for thinking the city through housing struggles. In sum, collaborative research embeds scholarship in the lives of residents, movements, and organizations, in their struggles for housing, in these complex practices central to life in Southern cities. **By Sophie Oldfield**

THE RESEARCH STUDIO

In October 1968 Denise Scott Brown, Robert Venturi, Steven Izenor, and thirteen students of architecture and design spent a week in Las Vegas studying its urban and architectural fabric. By means of photography, filming, and sketching, the group engaged with the quotidian landscape. After returning from the trip, for the remainder of the semester the students devised new methods of representing their findings with video, photography, collages, and drawings. Collaborative work and a combination of descriptive and propositional elements were brought together and eventually exhibited and discussed in the final presentations. The resulting exhibition and the book *Learning from Las Vegas* (1972) radically altered our perception of both the contemporary city and urban pedagogy. It not only became a central oeuvre of architectural theory influencing a generation of students and practitioners, but also set the foundation to the teaching format of the Research Studio.

Learning in the context of a research studio represented a radical change of the paradigm in academic pedagogy. The research studio breaks from the hierarchy of conventional lectures and seminars. Within the framework of mutual exchange, every member plays a dual role of simultaneously learning and teaching. Consequently, the professor becomes a curator, guide, or companion on a path of rich discoveries, rather than being the omniscient authority.

In the 1990s Rem Koolhaas started research studios at Harvard with "Project on the City," analyzing the contemporary city from a postmodernist perspective, and stressing the importance for architects to understand the context in which they are intervening. The Institute of Urban Research ETH Studio Basel, founded in 1999 by the architects Roger Diener, Jacques Herzog, Marcel Meili, and Pierre de Meuron, forms a continuation of this teaching method. Both these seminal urban research studios based their pedagogy on the Las Vegas studio and developed it further. Building on this innovative architectural pedagogy, our program transfers the studio into the urban humanities, infusing project-based, collaborative, and creative learning throughout the curriculum.

A key aim of our studio pedagogy is to develop a shared vocabulary among our students, hailing from a wide range of backgrounds and disciplines, from architecture and design to geography, anthropology, political science, cultural studies, and more. The studio introduces our students to basic research skills, including mapping, visual analysis, archival research, and fieldwork. Bringing together lectures, mapping, seminars, film screenings, photographic documentation, archival work, tutorials, drawings, field research, and collaborative workshops responds to the intricacy which urban research implies. Combining scientific analysis with individual experiences of the field allows us not only to convey existing knowledge, but also to produce new knowledge and alter perspectives on the urban question. The output of the

Research Studio, University of Basel, 2019 © Photo: Myriam Perret

students' work ranges from written and photographic essays to maps, drawings, diagrams, and videos. Attributing the same value to texts and visual material and demanding equivalent precision in their formation, both play vital roles as primary sources in knowledge production and as tools of communication. The research studio takes place in a shared (physical) space. Creating such a space for common learning and thinking allows not only the exchange but also the testing, evolving, and improvement of individual work. Every student and teacher in our program contributes to a toolbox of multiple methods, expertise, and experience. Thanks to this multitude of approaches, it becomes possible to cope with the complex intertwinement of social, political, economic, cultural, ecological, and spatial aspects of the built environment. The competencies in which we train to operate in a collaborative work environment, along with the need for mutual understanding and the skills of communication among different fields, are key capacities needed by any actor in the urban disciplines. In a productive interplay, the theoretical competencies of the humanities enhance the architectural and spatial abilities to engage with urban phenomena and vice versa. **By Manuel Herz and Myriam Perret**

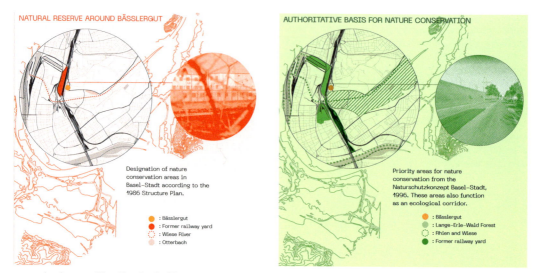

Landscape politics: Mapping the Bässlergut environment, 2020 © Alessandra Leta, Vivian Nhieu, and Jonas Adrian Baum

CRITICAL CARTOGRAPHY

Maps reveal, delimit, confirm, navigate, historicize, erase, anticipate, persuade, and, sometimes, even lie. Far from a scientific reading of mapping as an objective representation of a stable reality, our pedagogy explores the myriad of ways in which historical legacies of colonialism and imperialism continue to shape our gaze of the urban landscape—affecting our normative, political, and personal considerations of the relations among subjects, objects, and spaces. Maps can be understood as instruments of violence and terrains of power, asking us to explore the historical matrix within which mapping developed by looking at the epistemologies of various types of spatial and temporal maps that represent colonized, occupied, and otherwise marginalized frontiers and experiences. For this reason, maps also ask us to actively engage with resistance to this practice in the form of other traditions of mapping, including counter-cartographic contestations that make visible otherwise marginal experiences and hidden histories of violence. From this insight into the social relevance, politics, and ethics of mapping, new ways of engaging in a practical and creative aspect of cartography can emerge. Starting from the power relations in our own everyday environments, our pedagogy trains various hands-on techniques and technologies for mapping local relations in space and time. Experimenting with a range of mapping tools and interdisciplinary methods—including fieldwork, archival research, visual and material analysis, and remote sensing—we develop creative techniques to produce and represent alternative urban landscapes and overlapping cartographies. **By Shourideh C. Molavi**

EXPERIMENTING WITH PUBLICS

Our pedagogy provides a space to explore Cape Town's various publics, how they constitute themselves and how they take up space in the challenging environment of a post-apartheid city. In this course, we experiment with embodied research practices and alternative forms of knowing the city. Two themes shape our course pedagogy. "Sensing the City" locates and engages with publics produced through public art and performance. This theme asks questions about the kinds of audiences public art is created for, the places associated with these publics, and the assumptions about their aesthetic agency that drives public-facing art interventions in Cape Town. Through visiting, attending, and participating in (public) artworks, performances, and events, we trace the city's embodied aesthetics. In parallel, "Running the City" explores publics produced through varied forms of organized running in different parts of Cape Town. This theme provides a chance to engage public space through movement: a voluntary, mass participatory tradition in Cape Town. What do we see when we run, how do we engage, what are the ways in which running is a means to move collectively through the city? In this way, running becomes a lens on the city, its transformation, its liveliness, its mobilities and its conviviality. On club training runs and in races in different parts of the city, running is a means to move in and across Cape Town's segregated cityscape. In running, we participate, engaging and observing through this embodied, vibrant, mobile method. **By Sophie Oldfield and Anna Selmeczi**

Running the City, Exhibit, "A Race," Cape Town, 2018
© Photo: Sophie Oldfield

FINDING YOUR RESEARCH VOICE

The center piece of any postgraduate degree is the development of original research as the core of one's final thesis. The ethos of both Critical Urbanisms as a program and critical urbanism as its conceptual foundation builds from firsthand empirical engagement with contomporary urban issues, using a mix of conventional and experimental social science and humanities research methods. Finding a suitable topic is certainly important for producing a good thesis, but the ultimate goal of each individual research journey is finding one's own voice as a young scholar. To kick-start this process, we take our students on a three-day research design retreat. Using a tailor-made workshop methodology, we assist students in distilling their broad interests into workable research projects, matching them up with suitable supervisors, and strengthening their confidence in pursuing their passion. As one student recalls: "The lightness of the atmosphere created a space in which thematic conversations were suddenly easier to have. I feel more confident about my thesis, and I am looking forward to starting it. From something that put me under pressure it has become something I am more and more excited about." In combining intense and rigorous work with moments of camaraderie and fun, the research design workshop encapsulates the essence of our program, and is an integral part of igniting and amplifying the voices of a new generation of budding urban scholars and practitioners. **By Laura Nkula-Wenz and Sophie Oldfield**

A thesis workshop session, Fynbos Estate, South Africa, 2018
© Photo: Sophie Oldfield

CITY AS ARCHIVE

Beyond its common understanding as a collection of records evidencing the past, the archive offers a lens to grapple with urban questions of temporality, materiality, media, and knowledge. The city is made up of layers of social, cultural, and physical histories. Some of these have been privileged while others have been forgotten or silenced, or linger as traces. The urban therefore offers a promising object of study for practices of discrimination, objectification, control, contest, movement, reflection, and redefinition. Conceptualizing the city as an archive means approaching the city as a site of selective public and/or private memories, a physical collection of records shaped by various power dynamics, and a metaphor for holding knowledge. Historians tend to approach these existing archives as repositories of "primary sources," yet the materiality and media of the city itself can also be used as evidence in urban research. We begin with the premise that archives are not a collection of neutral records of events but rather that they shape difference and "otherness" with regard to gender, class, ethnicity, sexuality, and ability. Such ethnographic perspective on the role of archives prompts new imaginations of the city as archive, and thus new approaches to urban research as the production of archives. Starting from the at times violent bureaucratic machinery of government archives and the haunting absences of the colonial archive, we propose alternative ways of curating urban knowledge. These engaged forms of research can lead to producing new archives that speak from the voices of a range of marginalized or otherwise silenced interlocutors. Beyond producing oral histories of the city, we can also ask how material properties, textual records, and human testimonies speak differently about the city, its locality, and its global entanglements. From street signs to buildings, from dust to data, the city is an "open" archive offering an entry into its polymorphous social worlds.

By Kenny Cupers and Aylin Tschoepe

Unpacking Ilham Moubachir's *Feelings and Senses of a Changing City: A Soundscape,* 2021 © Tschoepe/Käser. In the City of Geneva, Ilham Moubachir engaged with an urban site that is undergoing transformation. The curated sound project conveys the negotiations of various human and nonhuman actors in urban space, giving a sense of the changes of the site over time. The sound files can be accessed through QR codes.

Urban everyday—visualizing vocabularies, Cape Town, 2019 © Photo: Alma Viviers

THE URBAN EVERYDAY

The "Urban Everyday" seminar exposes students to different discourses around how cities are built by people, movements, and organizations "from below." We draw on scholarly work that explores the city through ethnography and close readings of concrete ways in which people engage with, act in, and study the city. Methodologically, this body of literature is built on thick descriptions, intricate ways of narrating and analyzing cities.

Engaging a broad spectrum of everyday urban practices, we embrace the ordinary ways people make lives, encroach on land, challenge the state, and creatively claim a right to the city and access to its resources.

As such, the "Urban Everyday" seminar offers an entry point to city building that explores agency found in intersecting practices of occupation and adaptation, engagement and participation, resistance and protest, as well as waiting, encountering, and imagining the city. In tracking diverse forms of agency, we come to grips with the political substance of the city—its housing and land struggles, experiences of work, and strategies to make ends meet, questions of identity and belonging. We explore how all these experiences meet, compete with, and rub up against rights, policies, and state techniques.

In reflecting on this productive tension between structural forces and ordinary forms of agency, new vocabularies are necessary for describing contemporary Southern city dynamics and understanding how the urban everyday is an indispensable perspective for locating and producing urban theory from the South.

By Sophie Oldfield and Laura Nkula-Wenz

MATERIAL INVESTIGATIONS

When the state intervenes in the private realm of a family's home, it does so with the tools of administration, through regulations, by-laws, and ordinances. Though seemingly immaterial in themselves, they do come with their own physical macrocosm: official statements and payment notices printed on paper with institutional letterheads, identity cards and tags of government officials, passports or residency cards printed on cardboard or laminated in plastic, electricity and water meters that are often sealed, and of course the buildings themselves with their windows, doors, staircases, and roof tiling, with their layouts shaped by building codes.

These materialities are never neutral or innocent. The legibility of a fading name printed on a crumpled piece of paper can decide whether a family is entitled to government housing or not. The difference between a tiled roof and one made of corrugated iron is one of comfort and safety, but it can also carry significant political implications, depending on context and location. As demonstrated by many different projects in this book, such material dimension of governmental power can hold its own set of emotional and concrete responses by the residents affected. Conversely, studying the physical materialization can provide evidence of the power relationships that stand behind and shape these very materialities—especially in postcolonial contexts.

Interior decoration of a residential space in the Sahrawi refugee camp "Boujdour," in southwest Algeria, 2012 © Photo: Manuel Herz

What story can a single brick tell of the aspirations of a working-class family when they constructed their new home? What is the significance when a refugee family living in exile in the Sahrawi camps in Algeria switches from textiles as wall decorations to stucco and plaster?

In our pedagogy and research-led student projects, we use "materiality" as a category to investigate spatial, political, and historical urban relations. Traditionally, a materialist discourse can refer to the nature of being in a material sense. It can also mean a certain emphasis on material cultures tuned to the nature of objects, things, artifacts, and spaces. This approach becomes a way to study the dynamic constituent within the formation of human subjectivities and human social structures through labor, architecture, relations of production and commodification, and conflict. Our pedagogies make use of these notions as a platform to expand the debate around the epistemic power of materiality, beyond the sphere of dialectical materialism, post-structuralism, and phenomenologist traditions. We attempt to articulate and bring together in a hitherto less familiar way interpretations and investigations of the material world that are traditionally in disagreement with one another, which offer divergent readings of the built/lived environment, and eventually subject/object relations and conflict. We treat materiality as congealed sets of social and political relations, objects in which politics lie dormant. This frame allows us to demonstrate how the cultural, social, and political depend on the material world (natural and built) as much as they depend on human actors. Using the framework of spatial research, we explore the notion of materiality as the basis from which to understand the formation of power structures as spatial arrangements where territorial projects, architecture, urbanism, and human bodies intertwine. Material investigations therefore open up many avenues of experience and on the margins and the peripheries of situations that challenge material arrangements of power. By bringing "buried" or "hidden" materialities to the surface, we aim to unveil particular and seemingly anonymous events and spaces, which at some point are made visible, intelligible, and therefore political by societies. **By Emilio Distretti and Manuel Herz**

URBANISM ACROSS GEOGRAPHIES

Running parallel to the "Urbanism from the South" track, "Urbanism across Geographies" is a track initiated in 2021 that examines the urban present from a local context, while seeking to make broader connections across the dividing borders. In examining the tensions that link local practices and realities with global structures, we pay particular attention to historical colonial and imperial legacies, and to trans-local processes that cross the imagined "Global North" and "Global South" divide. We focus on landscapes and urban spaces as both objects of investigation and sites of intervention—the very medium within which movement takes place and through which power and daily resistance are represented and exerted by communities. With this, we engage with sites in and around the city that interrogate borders, power, territory, and the global circulation of people, ideas, goods, identities, and solidarities. In a first iteration of this new pedagogical track in 2021, the focus has been on colonial infrastructures, confiscated properties, and militarized environments in Sicily. These reflect the proximity that exists, and has always existed, among the imagined regions known as the "Mediterranean," the "Middle East," "Africa," and "Europe." Using the notion of the Black Mediterranean, we have worked closely with practitioners on the ground to explore key landscapes and urban spaces in and around Palermo that speak to Sicily as a cultural, architectural, and environmental intersection of these regions. With this, we examine how the urban present and racialized inequalities experienced by communities in these spaces are linked to colonial legacies and regional hierarchies of power. The methods we mobilize include interviewing, participant observation, visual and spatial analysis, mapping, and direct action. **By Shourideh C. Molavi**

Final public event of the first Urbanism across Geographies track in Palermo, 2021 © Luca Pfeiffer, Alessandra Leta, Vivian Nhieu, Ayesha Schnell and Karin Gromann

Ways of Knowing the Ci[ty]

Making Tensions Productive

by Sophie Oldfield and Laura Nkula-Wenz

Cities generate and are produced in different and contradictory knowledge systems, from state logics and capital regimes to the lifeworlds of residents, shaped by the built environment, in movements and mobilizations.

Such transversal logics and conflicting rationalities generate productive tensions in old and new technologies of governance and regulation, in material and political dynamics of dispossession and mobilization, and in complex sociocultural and economic logics. At the same time, cities assail our senses, shaping them in the sounds, languages, smells, temperatures, tempos of the streets, varied public cultures, and norms and practices that make up urban places and city publics. How can we as critical urbanists embrace these diverse ways of knowing? How can we pay attention to the multiplicity of experience, material and sensual, that shapes the ways in which we might know the city?

In engaging such complex dynamics as productive tensions, we expand the project and practice of urban studies and our research agenda, opening up dimensions of the city that are material, aesthetic, and performative, constituted in modes of inhabiting and moving through city spaces. This approach to studying cities reveals diverse ways of knowing: a world of interesting and provocative methods that take seriously notions that affect the sensory and the emotive, as well as the material. Through it we can embrace alternative ways of knowing that sit amid the individual and collective, the public and private, the aesthetic and the felt. Urbanists can creatively expand ways of representing embodied experiences of diverse city spaces, as well as their politics and publics: in narrative and visual form, in varied creative genres and mediums, in interventions that are experimental. Through these experimental practices, urban scholarship is deepened in incisive and contextually rich ways.

The complexities of cities challenge and inspire urbanists to contend with diverse ways of knowing the city, displacing planning and policy as primary and singular interfaces for understanding and engaging the city, as well as the state-citizen encounters that shape it. Consequently, we built our pedagogy from an interdisciplinary genealogy of ideas, from Amin and Thrift's theoretical provocations for "seeing the city,"[1] via Kathleen Stewart's creative strategies for bringing into view "ordinary affects,"[2] to Jennifer Robinson's provocation to engage comparatively with a "world of cities."[3] As Simone and Pieterse[4] suggest, the urban majority, city residents, pass time, claim rights, make ends meet, dwell, and dream in ordinary everyday ways. Neither "clandestine" nor "isolated," these ordinary forms of city life are everyday urban practices which Teresa Caldeira suggests "interact with the state and its institutions, but usually in transversal ways."[5] These are the types of sites in which we locate our approach to critical urbanism. It is the daily urban experiences that make visible the ordinary ways in which residents negotiate their lives and livelihoods, in their homes and across different neighborhoods. In these spaces, we can engage with the diverse ways in which the state meets and engages its citizens, through institutions and policies, steeped in different political economies, as well as entrenched logics of violence, inequality, and injustice.

Paying close attention to everyday urban dynamics and the lived experiences of ordinary city dwellers lies at the heart of our pedagogical philosophy, which values and incorporates different knowledge systems and modes of knowledge production. In line with the epistemological premises of "Southern Theory," knowledge produced in and through everyday ordinary urban practices "from below" undergirds how we can understand and theorize the city. We enter this debate through a range of common and intersecting urban practices performed by individuals, organizations, and social movements; for instance, protesting, waiting, occupying, participating, and imagining. Building our pedagogical journey around these everyday practices allows us and our students to explore different forms of agency and build an alternative conceptual vocabulary vis-à-vis the urban theory canon. In tracking diverse and at times contentious forms of agency, our pedagogy engages transversal logics, which nonetheless remain intimately intertwined with notions of the state and market logics. This also allows us to see the very substance of the city, its housing, land, and labor struggles, individual and collective strategies to making ends meet, as well as questions of identity and belonging. These experiences frequently clash, compete with, and rub up against rights, policies, and state techniques as often prescriptive, government-driven, top-down processes. In other words, we proactively embrace the inherent tensions between structural forces—for instance, the state or capital—with forms of agency reflected in claims of citizenship, collective political actions, and, invoking Asef Bayat, ordinary acts of encroachment.[6] While waiting, participating, protesting, remembering, and so on occur and can be observed as everyday urban acts, their specific configuration, their logics, and their transversal nature are harder to grasp.

"Inherently unstable and contingent,"[7] as Teresa Caldeira argues, grasping these transversal logics requires methodologies and pedagogies open to experimentation, to diverse ways of knowing the city, and to embodied forms of knowledge production. The complexity of contemporary cities calls for creative and experimental research and representations that are immersed in ordinary acts: in the sounds and smells of homes and streets, in cultural production and embodied practices like walking and running the city, in individual and family stories and shared city histories. Hence, in the dynamism of the everyday, through embodied ways of knowing, we can embrace the contradictions, creativity, and complexity rooted in the transversal logics that shape everyday urban life.

It has been a beautiful challenge to design and build a bespoke pedagogy that intentionally plunges us and our students into diverse methods and spaces of the city. Different ways of knowing require creative and committed research, agile and innovative methods; what Jennifer Robinson and Ananya Roy articulate as "alternative modes of inquiry and new geographies of theory."[8] Therefore, our approach has been built across our individual disciplinary traditions and passions for urban research, grounded in a shared ethos of experimentation.

Experimenting is central to our pedagogy. From the conventional to the absurd, we have created opportunities for trying out a variety of methods, from sensing and running in the city to experimenting with publics and material investigations. In this mix, we prioritized the actual doing of method, providing a set of opportunities to reflect on these experiences, their affective elements, and the embodied and relational things that creative research approaches impel us to engage. In paying attention to embodiment, for instance, both our own and that of others, we open up forms of research where we become active participants, shifting the objects and subjects of research, along with our ways of knowing and representing them. In practicing embodied ways of knowing the city, we pay attention to senses, to modes of moving, to the material and social spaces we inhabit, and to the ways in which subjectivities are shaped and in turn are remaking contemporary cities.

In our pedagogy, we are alert and attentive to context, immersing ourselves in different city spaces—through attending public events, participating in exhibitions, holding debates, creating artworks, and visiting contested sites. This is a pedagogy through which we *confront* the always partial nature of our knowledge with ways of tracing the city's embodied aesthetics, exploring the different publics produced through varied forms of mobility. To work through these partialities, to relate to and build knowledge from them, we track what we and others see and feel when we run, walk, and move collectively through the city—on foot or on public transport. Through a practice built around sense and sense-making, we engage the city as an aesthetic order—an order made up of layered patterns that define the distribution of sensory experience among those who regularly inhabit and pass through urban space. In turn, we can engage and confront accepted narratives and visualizations of the city with other ways of knowing, with diverse "publics"—the collective political subject and shared spaces of the city—that give shape to these context-specific patterns of distribution.

In this mix, we prioritize and valorize ways to *traverse* spaces and scales, modes of inhabiting and knowing, discourses and forms of power shaped in and produced by diverse city actors. Our pedagogy encourages students to experiment, to think out of disciplinary boxes, to work across research methods. In making visible transversal logics, engaging with the urban everyday inspires on a methodological level a politics of knowledge production that insists that ordinary acts are a significant foundation for the making of urban theory. These intimate and multisensorial encounters provide additional depth and texture to hard-fought questions around what kind of and whose knowledge is usually valued when we study the urban. Ultimately, engaging with ordinary acts and actors stretches our imaginations, extending what constitutes legitimate urban knowledge, a move that disrupts and expands the urban studies canon. In sum, a focus on both everyday experiences and embodied methods helps us and our students broach pivotal topics around decolonial scholarship and the right to the city from relatable and exciting new vantage points.

The rich and provocative ways in which students have embraced varied ways of knowing and have reshaped the narrative and visual forms of their urban work are explored in the "Voices" section and visuals that follow this introduction. Naomi Samake engages critically with dark and light, the literal access to electricity or lack thereof, that shapes the varied visibilities of lifeworlds in the Accra airport area. "Sewing Threads" by Diana Vazquez-Martinez is an exquisitely rendered piece of art inspired by "Sensing the City" in Cape Town. This challenge of the sensed and the felt is taken up by Linda Wermuth in her rendering of running—the literal and tactile moving across Cape Town's variegated city spaces. And Lee Wolf's "The Ideal Urban Experience" brings this mix together in poetic form.

The individual essays that follow are inspired by everyday realities and encounters. James Clacherty's "The State at Home" embraces the lived experience of state bureaucracy in the context of precarious housing in Cape Town. Jacob Geuder reflects on video activism, which makes police violence visible: a key strategy in mobilizing a right to the city in Rio de Janeiro. Thomas Betschart tracks the ways in which the Ethiopian state embodies and builds a nation through the installation of large-scale road infrastructure. Isabella Baranyk's "Lubricating Logistics" focuses on the lived experience of truck drivers, a crucial cog in the global logistics flowing from Accra ports out to the world and back. Saad Amira renders visible the ways Palestinian villagers in the West Bank secure resources and farm in the face of settler-colonial ecological strategies of the Israeli state. In the final piece in this section, Laura Nkula-Wenz examines the ways in which a global discourse of design lands in Cape Town, spawning contradictory forms of local world-making. The pieces in this section share research built through varied methods, experimenting with ways of knowing found in the productive tensions that create our everyday lifeworlds at the intersection of different forms of state power, and the various flows that link the local and the global.

---

[1] Ash Amin and Nigel Thrift, *Cities: Reimagining the Urban* (Cambridge: Polity Press, 2002).
[2] Kathleen Stewart, *Ordinary Affects* (Durham: Duke University Press, 2007).
[3] Jennifer Robinson, "Cities in a World of Cities: The Comparative Gesture," *International Journal of Urban and Regional Research* 35, no. 1 (2011): 1–23.
[4] AbdouMaliq Simone and Edgar Pieterse, *New Urban Worlds: Inhabiting Dissonant Times* (Cambridge: John Wiley & Sons, 2018).
[5] Teresa Caldeira, "Peripheral Urbanization: Autoconstruction, Transversal Logics, and Politics in Cities of the Global South," *Environment and Planning D: Society and Space* 35, no. 1 (2017): 3.
[6] Asef Bayat, *Life as Politics: How Ordinary People Change the Middle East* (Stanford: Stanford University Press, 2010).
[7] Caldeira (see note 5).
[8] Jennifer Robinson and Ananya Roy, "Debate on Global Urbanisms and the Nature of Urban Theory," *International Journal of Urban and Regional Research* 40, no. 1 (2016): 181-186.

DARK AND LIGHT AT AIRPORT CITY

Lighting infrastructures and various levels of luminosity symbolically trigger local forms of inequality and instability. In 2015 Ghana experienced persistent, irregular, and unpredictable periods of electrical outages, and inherited the name Dumsor—an expression in the regional language Twi meaning "turn the lights on." By studying the materiality of light in the more recent world-class development of the Accra Airport City (AAC), my

Amelia's temporary food stand, 2019 © Naomi Samake

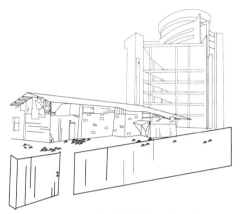

Temporary housing, 2019 © Naomi Samake

research explored the luminosity that exudes from intended and planned street, decorative, and security fixtures, and the exuded luminosity from these and AAC's buildings at night. These light infrastructures materialize a range of boundaries and epitomize the inequalities embedded in the built environment and local memories.

Light, while becoming an accessory to modernity, also becomes a moral and political reordering of social and spatial control. As Ananya Roy[1] critically notes, it is important for the world-class city to be understood beyond its iconic facade. The world-class tendency to illuminate what should be seen and erase what is less desired through the absence of light fuels strategies of calculated invisibility.[2] During my research, it became evident that local practices and conditions such as street-food vending and fixed-term labor agreements (among migrant workers) seep into AAC and patch the holes and cracks of the world-class city. From Monday to Saturday, Amelia packs her large steel and aluminum pots, prepares rice and beans as well as bundles of plantains, and feeds daily visitors and employees in AAC. By eleven o'clock, plantains are roasting on a wired sheet, heated by lit charcoal, and beans and rice are being kept warm on a portable mini-propane stove. Construction workers, among others, take breaks at Amelia's stand. Many of the construction workers I had the privilege of speaking with stay "on site" during the week or even throughout the duration of their employment—"on site" meaning in this temporary housing structure that has little to no water or electrical facilities. Construction workers here have come from distant places, some even from outside of the greater Accra region. The local employment standard of contractors not providing accommodation for their workers is a reality here. In effect, human infrastructures, like construction workers, ultimately shelter in the cracks and crevasses of the plan.

Nevertheless, it is quiet encroachments[3] such as the practices sketched here, within and beyond the existing light infrastructure, that help facilitate and maintain the choreography of AAC. In sequence to this world-class city, as the lights are turned on around six or seven o'clock in the evening, street-food vendors, construction workers, and security guards, among other human infrastructures that motorize AAC, are gone. These practices and norms challenge on a micro level

Accra Airport City, 2019 © Naomi Samake

the intended portrait of a world-class city, and illuminate small contestations of the ideologies fostered by a postcolonial, modern Ghana. And while AAC aspires to produce a basic sensual environment, light becomes the material border that separates the seen from the unseen, the good from the bad, and the granted from the denied. **By Naomi Samake**

---

[1] Ananya Roy, "The Blockade of the World-Class City: Dialectical Images of Indian Urbanism," in Ananya Roy and Aihwa Ong (eds.), *Worlding Cities: Asian Experiments and the Art of Being Global: Studies in Urban and Social Change* (Malden, MA: Wiley-Blackwell, 2011), 259–278.
[2] Tim Edensor, "The Gloomy City: Rethinking the Relationship between Light and Dark," *Urban Studies* 52, no. 3 (2013): 422–438.
[3] Richard Ballard, "Geographies of Development III: Militancy, Insurgency, Encroachment and Development by the Poor," *Progress in Human Geography* 39, no. 2 (2015): 214–224.

SEWING THREADS

"Sensing the City" was a course taught at the University of Cape Town that aimed, through different exercises, to develop new ways of perceiving the city by paying special attention to the sensory experiences in it. This process of sensory knowledge inspired me personally to create *Sewing Threads*.

In particular, as I explored the railway transport in Cape Town through photography and listening to sound, I began to wonder what form the results of sensory knowledge take in urban studies and how it is currently used. In this sense I took the name "Sewing Threads" literally and I used colored threads, thinking of them as sensory knowledge and as the powerful ideas sewn together and transmitted through books—the sources of knowledge that we as urbanists produce.

The book sews together in a collage form the music and conversations I heard in railway stations, the metal-on-metal clanging of the train approaching or the noise it made when I was on it, the feeling of tension at peak hour, the feeling of insecurity in empty and dark spaces, the description of smells, and my thoughts while I waited a long time for the train. This way of approaching the city increased my sensitivity, but most of all it made me realize that, although emotions may seem intangible and ephemeral, they can be captured, and as urbanists this is our main challenge.

By crafting this piece, I realized that the street is what urbanists should pay more attention to, building from the information that affects our senses. Agreeing with Pieterse (2013),[1] we as urbanists can embrace affect in popular practices across the city, as it is through the development of these registers that we might then begin to understand the diverse forms of creativity and conflict that shape the real city and encourage commitment to it. Being an architect and a critical urbanist makes me value what one branch offers to the other, and awakens my interest in not only producing written works, but also exploring other forms of representation of the city. **By Diana Vazquez-Martinez**

[1] Edgar Pieterse, "Grasping the Unknowable: Coming to Grips with African Urbanisms," in E. A. Pieterse and A. M. Simone, *Rogue Urbanism: Emergent African Cities* (Johannesburg: Jacana Media, 2013).

Representing city movements, *Sewing Threads,* 2019 © Photo: Diana Vazquez-Martinez

Representing city movements, *Sewing Threads*, 2019 © Photo: Diana Vazquez-Martinez

THE RACE, AN EXHIBIT

Experimenting with publics through the lens of sports or, more precisely, through running, offers a whole new spectrum of research tools for thinking of the urban. It not only forces us to think through what we see, but ultimately activates all our senses. Suddenly, one becomes fully aware of the ground one runs on. A sandy ground is indeed an obstacle compared to a paved road. Different buildings turn into landmarks: exactly here, I crossed the 5 km line. The city becomes the playground of the runner who repurposes its preexisting functions. Most importantly, as Murakami wrote in his book *What I Talk About When I Talk About Running*,[1] you only need a pair of running shoes to start your running journey. Or, as I would put it: your athletic research journey.

In the course of the "Experimenting with Publics" class at the University of Cape Town, students had the chance to join the Itheko Sport Athletic Club. The club met every week, and we ran together in the streets of Cape Town's Southern Suburbs. In order to collect and also illustrate the variety of individual experiences of thinking the city through running, we collected and exhibited bits and pieces of those runs and races with the running club. The result was a diverse assemblage of impressions and sensations made visible in a creative way. The work produced included videos, creative posters, and performances with running objects, as well as an interactive piece about the materiality of the surfaces one runs on.

That class beautifully showed that considering different and perhaps not so familiar research tools may result in productive ways of knowing the city. It opens up the possibility of leaving the typical academic environment and diving into the everyday life of the city.

By Linda Wermuth

[1] Haruki Murakami, *What I Talk About When I Talk About Running: A Memoir* (New York: Vintage House, 2008).

Most people cannot really imagine a place
When you just tell them what it looks like.
Our task was to use our artifacts to say something
about CPT.

With the following words,
I therefore want to figure out,
For myself,
What is the *ideal* urban experience?
What is the essence of CPT?

During this process, I am both creator and audience.
Looking, listening, trying to smell, at times also touching.

The longer I stay in this city,
The more I get the feeling that
I must invite the unease
I must learn to make the unfamiliar
Familiar.
Welcome the things that are uncomfortable.

I found out that you cannot protect yourself
from this city forever.
So what happens when you let your guard down?
When you walk alone?
Alone at night?
When you let the stranger talk to you?
When you sit and wait?

There occurs a feeling of *not quite,*
Everything is there for you to see,
But you do not know how to make use of it
Just yet.

There is the anger and the helplessness
when a stranger asks you for something,
Speaking incomprehensibly and not loud enough.
You cannot hear him.
You pretend
Not to hear him.

The movement of nature caused by the wind.
Incredibly many beautiful people.
Sunlight and shade.
The smell of a car's insides.

A guy I met here told me: this city stretches you.
And it really really really stretches you.
But when you let yourself be stretched,
You discover things.

There are the DJs that move
Their record shop, their friends, their drinks,
their self-painted benches
Out onto the street on *Some Sundays.*

There is the *Bus for Us*.
Us for us.
You see people wearing the warmest coats,
Sunshine or rain,
Because—apparently—it's winter.

You also hear a lot in this city.
A lot of different opinions
On the same thing.
Traffic starts at 2:30 and lasts until 5:30. If you leave
around three it's fine.
No, no, after six the streets are fine.
You know, the weather is different in Obz.
It's because of the mountain.

Then there are those strange days,
When it's foggy and Table Mountain is missing
Because he is hiding behind the clouds.
I find that there are other things also missing in this city:
The night,
People from my age group,
Bicycles,
Smells.

Smells are coupled with emotions.
And as there are no smells in this city,
There are also no emotions.
Or maybe too many of both.

In Cape Town,
Sensing the city means something different to each of us.
For you, it might be the taste of yet another piece
of carrot cake.
For you, it might be hearing a new song that is perfect.
For you, it might be the mind-numbing noises
on Main Road.
For you, it might be the first time you smell urine
in the streets.
And for you,
It might be playing the tambourine on Lion's Head,
The wind blowing through your curls.

Whether we like it or not, our senses are always there.
They are what guides us,
What makes us experience this city
And this city life.

It's true,
Sensing the city does not equal feeling the city.
But sensing this city
Sure makes you feel.

THE IDEAL URBAN EXPERIENCE

This poem was created for the final exhibition of the course "Experimenting with Publics—Sensing the City" that I participated in at the University of Cape Town's African Centre for Cities, taught by Anna Selmeczi in 2019. The aim of this course was to grapple with the concept of having and behaving like an audience: in our case, specifically, an audience to the city. What are the ways in which the urban can be experienced, besides the common walking and seeing of it? On our journey to find answers, we came upon sociocritical sound installations, encountered expressive public art, danced at exuberant concerts in extraordinary locations, and even found the photographer (and maybe a new passion) within ourselves. To round this off, we shared lively discussions about the various meanings of sensing and experiencing *anything,* ranging from smaller things like smells to larger phenomena such as prejudice. However, our little group always circled back to the observation that sensing the urban is in the end an individual experience and thus remains unique to each of us. In what follows, I put into words my own personal definition of experiencing this beautifully ugly city that is Cape Town. **By Lee Wolf**

The State at Home: Housing and Uncertainty in Eastridge, Cape Town

By James Clacherty

Imagined Homes and Concrete Houses

For nineteen years, Fatima and her family have been living in Eastridge, Mitchells Plain, in a house to which they have no legal claim. As a South African citizen, Fatima has a right to access housing. When she applied to the Eastridge housing scheme in 1999, she believed that the state, which commissioned the construction of the houses by the Cape Town Community Housing Company (CTCHC), was meeting its constitutional obligation to ensure that right. Instead, Fatima and the majority of her neighbors have spent the last nineteen years in conflict with the CTCHC. They have protested what they saw as unfair payment increases, have attempted to take the CTCHC to court, have challenged evictions, and have participated in a payment boycott. All of this has led to Fatima and her neighbors being declared illegal occupants of their houses by the CTCHC.

In a favorite spot in the kitchen, Eastridge, Cape Town, 2018 © Photo: James Clacherty

Within this contentious context, Fatima's nook by the stove represents the comfort and ordered predictability that she and her family have tried so hard to create in their home. She spends hours standing here cooking and watching people walk by her front window, keeping track of the goings-on in her home and on the street outside. The work that goes into creating these familiar spaces and recurring domestic tasks belongs to Fatima's imagination of a home as something that endures through time. A place where she feels in control of the world. This imagination comes into uncomfortable contact with the bureaucratic category of illegal occupant, and the uncertainty and anxiety that this status creates.

The Imagined State and the Lived State

One block away from Fatima live Wayne and his family. On my visits to his home, Wayne tells me long stories about his relationship with the CTCHC and the City of Cape Town government. The state appears in Wayne's stories frequently: in his excited anticipation at the prospect of becoming a homeowner, as well as in his experiences of disappointment, frustration, and anger when this status was withheld from him. Wayne has a detailed understanding of his entitlement to state housing and is keenly aware of the state's failure to ensure this access to housing for his family and his neighbors. Within this awareness is a tension between the state as it could be and the state as it actually is.

In Wayne's explanation, the state appears as a collection of different entities that act both as conduits for the realization of socioeconomic rights and as obstacles to them. In order to get by from day to day, he and other residents like him have to navigate a complex network of state institutions and agents: from the unresponsive offices of the CTCHC to the City of Cape Town rates office, from lawyers serving Notice of Payment Default letters to municipal technicians arriving to turn off your water, from long queues outside the Home Affairs office to court cases that overrule eviction orders. These encounters can become overwhelming and destabilizing for the residents, as their very futures are dependent on how well they can negotiate this shifting, often contradictory network.

In their attempts to make sense of the multiple institutions and agents that make up the state and deal with the uncertainties that these encounters create, the residents develop strategies that rely on mundane tasks oriented toward the house. Painting the living room walls, tiling floors, replacing rickety doors, carefully tidying the house and arranging the objects within it, as well as the unceasing, cyclical tasks of housework and the maintenance of a daily routine all become ways of coping with uncertainty. The house becomes a space within and through which the residents figure out and express their sense of self in relation to the ongoing project of the state. Residents invest in their houses so that they match their own sense of dignity, and in so doing resist their bureaucratic construction as unlawful occupants or as ungrateful freeloaders.

Homemaking—State-Making: A Key Finding

Acts directed at bringing about the ideal home—slow incremental improvements such as building flowerbeds, hanging curtains, polishing kitchenware, or even just acts of imagining the ideal home—are, on the one hand, a way for the residents to assert ownership over their houses and make them their own, and, on the other hand, an assertion of political personhood. Acts of homemaking become an assertion of the dignity and respectability that is denied them by the state when it withholds tenure to their houses and relegates them to the delinquent category of "illegal occupant." The imagining of the ideal home and the flawed state that frustrates the achievement of this ideal are in constant tension with each other.

A family's renovated new front door, Eastridge, Cape Town, 2018 © Photo: James Clacherty

In their everyday encounters with the state, the residents are confronted with the actual, flawed state that obstructs their access to housing and places them in the bureaucratic category of illegal occupant. The residents feel excluded from the moral community of the state and are denied the entitlements due to them as members of this community. Homemaking practices are, in this context, an attempt to assert a different kind of identity—that of a respectable, contributing member of society who deserves to have their rights recognized. In this way, the imagination of the ideal home and the measures taken to achieve that ideal home, despite limited resources and lack of tenure, are at the same time an imagining of a different kind of relationship to the state—a more caring relationship in which the state behaves transparently and democratically.

Through their encounters with the state and its project of housing delivery during the nineteen years they have lived in Eastridge, residents have developed two concurrent understandings of the state: one of the inadequate, contradictory state that obstructs their access to housing and their sense of belonging to a community of rights-bearing subjects, and the other of the ideal potential state that protects their rights and behaves transparently and democratically to ensure that all citizens are treated with the respect and dignity they deserve. Because of the link between homeownership and citizenship in the experiences of the Eastridge residents, imagining an enduring home and creating a sense of order and ordinariness in that home—despite their extraordinary unlawful status—is a way of rejecting a status quo that creates instability and uncertainty and undermines the residents' image of themselves as homeowners and as citizens deserving of respect.

The Research Journey
This piece of research emerges out of an ongoing collaborative project between the Eastridge Community Committee, the Western Cape Anti-Eviction Campaign (AEC), and Dr. Sophie Oldfield and Dr. Anna Selmeczi from the African Centre for Cities. The Eastridge Committee approached the AEC asking for help in their struggles with the CTCHC. The AEC in turn approached Dr. Oldfield and Dr. Selmeczi, asking them to manage a research project to gather information about the residents' houses, their legal status in the houses, and the history of their engagement with the CTCHC, with the aim of building a case for the residents to be able to negotiate transfer of the title deeds to their houses.

Electricity receipts, stuffed in a drawer, Eastridge, Cape Town, 2018 © Photo: James Clacherty

Through engaging with a number of Eastridge residents and collecting histories of their engagement with the CTCHC, the complex, often contradictory logics of navigating state institutions slowly began to emerge. What emerged did not quite fit within the schema of "conflicting rationalities," nor with the idea of contradictory knowledge systems. The Eastridge residents are knowledgeable about state rationalities and regimes of power; they understand bureaucratic knowledge systems, and are highly adept at navigating the impacts that these have on their everyday lifeworlds.

Many of the considerations for how I approached this research project emerged out of a previous research project, the fieldwork phase of which was largely unsuccessful relative to my aims. During this project I wanted to be particularly rigorous about my data collection and my engagements with the residents and the research site at large. The aim was to keep the fine details of the individual experiences of the residents at the center of the research project, and then later really ground my analysis in these experiences. The reason for this is that "the state" and "citizenship" are such large and easily taken for granted concepts, and I wanted to focus on the way these entities emerged in the lived experience of the residents through their interactions with their houses.

By continuously coming back to the stories I was told by the residents and centering the seemingly mundane details around which they structured their narratives of engagement with the CTCHC and various other elements of the state project, a much richer, more complex and layered story emerged. It was in stories I was told about how long it took one family to paint the walls of their bedrooms, or the piles of unopened envelopes from the CTCHC, or the challenge of making friends and building a community in a new neighborhood that the messy reality of the state emerged—not in any questions I could have asked about their understanding of citizenship or their opinion on housing policy. Through this approach I was led to focus on the materiality of the houses—the crumbling bricks, the newly fitted kitchen units, the collections of family photographs, the drawers full of receipts and bills—and the relationships that formed around these material objects. This wasn't something I had expected to be so significant, but it had the effect of grounding the abstract workings of the state project in the tangible lived reality of the residents. High fences and the rituals of vigilance were experienced as symbols of abandonment. Collections of receipts for housing payments became talismans of faith in the judicial system that they hoped would one day put everything right.

It is exactly these relationships with material objects—letters, fences, walls, floors, and light fittings—that allow us to see the intimate ways in which the actual complex, contradictory lived state winds itself intimately into people's lives or bumps disruptively into their imagined futures.

A Takeaway from the Process

When I started thinking about how I might present the thesis that this research contributed to, my first impulse was to include a map of Eastridge at the very beginning to give the reader some context and a sense of the space they would be reading about. I very quickly realized that this would be an entirely inappropriate point of departure for the story. Instead, I started with the photograph that also appears at the beginning of this piece: Fatima resting comfortably in her nook in the kitchen. This story is one that moves from the small scale to the large. The significance of this research for me, and a key takeaway from the research process, is that it is in the minute details that the larger themes emerge. One must beware of moving too quickly to the big concepts, and must constantly return to the small details at the heart of the story. It is in these everyday details that the larger scale of the state appears.

The state project becomes an intimate part of people's lives. They encounter its various elements on a day-to-day basis and respond to it in strongly emotional and corporeal ways. If we are to understand these processes of state formation and reproduction and the process of citizen subjectification in a way that engages honestly with their complexity, we need to be sure not to lose sight of the spaces in which these processes become most real and where they are most keenly felt: in the everyday lives and homes of ordinary people trying to cope with extraordinary circumstances.

Video Activism as Bottom-Up City Making
By Jacob Geuder

"Peace without a voice is not peace, it is fear"; these were the words on a favela resident's poster at a protest filmed in Maré, Rio de Janeiro, in February 2015, after a series of lethal police attacks that left eleven victims dead or injured. The police responded to this street demonstration with live ammunition, injuring at least one of the activists in the protest.[1] Since the early 2010s, the exponential growth in the availability of smartphones and social media in Brazil and South Africa has increased the number of potential videographers dramatically. With the importance of filming as a "repertoire of contention" for urban movements and urban citizens, video activism has become a critical way to make visible the realities of city life for those who bear the brunt of systems of violence and marginalization. Videographers' audiovisual testimonies make visible evidence of violence, showing the ways in which violence is inextricably entangled with city space. Video activism has become a key repertoire in struggles for a right to the city in the twenty-first century. This short essay builds on my PhD, "Visualizing Urban Struggles: Video Activism as Utopian Practice," organized in close collaboration

Video activists filming a demonstration, Rio de Janeiro, 2015 © Photo: Jacob Geuder

with individual video activists and collectives in Rio de Janeiro and Cape Town. Here, I show how video production emerges from specific city contexts and struggles in Rio and in Cape Town, navigated through a simultaneity of activism on the street and on the net. I explore the ways in which this medium exposes critical and powerful structures and symbols of violence that shape activism and city life. I draw on this work to reflect on the utopian potential of video activism and its ambivalent position, caught between the commodification of online networks by for-profit social media and the multilayered levels of violence played out on the streets. Both these dynamics shape the ways in which video activism works to further bottom-up struggles for a right to the city.

The Simultaneity of the Streets and the Net
Every video has a story, shaped by global technologies, rooted in the city, at times able to challenge and at others to reproduce the deep divisions inscribed into Cape Town and Rio de Janeiro. Through interviews, conversations, and observation, in this research I unravel what "doing video activism" means on the ground for video activists. Interviewees repeatedly emphasized the intermingling of the streets and on the net in their experiences. Commenting on the inextricable infiltration of the streets and the net during the *Jornadas de Junho* in Brazil, Esther Solano, professor for media studies, argues: "There is no way of studying the protest without studying the web. The web and the streets are two sides of the same coin."

The links between mobilization on the streets and online reflections make it critical to understand the particular histories of urban social movements in order to grasp the emergence of video activist scenes. For example, in Rio, contemporary forms of video activism can be understood only in the context of the massive protest wave of the *Jornadas de Junho* in 2013 that swept through the streets of the "marvelous city" and in which media became a major "battleground." The street protests articulated a critique of neoliberal urbanization, catalyzed by developments linked to the FIFA World Cup 2014 and the Olympic Games 2016. The investment of billions into stadiums and infrastructure benefitting the already privileged stood in stark contrast to decaying public health and education systems. When a price rise for public transport fares was announced in early 2013, the anger and frustration boiled over into public unrest. The police responded with heavy-handed repression of protests, simultaneously supported and reinforced by the mass media. The media giant Globo, at the forefront of Brazilian corporate media, ran a campaign, for instance, to stigmatize the demonstrations of the *Jornadas de Junho* as "vandalism," "looting," "rioting," and "terrorism." Owned by five influential Brazilian families, this corporation was founded as a TV station in 1965 with the support of the military dictatorship then governing the country. As one of the biggest TV networks worldwide today, Globo has since continued to play a significant role in favoring right-wing and conservative politics in Brazil. In reaction to Globo's stigmatizing of protesters as vandals, on an unprecedented scale, activists in Brazil took cameras into their own hands to produce audiovisual representation "from within" movements and protests. The aim of that video work was to make visible and sharable videos of the police attacking unarmed protesters: to "return the gaze," so to speak. In a remarkable act of communicative autogestion—self-management—they put into practice the Indymedia slogan "don't hate the media, be the media."

There is a dialectical relationship between video activism and mobilization of urban movements. On the one hand, the prominence of contemporary forms of video activism has shaped the counternarratives produced by and drawn on by movements since 2013. Videos have amplified protesters' voices, presented evidence of police violence, and deconstructed and contested hegemonic narratives of activist "vandalism." At the same time, video activism collectives in Rio have been inspired and shaped by activism in 2013. Many of the collectives that practice video activism emerged in response to the heavy repression experienced at street protests. Hence, the increased availability of global technological innovations such as smartphones and social media alone are necessary but insufficient to explain the organization of bottom-up video activism in Rio de Janeiro. As digital and material spheres of activism mutually infiltrate each other in the production of online videos, it is necessary to consider local specificities as much as the global technologies that shape video activism.

Exposing Violence and Vulnerability
Videos have the power to expose violence, its contexts, perpetrators, symbols, and structures. To audiovisually record a perpetrator physically harming a victim has become easier than ever before with new communication tools at hand. For example, an eyewitness video recording the brutal humiliation of a man on the streets of Cape Town went viral on October 6, 2014.[2] Filmed from an office space, the video shows how a group of police officers stopped a Black man in his car, forced him to strip naked on the open street, and then beat him up, showing viscerally visible heavy police boots hitting him in his genitals. In making videos, citizens and activists oscillate between power and vulnerability. The videographer who recorded the humiliation and beating of the Black man by Cape Town police officers, for example, recounted that the same officers came knocking at her door when they realized they had been recorded. In this case she did not suffer immediate retaliation, but in many other cases police officers have not been shy to threaten eyewitnesses filming.

Since violence is not always as graphic, situational, and evident as in the case above, video activist collectives have produced short documentaries that call out structural and symbolic violence on the city's urban margins, making it visible and public. For example, the MIC Collective in Rio de Janeiro published a seven-minute video which addresses the assassination of Jhonata by "Pacifiying Police" in Rio's favela *Morro de Catrumbi*.[3] By piecing together eyewitness footage, an interview with Jhonata's mother, and snippets of press reports, the video demonstrates the racism inherent in Brazilian police violence. The police claimed that they had shot the sixteen-year-old boy because they had "confused" a bag of popcorn he was holding with drugs. The video shares Jhonata's mother's despair, as she explains she sent her son to get the popcorn for a birthday party the following day. The video then skips to a sequence of newspaper articles that offer other examples of police claiming to "confuse" arbitrary objects—such as a hydraulic pump, a skateboard, a phone, or a drilling machine—for weapons. The number of residents killed by police in such circumstances in Rio's favelas is staggering. In contrast, there is no single case of such "confusion" in which police officers have killed a white resident in one of Rio's wealthy neighborhoods. The death of Jhonata, as the video makes clear, is not a single incident or simply a product of confusion.

Violence is more cumulative and complex than a single type of incident. Structures of violence embedded in systemic marginalization are often equally harmful, though less visible. New technologies at hand increase the possibilities to film and engage these structural realities, but they require know-how and organization. Consequently, many videographers have organized themselves in video activist collectives to

Bloodstains of Jhonata on a bag of popcorn, Rio de Janeiro, 2016
© André Miguéis, Mídia Independente Coletiva
https://www.youtube.com/watch?v=bFIKP-IWnm8&t=43s

build networks, save footage, bring together and protect individual videographers in marginalized urban areas, and create and sustain channels to distribute videos. Recording can be dangerous—a "death sentence," as one video activist explained to me while we were sitting in a café at the entrance to one of the biggest favelas in Rio's North Zone.

Distributing Videos for Profit: Social Media and Institutional Irresponsibility
For-profit social media play an ambivalent role as gatekeepers for bottom-up video production. On the one hand, they offer avenues for urban movements as well as urban citizens to disseminate content, which amplifies their voices and forms of mobilization, and their critique of violence. These online platforms enable urban citizens to circumvent traditional gatekeepers in journalism, such as Globo in Brazil. On the other hand, the dissemination of bottom-up video production through

these channels incorporates them into a profit-driven logic that can all too easily undermine the emancipatory claims and demands of urban movements. Interviewees repeatedly expressed their frustration with social media companies and their decision-making, which is not politically accountable. Corporate social media are the center in the systems of "communicative capitalism," "data colonialism," and "digital capitalism" that monopolize profits and concentrate decision-making power, hence undermining bottom-up video activists struggling for the recognition of urban citizenship rights, pushing for commons rather than commodification, and working toward a bottom-up autogestion rather than top-down algorithmic governance.

Poster at a street protest in Maré, Rio de Janeiro, 2015 © André Miguéis, Mídia Independente Coletiva
https://www.youtube.com/watch?v=vH0r460o3_c

"To not have money is a crime," Rio de Janeiro, 2015 © Photo: Jacob Geuder

Initially, video activist collectives in Rio established channels for the distribution of activist videos on the sites of corporate social media such as Facebook, YouTube, and Twitter. Once sufficiently organized, the MIC Collective built its own websites to be independent from the oligopolies of YouTube and Facebook. They aimed to bypass these corporate exploitative models and evade censorship, while retaining their nonhierarchical, inclusive, and independent form of organization. While these initiatives safeguarded the collectives' legitimacy and street credibility, it proved impossible to sustain the levels of work and infrastructure to run a website, and in 2016 the MIC Collective returned to using the platforms of corporate social media. While video activists dedicated to visualizing urban struggles increasingly felt the economic pressure of decreasing incomes due to their time and commitment invested in sustaining video activism, the corporate social media giants multiplied their revenues. The power imbalance between top-down digital powerhouses and bottom-up video activists continues to grow, while courageous videographers make audiovisuals work for people, not for profit.

Utopian Practices of Video Activism

In short, digital communication has become urbanized, its digital threads woven into our twenty-first-century cities. Video activists working toward the "concrete utopia" of a radically democratized communication play a key role in bottom-up city-making that is critical not only in Rio de Janeiro and cities like it, but across the world. However, video activism cannot operate outside the contradictions that the system of neoliberal capitalism imposes in the streets and on the net. To find a voice in urban struggles at the margins, video activists themselves are constantly oscillating between the streets and the net, exposing and engaging power and vulnerability at the same time.

[1] Mídia Independente Coletiva, "Rebelião no Complexo da Maré – RJ," YouTube video, 7:35, February 26, 2015, https://www.youtube.com/watch?v=vH0r460o3_c.

[2] grantzax, "More cape town police brutality – March 07, 2014," YouTube video, 2:02, March 7, 2014, https://www.youtube.com/watch?v=ntdXgRcC9SY.

[3] Mídia Independente Coletiva, "No Leblon a PM não se confunde," YouTube video, 6:30, July 21, 2016, https://www.youtube.com/watch?v=bFIKP-IWnm8&t=43s.

Ethiopian Intersections of Road Development

By Thomas Betschart

Roads are a crucial component of the assemblages of infrastructures that facilitate the movement of things in our daily lives. Globalization is not possible without tarmac. Their *raison d'être* seems so mundane and self-evident that in contemporary urban surroundings one will only bother thinking about them once their functionality is obstructed—due to maintenance or when traffic exceeds available capacities during rush hour. We tend to forget that roads once had to be built in places that were previously difficult to access, and that their coming into being transformed entire geographies, lifestyles, politics, and economies, while reshuffling existing hierarchies, accelerating development, and fostering new modes of communication and exchange.[1]

Roads have gained much attention in archaeological and historical studies, due to their crucial role in the building of ancient empires and trade routes. Historical engagements with modernity have seen the emergence of a new mobile social class, as well as the transformation of social relationships and the installment of new bureaucratic forms of governance.[2] Since the beginning of the nineteenth century, the construction of road infrastructure has proliferated at an increasing speed, guided by a desire to establish hegemonic powers that finally led to the establishment of neoliberal political rationales in our contemporary world of extended urbanization.[3] This can be seen, for example, through the contemporary planning and establishment of new trade corridors along the East African seaboard that links peripheral sites of extraction and production with the global centers of trade and consumption, such as Kenya's flagship LAPSSET Corridor Project, Ethiopia's Addis Ababa-Djibouti Railway, or the current upgrade of the Addis-Nairobi corridor. As planned state logistics and transportation infrastructures are deployed, used, and contested, they create local urban environments that are the result of specific localities and practices. Tracing roads and the commodity chains they facilitate reveals the multitude of entangled layers and structural contradictions in the interconnected geographies of our time, shedding light on emerging geographies of inclusion and exclusion.

Airport Road, Hawassa, 2019 © Photo: Thomas Betschart

Ethiopia is a multiethnic state and it builds on a century-long history of state-driven development. This was initially sparked by the imperial unification of Ethiopia by Emperor Tewodros II in the mid-nineteenth century, followed by his imperial successors, later by the Leninist-Marxist rule of the DERG (Amharic for committee) (1973–1991), and then by the Ethiopian People's Democratic Revolutionary Front under Tigrayan domination (1991–2018). Throughout these different periods, power and territorial consolidation came into being through the construction of roads that established connectivity as well as militarized urban centers. All Ethiopian governments' means of exerting power have been closely connected to the provision of infrastructure, as it directed their urban expansion through the planning of transportation corridors and the drawing of political legitimacy from the provision of infrastructure as the primary means for fighting poverty.[4]

Public infrastructure development in Ethiopia has seen massive upscaling in recent years, with ambitious endeavors such as the building of the Grand Ethiopian Renaissance Dam, the Addis Ababa-Djibouti Railway, the Addis Ababa Light Rail, the planning of expressways, the increasingly prominent role of the state-owned Ethiopian Airlines in global air travel, the construction of roads that connect peripheries to urban centers, and the establishment of dry ports and industrial parks. The latter, built, financed, and operated predominantly by Chinese contractors, reflect the nation's partial strategy to follow what has become known as the "Chinese model of development." This refers to the installment of industrial growth poles, taking advantage of low labor costs and integrating Ethiopia's production sector into the global economy through foreign direct investments and infrastructure development.[5]

During my time in Ethiopia, some of my liveliest discussions circled around the topic of infrastructure. It appears that the built environment, especially the prominent state projects mentioned above, is a hot topic in the restaurants and cafés of Addis Ababa, Hawassa, Bahir Dar, and Mekelle. After all, in these cities it is nearly impossible to ignore the scaffoldings supporting the many skyscrapers that are shooting out of the ground at miraculous speed, or the transformation of streets into bright and fluorescent urban corridors of sound, light, and traffic, which ensure Ethiopia's arrival in the twenty-first century of consumer capitalism can hardly go unnoticed. As an Addis Ababa–based sociologist told me: "Ethiopia seeks its common identity by means of constructing itself."

Ethiopia continues to change at a fast pace. It elected a democratic federal government in early 2018 after three years of violent protests, ending a twenty-seven-year-long autocratic regime founded on ethnicity-based politics. Still, the nation remains far from being politically consolidated, as is evident through ongoing regional struggles for more sovereignty and persistent tensions along ethnopolitical lines, as currently seen through the violent crisis raging in Ethiopia's northern region of Tigray.

In November 2019 the Sidama region became Ethiopia's tenth regional state, after months of ongoing negotiations and violent turmoil. Formerly integrated into Ethiopia's Southern Nations, Nationalities, and People's Region, the lush area lies along the Addis-Nairobi corridor and is famous for its cash crops and coffee export. Its accessibility has turned the region into a rapidly urbanizing region that attracts investments, industrialization, and an ever-expanding tertiary sector. It is indeed fascinating to see how Hawassa, Sidama's capital, has been reshaped by the recently built cobblestone roads, which have turned residential areas into lively markets and service compounds. Monuments reflecting its ethnic heritage have been erected, and the city has become a hub for the production of garments, provision of governmental services, and a trade hub for agricultural commodities. As a consequence, the rich and politically connected upper class has constructed its villas on the nearby shores of Lake Awa. Upon my arrival in Hawassa in June 2019, protesters had installed signs along the roads, stating Sidama's independence, while the protests sparked military repressions leading to a state of emergency in the region at the time. Dozens were killed, hundreds injured, and public life came to a halt as the military patrolled the streets. Contradicting rumors spread and it became hard to tell whose rioting and whose violence lit the initial sparks. The conflict in Sidama could be framed as the expression of reshifting power dynamics in a politically volatile and ethnopolitically charged environment. The background of this story is, however, more complicated, as opinions, viewpoints, and analyses diverged. Nonetheless, the fact that roads played a crucial role in sparking and fostering this particular conflict was a shared opinion among different parties and commentators.

I meet with Ayele[5] at Washington Hotel in Addis Ababa's bustling Bole District in June 2019. The prominent journalist and scholar of crisis studies wanted to meet me here, at the exact site of the assassination of a leading military representative just one month earlier. The general had tried to seize control of the northern state of Amhara. Ayele is well-known throughout Ethiopia, and he understands its current conflicts. "What I am about to tell you would have sent me to jail just one year ago," he confides. However, after three cups of coffee we both feel comfortable enough to move on to discussing the political situation in Sidama and the reasons for the popular uprising. Ayele emphasizes that infrastructure takes center stage in this conflict. Sidama is considered to have comparatively reliable roads and electric grids, as well as solid productive capacities of cash crops, high levels of industrialization, and good interregional connectivity: "Roads mean business and production, while tax autonomy means that the subsidization of other regions comes to an end, which leads to more roads, more business, and more opportunities in Sidama," states Ayele. Furthermore, roads also hold the key to political agency, acting as a tool to exert power and state control. Resistance against the government forms along the roads, while the same infrastructure becomes militarized, surveilled, and strictly controlled in order to suppress insurgencies.

Airport Road, Hawassa, 2019 © Photo: Thomas Betschart

Ayele is convinced that the volatile situation in Ethiopia should be understood as a scramble for resources and agency along ethnic lines. Sidama, with its current dynamics, is therefore at the forefront of changing the status quo, and aiming at generating more autonomous resources for developing its urban infrastructure. Tracing the roads in this specific region provides a viable methodology for understanding the lived realities, political negotiations, militarized control, global entanglements, (shadow-)logistics, practical norms, and the history of development that undergird urban life with all its consequences. Apart from understanding who controls and uses the roads, encounters on the tarmac lead to insights into socioeconomic entanglements and their dispersion. Large areas in Sidama have only recently been connected by road to other regions, while its western hinterlands still remain disconnected from the global flows of commodities. This reveals some of its ambiguous developmental pathways and uneven geographical outcomes.

Recently built roads have led to the establishment of newly built communities and towns, such as Dore Bafana, a town with 8,000 inhabitants west of Lake Awa. Although it only emerged over the past ten years, it is already a logistic hub for agricultural goods, where information is exchanged and where novel urban lifeworlds become enmeshed with traditional rural practices. Access to the Internet provides real-time information on market ratios such as donkeys, which carry the bulk of cash crops into the urban sub-centers and are crucial to the supply chains that export the Khat, coffee, and maize that grows in the fertile hinterlands. Nearby, what has now become Africa's largest industrial park was built by a Chinese construction company under the precondition of prior road construction, which in most cases was also outsourced by the federal government to Chinese contractors. The factories' strictly surveilled working surroundings now form a precariously low-paid urban working class that absorbs migrants and commuters from the peripheries and sub-centers such as Dore Bafana, thus changing the face of the urban while new practices emerge and manifest in the built environment and urban culture. Some kilometers apart, a new urban elite with political affiliations is emerging, while it redirects road construction to plots of land it acquired, fostering land speculation based on anticipated real estate windfalls.[6]

The southern regions of Sidama are characterized by disruption, while donors such as Irish Aid, along with their aspirations to establish connectivity, have been expelled in 2002. This was done in order to suppress development, so as to ensure centralized political control and to direct the export of cash crops through the center of Ethiopia, blocking alternative routes through Kenya. These are now served by a wide network of incremental shadow logistics and smugglers, bypassing Ethiopian tax authorities. Above these conflicting realities hovers the sphere of international geopolitics. China is the most prominent but not sole investor in Ethiopia, and it constructs the majority of large-scale infrastructure such as expressways and industrial parks. Along with its plans, designs, and visions, it brings its state-owned construction companies, workers, commodities, soft power, political cooperation, and monetary dependencies. In Ethiopia's state developmentalist context, the multiethnic nation state has always drawn its legitimacy from the provision of infrastructure. Rooted in the imperial, socialist, and postrevolutionary history of the nation, rent-seeking for the funding of massive infrastructure endeavors, such as roads, is still at the core of Ethiopia's national and international governance, marking it as one of the clearest examples of state developmentalism.[7] Roads therefore play the most crucial role in the reciprocal negotiations of access to resources owned by the state or

During the last decade motorcycle fleets have been privately established, connecting the rural hinterlands to their agricultural centers. The cities ban motorcycles within their perimeters during times of political tensions. They are regarded as a threat to security and a major conveyor of political resistance, Hawassa, 2019 © Photo: Thomas Betschart

the regions. They direct the flows of capital, goods, people, and urbanization, and represent the most powerful tool in planning the nation's future topography.

Flows as well as disruptions in the movement of people, commodities, and information reveal the tensions, conflicting realities, as well as the multitudes of knowledge systems and practices that produce and are produced by urban space. By understanding "spaces of friction" as constitutive elements of the urban, we can see how they interlace territorial regimes and form the basis for negotiating power and agency in Ethiopia's current political and geographic transformation. One day, these new roads and the contestation they created might just become invisible—as is the fate of much of our mundane urban infrastructure. However, their impact on the nation, its people, and their lived realities will surely remain a determining factor for Ethiopia's future transformation.

[1] Penny Harvey and Hannah Knox, "The Enchantments of Infrastructure," *Mobilities* 7, no. 4 (2012): 521–536, doi:10.1080/17450101.2012.718935.

[2] Jo Guldi, *Roads to Power: Britain Invents the Infrastructure State* (Cambridge, MA: Harvard University Press, 2012).

[3] Andy Merrifield, "The Urban Question under Planetary Urbanization," *International Journal of Urban and Regional Research* 37, no. 3 (2013): 909–922.

[4] "The World Bank in Ethiopia," The World Bank, accessed July 22, 2020, https://www.worldbank.org/en/country/ethiopia/overview.

[5] Personal communication.

[6] Daniel Mains and Eshetayehu Kinfu Tesfaye, "Making the City of Nations and Nationalities: The Politics of Ethnicity and Roads in Hawassa, Ethiopia," *The Journal of Modern African Studies* 54, no. 4 (2016): 645–669, doi:10.1017/S0022278X16000562.

[7] Christopher Clapham, "The Ethiopian Developmental State," *Third World Quarterly* 39, no. 6 (2018): 1151–1165, doi:10.1080/01436597.2017.1328982.

[8] Emanuele Fantini, "Developmental State, Economic Transformation and Social Diversification in Ethiopia," ISPI Analysis 163 2013, accessed July 10, 2020, https://www.ispionline.it/sites/default/files/pubblicazioni/analysis_163_2013.pdf.

Lubricating Logistics
By Isabella Baranyk

Inside of the newest terminal of Tema Harbor near Accra, Ghana, cranes, lifts, and trucks move containers through the network with speed and precision. Just beyond the terminal's gates lies Glory Oil Filling Station, whose lot is filled with parked trucks. Their drivers are not here for gasoline; they're here waiting for permission to enter the port, pick up or drop off a container, and carry on. Tema is known to be one of the most active and reliable ports in the region, with the capacity to process more than 2,000 containers daily.[1] But these drivers have been waiting all day. Many will continue to wait through the night and into the following days and weeks.

Glory Oil Filling Station, Tema, Ghana, 2019
© Photo: Isabella Baranyk

Tema Port, Tema, Ghana, 2019
© Photo: Isabella Baranyk

How is it possible that these two temporal realities—one in which containers are moved through a space with engineered quickness, and another in which the human bodies partially responsible for their movement are stagnated—exist within a few hundred meters of each other? In her book *Extrastatecraft: The Power of Infrastructure Space,* Keller Easterling describes the market as a major lubricating force behind the proliferation of contemporary infrastructure space.[2] At Tema, that same lubricant seeps into the port and informs the creation of quick logistics fashioned from the same slick material. On the dusty road behind, market logic means indeterminant periods of latency between jobs for the truck drivers. Shrunk in lubrication and stretched in the dirt, time is a resource to be conserved and expended in accordance with the market. It has material consequences that take shape in the port and along the street behind it.

The role of time and the market in organizing material conditions at Tema Harbor is part of a larger process through which time became meticulously standardized to aid capitalist globalization. As European powers scrambled to establish colonial outposts of trade and extraction in the rest of the world, technologies such as railroads and steam ships had expanded the scale and shrunk the speed at which trade took place. They also required a degree of standardization to work effectively. Twenty-six nations convened at the 1884 International Meridian Conference to determine a prime meridian—the first step to establishing global time. They selected Greenwich, England, as the site of the new line, furthering the British Empire's attempted control of world order. The line originated in Greenwich and extended north and south to girdle the globe, and it also happened to pass through Accra.

By that period, following decades of earlier land invasion and seizure, most of the present nation of Ghana had been established as an official British colony—the Gold Coast—for seventeen years. Colonial authorities in the Gold Coast were soon synching Accra's clock to Greenwich by telegraph every day, with precise results.[3] Time was also experienced intimately by Gold Coast locals. For missionaries, educators, and capitalists alike, enforcement of rational time on local laborers was a means of expressing supremacy and ensuring the highest wealth extraction possible.[4] Laboring bodies were expected to work according to the clock, a tool of the colonial regime opposed to all other understandings of work and leisure, at the threat of violence.[5] The mechanical clock was another tool used by British imperialists to enforce power over laborers, and it displaced those bodies from the rhythms around which life had previously been constituted.

British colonists during that time had become well aware that time is money, and that with standardization comes speed. By the 1920s, an accumulation of products for export had exposed the inadequacy of the existing port's infrastructure speed.[6] Rather than retrofitting the old ports, colonial leadership determined that it was necessary to build a new one—Tema—to be created in the efficiency-informed, updated topology that had blossomed under global capitalism. When Ghana became an independent nation, those same standardized spatial logics used at Tema Harbor were still needed in order to play nice with international trade, but this time to bring security to the nation and its people, representing a "totalizing vision of national life and prosperity" under President Kwame Nkrumah.[7] Despite the port's initial success after its 1961 opening,[8] agricultural crises and political instability in the nation caused it to be "marked by stagnation and inefficiency" in the decades that followed.[9] By the 1990s, the port had fallen into disrepair.[10]

During this lull, ports around the world were shaped by containerization, which intensified standardization and expanded its reach well beyond the confines of the port. Containers create identical encasement for irregularly shaped and sized goods to be shipped, and allow for the engineering of entire logistical systems and technologies that utilize their uniformity to maximize efficiency. In 2002, the Japan International Cooperation Agency revitalized Tema Harbor, building warehouses, cranes, and the complete container infrastructure.[11] In the summer of 2019, a third, larger terminal was opened at Tema Harbor, operated by Meridian Port Services, which is primarily made up of Maersk, one of the world's leading shipping companies, and Bollore, a French logistics company which operates twenty-one other ports in Africa alone as part of its "Port Terminal Network."[12] Under a highly automated and surveilled process that mirrors other international ports operated by Bollore and a number of other similar companies, bodies of truck drivers, along with containers, are inscribed in automated efficiency flows.

Frank at Glory Oil, Tema, 2019 © Photo: Isabella Baranyk

Outside of the barricaded gates of the port, the relentlessness of speed and reconfiguration of space in its service seems to lose its grip. Meridian Road connects the port facilities to the surrounding community, logistics offices, and the rest of the road network. It is also used for parking, both permitted and illegal, as drivers wait to enter the port. Glory Oil Filling Station sits at one end of that street, characterized by a nearly ceaseless traffic jam of trucks. I arrive at the filling station in the morning and am promptly invited to sit with Frank, a truck driver in his early twenties. He has arrived hours earlier, responding to a call from the control agent he works with saying there would be a load for him to pick up. He has come from his home in northern Accra, about an hour's commute. His container could be ready at any point between now and the next few days, but the expectation for him to enter the port within a small appointment window and confirm the pickup quickly with his boss means that he needs to stay near the truck. Regardless of when the call arrives, Frank will not be compensated for his time spent waiting, and will be paid only for completing the job.

Frank and I have been sitting on a wooden bench under the shade of the convenience store's awning. His yellow truck is to our right, parked on the station's grass and facing the street. From this position we can see about a dozen other parked trucks and many of their drivers chatting in small groups around the perimeter of the lot. Frank is certain that the others are napping inside their vehicles. Without a smartphone, Frank tells me, these hours and days of waiting are just that: waiting. Over and over, he uses the word "nothing," with a tone far more neutral than frustrated or disheartened, to describe what he does here.

Even with all the waiting, Frank says his work "isn't bad."[13] In his book *On Waiting,* Harold Schweizer describes time as the world's key "organizing principle" from the twentieth century onward.[14] He asserts that for the individual, waiting is an unpleasurable experience with a lost opportunity cost: "What really matters is the cost of one's waiting experience, not just in money but in frustration, anger, and other stresses."[15] Attempting to reconcile Schweizer's understanding of waiting with Frank's produces new tensions.

It's not, of course, as if Frank is unconcerned with or oblivious to the inconvenience of waiting. He tells me that he prefers picking up loads at Terminal Three because, despite the system's privacy-invading security measures, he knows that when he does finally enter, he will be in and out within thirty minutes.

On the other end of Meridian Road lies Community 5000, an informal neighborhood encompassing self-built homes and the skeleton of a multistory concrete building on a dirt lot. I am visiting Paul, a logistics employee whose small company is suffering from lack of traffic in Tema Harbor's older terminals. Paul tells me that the inhabitants of Community 5000 all come from the same Muslim tribe many hours away in the north. The waiting experience of Community 5000's truckers spans weeks. Truckers arrive from the north anticipating a job, and until that job materializes, they stay. Whether here in Tema or on the road, drivers and their mates

Drivers with their trucks, Community 5000, 2019
© Photo: Isabella Baranyk

The bed in Masud's truck, 2019
© Photo: Isabella Baranyk

sleep on the thinly-padded beds in their trucks. Masud, who's been driving for nine years, mentions his back pain and the Truckers Union's refusal to contribute to his medication costs as he shows me the inside of his truck.

Masud focuses our conversation on the ways in which he and his colleagues struggle as they wait. Here on the dirt lot, heavy rain can flood the place for days. The trucks sink into the mud, and mosquitoes multiply. Our talk of waiting is steeped with a sense of economic decline and hardship. Masud explains that the new terminal, with its expensive technology and high-profile contractors, promised work, but its blazing success hasn't translated to helping the drivers. While time continues to speed up inside the port, its slowness for the truckers carries with it time spent far away from family, uncomfortable living conditions with negative health effects, lack of pay, and economic stagnation. Here, yet another type of time has spurred an economy. Community 5000's women cook their home tribe's cuisine to sell to the truckers next door, offering a taste of home at an affordable price.

Like Frank, Masud is not making any money, and he's far away from his family, waiting for a job that may never come. Unlike Frank, Masud expresses to me the disagreeable conditions of his waiting period. The understanding of time as a value commodity under capitalism is something that must be learned.[16] Laborers receive the marketing messages of the new port's success, the jobs it has created, and the prosperity it brings to the nation, but they don't feel it themselves. They are asked to buy into the same moralizing understandings of work and development by which the port operates—the laws that speed it up—but until they enter the port to be processed alongside containers, the same temporal logics do not apply to them. The experience of time here is a temporal paradox caused by capitalist excess, in which laborers are expected to uphold the belief in standardized, universal, ever-quickening time for profit. They simultaneously live in a temporal zone where complacency, with entire stretches of life lived in waiting, is necessary for survival. This is what it means to *inhabit* spacetime plurality, to be part of an inconsistent modulation between worship of the clock's incessant beat and faith that one day the dream it promises will be realized.

[1] "Operational Launching of MPS Terminal 3: Docking of the First Commercial Vessel," Meridian Port Services, accessed July 3, 2019, https://dailyguidenetwork.com/operational-launching-of-mps-terminal-3-docking-of-the-first-commercial-vessel.

[2] Keller Easterling, *Extrastatecraft: The Power of Infrastructure Space* (New York: Verso, 2016).

[3] John Milne, "Civil Time," *The Geographical Journal* 13, no. 2 (1899).

[4] Vanessa Ogle, *The Global Transformation of Time: 1870–1950* (Cambridge, MA: Harvard University Press, 2015), 8.

[5] Ibid, 93–94.

[6] E. C. Kirchherr, "Tema 1951–1962: The Evolution of a Planned City in West Africa," *Urban Studies* 5, no. 2 (1968): 208.

[7] Brenda Chalfin, "Recasting maritime governance in Ghana: The Neo-Developmental State and the Port of Tema," *The Journal of Modern African Studies* (2010): 576.

[8] David Hilling, "Tema—The Geography of a New Port," *Geography* 51, no. 2 (1966): 120.

[9] Chalfin (see note 7), 578.

[10] Ibid.

[11] Ibid, 583.

[12] "Bolloré Ports," accessed September 3, 2019, https://www.bollore-ports.com/en.html.

[13] Frank. Waiting at Glory Oil, November 8, 2019.

[14] Harold Schweizer, *On Waiting* (London: Routledge, 2008), 4.

[15] Ibid.

[16] E. P. Thompson, "Time, Work-Discipline, and Industrial Capitalism," *Past & Present* 38 (1967): 86.

Slow Violence in Palestine
By Saad Amira

Our story begins in a small village at the heart of Palestine, Iskaka of Salfit district. Like any other Palestinian place, it has been under different modes of Zionist colonial domination. In the last fifteen years, an additional layer of rule crystalized when a newcomer joined the ranks and file of the Israeli state. This time it was an animal—a wild boar—introduced to the West Bank by the Israeli state. Within the space of a few years this animal has bred, its ever-growing presence an epidemic, an animalized technology, which has incrementally afflicted the everyday subsistence of Palestinian families and communities. Protecting agricultural produce from wild boars has proved impossible, especially considering Israeli restrictions and the minimal support from the Palestinian Authority. As a result, a long tradition of seasonal agriculture, especially in summer, has been nearly destroyed, and with it, a particular Palestinian lifestyle. The destruction of this lifeline has not affected solely village modes of production. It has entailed a set of overlapping regimes of violence that work in tandem, interweaving Israeli forms of colonial rule with the Palestinian Authority's politics of corruption, lethargy, and de-developmental strategies. In this essay, I use Rob Nixon's[1] notion of slow violence to gauge the long-term development of settler colonialism through the terrain of political ecology. Here, following William Cronon,[2] I provide a real-time exploration of the historical and environmental processes which shape this particular settler colonial project and its lived realities.

Through the entry and spread of wild boars, village life in Salfit district has been transformed in profound and complex ways—a novel and challenging political-ecological reality. In the village of Deir Istiya, a woman narrated to me how she sold her dowry—gold accessories worth around 3,000 US dollars—to buy a small plot of land in her village. She made this decision in order to uplift her family, which relied solely on her husband's daily labor for survival. On that land she planted olive trees. However, in the olive season, she was attacked by a wild boar, nearly sustaining a fatal injury. Traumatized by this experience, she felt terrorized and disempowered, unable to continue farming her land. This attack led to her abandoning the plot, which at the time we spoke had transformed back into wilderness. In an adjacent village, another woman lamented the incremental confinement to their homes that she and her neighbors face due to fear of being attacked by a boar. This creeping and growing reality has curtailed women's mobility, ending a plethora of seasonal and leisure activities which connected them to neighboring villages, as well as to Palestinian guerrilla fighters, once active in these spaces.

Wild boars thrive, feeding on agricultural plots and on the waste from settlements. A community religious figure in another village spoke to me about his relative, a young pregnant woman, who had experienced a novel, mushrooming skin disease, a condition never heard of before in this area, which jeopardized her health and her pregnancy. Its source in his community was the running sewage of Slafit district and the adjacent Ariel settlement—areas of Israeli settlement—which infiltrate the village space. Waste flowing from these settlements has created a lake of sewage in his village. This sewage and its toxic effects have profoundly impacted Palestinian village people's leisure, health, and well-being. This lake pours into a valley, now named locally the valley of sewage. It is in this confluence of conditions in which wild boars, leishmania disease, and other airborne diseases spread.

Wild boars feed on the waste of encroaching Israeli settlements. They thrive, I argue, in the failed developmental modes of the Palestinian Authority. While Israeli experts, soldiers, and petty Palestinian bureaucrats supposedly grapple with strategic political dimensions of occupation in the West Bank, wild boars are an overlooked weapon that enables long-term rule. The significance of the wild boar's violent presence in the micro-level social practices that sustain everyday life for Palestinian villagers is not engaged on the political level. It is this silence on wild boars, their invisibility in political debate, that makes this slow encroaching epidemic a symptom of a larger settler colonial reality. Wild boars and the sewage and waste on which they feed and thrive are an exceptional political force, one that permeates through the body and the landscape, effecting change on the ground. Against this backdrop, common debates on "the proletarianization of Palestinian villagers" become devoid of meaning. Most importantly, wild boars feed on, and in turn destroy, memories, landscapes, and leisure—the intimate spaces of Palestinian village life. The striking political silence on their growing destructive presence is the context in which they are agents and symptoms of an ever-encroaching settler colonialism, not bounded by the fine-tuned models of architects, statesmen, and politicians.

The project to make such forms of slow violence in Palestine visible entails work at the village level. Here I have employed research methodologies that offer nuanced focus and entry points to engage the dynamic and multiple forms of power and resistance that shape and constrain lives and livelihoods in Iskaka and in neighboring villages in Salfit district in the heart of the West Bank. My ethnographic research in this area built on conducting semistructured interviews and observing and participating in daily life from 2017 to the present. This approach and rootedness in the village and in this region has enabled me to devise interdisciplinary theoretical and methodological frameworks, rooted in and driven by the discourse and bodily mobility of villagers themselves. As the research developed, some of my frameworks were challenged or lost value, while others I could develop further, expanding them in the context and rhythms of forms of mobility and their constraints that shape daily life in the village. This approach has allowed me to track village mobility as the thread that connects all the symptoms, processes, power structures, infrastructure, and resistance in and around Iskaka. It is these forms of mobility and their loss that are the face of its antithesis, the "slow violence" at the heart of the asymmetric settler colonial project in Palestine.

Instead of seeking generic theories of mobility, if such exist, in this project I ground my understanding of mobility in its temporal and spatial practices in Iskaka. In doing so, I contribute to illuminating the workings of settler colonialism. Through political ecology, I juxtapose and inter-relate the daily rupturing of Palestinian indigenous livelihoods and lifestyles with the development of the settler colonial project. It is in this space that (im)mobility becomes a key scale at which invasion as structure—and not an event—is experienced, as suggested by Wolfe.[3] In short, the tactics, strategies, and forms of resistance that are evident in daily village practices and experiences make visible and demonstrate the destruction of mobility, the losses of production, the shifting of leisure, and the remaking of intimacy. In these spaces, the invasive structure of settler colonialism can be illuminated in Iskaka, tracked in different forms of bodily mobility and immobility.

Narrated through the stories of villagers, I map out the spatial and temporal power of settler colonial architecture, the ways it produces and constrains space, and its shaping of the infrastructure of daily experience. Placing their narratives at the heart of this analysis situates Palestinian villagers as agents of knowledge, and as agents in this power production, evident in the ways in which they interact with, resist, and acquiesce to settler colonial processes. This is a critical political and epistemological step that builds on Palestinian voices, experiences, and bodily negotiations. Through this approach, research can build on Palestinian village views and practices, these complex subjectivities that are essential to contest settler colonialism now and in the future. By centering research in this way, we avoid the risk of reducing Palestinian bodies to numbers, or to a geographic statistical figure, easily managed and written over. In this way, the spirit of settler colonialism as a linear historical progression is challenged. While the settler, as a foreign body, can engender certain political and architectural spaces, the narration of indigenous movement and immobility as social space

A footpath leading out of Iskaka Village, 2019
© Photo: Saad Amira

complicates this political narrative. It renders settler colonial spaces as bumpy, uncertain, and changing, and most importantly, as reversible. By building this analysis through engaging the social life of the village, I place at its center an indigenous Palestinian political project to destabilize the political project of settler colonialism.

Settler colonialism reads Iskaka's pristine village space in powerful ways, naming its "architectural forms," labeling it a "ghetto" or a "slum," a poverty-stricken Palestinian or Arab neighborhood adjacent to the Ariel settlement city. Yet, these inscriptions and acts, although powerful and controlling, do not eliminate or erase daily Palestinian

A view of Iskaka Village, West Bank, 2019 © Photo: Saad Amira

village life and its mindscapes. Instead, through this work, I explore the agency Palestinian villagers carve out in the face of slow violence. Although the settler colonial project and its volatile modes of security dominate Palestinian spaces literally and politically, Palestinian communities persist; they are present. In resisting, villagers shift their forms of mobility, producing embodied social spaces, surviving, albeit in asymmetric ways. These practices are critical. They challenge and disrupt readings of settler colonialism that depart from an architectural and infrastructural lens centered on settler power. Weizman's[4] (and others') approach to forensic architecture too easily privileges the power of settler colonialism, imbuing with stability and permanence acts of the Israeli state. Lost in this mix are the everyday ways in which Palestinian villagers nonetheless move and live. Palestinian village life always exceeds a collection of buildings of materials, whose movement can be "forcibly arranged" in the way a military commander "constructs" and dreams about the future. Let the military commander dream. Let us extricate social phenomenon from political projects of genocide which begin when the colonized internalize the infallibility of the colonizer.

[1] Rob Nixon, *Slow Violence and the Environmentalism of the Poor* (Cambridge, MA: Harvard University Press, 2011).
[2] William Cronon, *Changes in the Land: Indians, Colonists, and the Ecology of New England* (New York: Hill and Wang, 1983).
[3] Patrick Wolfe, "Settler Colonialism and the Elimination of the Native," *US: Journal of Genocide Research* 8, no. 4 (2006).
[4] Eyal Weizman, *The Geography of Occupation* (Barcelona: Center for Contemporary Studies, 2004).

Worlding Design
By Laura Nkula-Wenz

In reality, the tarmac just stops, midair, in a straight-cut edge. But in this montage, two bright yellow beams effortlessly connect to the gray concrete, tracing a wide, elegant curve before twisting and turning to form the number 2014. Cape Town's "unfinished highway" has towered over the city's CBD for more than four decades. Proposed in the 1960s, during the heyday of apartheid's nefarious modernist planning agenda, it was part of a ring-road concept that was to connect the newly reclaimed Foreshore with the seaside resorts along the Atlantic Seaboard. However, not all the freeways were completed, as funding ran out and construction stopped in 1977. Since then, Cape Town's "road to nowhere" has loomed large as an unintentional monument for the city's persistent sociospatial disconnects—a stark reminder of just how deeply racism and inequality remain etched onto the skin of the city. And yet, few things better embody generative potentialities and aspiration than unfinished infrastructure. Indeed, one would have been hard-pressed to find a more fitting image than the unfinished flyover to visualize Cape Town's emotive bid to become the World Design Capital in 2014[1] (WDC 2014) with the motto "Separated by apartheid, reconnected by design."

The city's WDC 2014 bid logo, its number filling the gap in the unfinished highway, Cape Town, 2013 © Photo: Laura Nkula

Tracing those *politics of becoming*, I have been interested in how globally popular urban development imperatives—to be smart, creative, sustainable, and resilient—have been grounded, refracted, and merged with local governmentalities to drive the reincarnation of Cape Town as the first African design city. After all, "superlatives and 'firsts' are rhetorical devices that prepare the reader for a theoretical move—the assertion that the city is a paradigm. Not just unique or exemplary, the city being discussed contains and portends the future."[2] In turn, the World Design Capital bid provided Cape Town with a unique platform to not only formulate its own aspirational politics but to also assume an authoritative voice for "African design" as a whole. This is intriguing because, from the bitter almond hedges planted by Jan van Riebeek to keep Indigenous Khoisan herders out of the recently occupied Cape Colony to frequent off-the-cuff remarks by locals and tourists alike about how Cape Town is Africa's most European city, Cape Town has always been at odds with its location. In turn, questions about how Africa is engaged, conceived, and received in the Cape and how the city positions itself on the continent are vigorously debated over "with the regularity and ferocity of the south-easterly winds."[3] So the WDC accolade provided a prime opportunity to revisit the forever contentious issue of how Cape Town relates to itself as an African city, not just a city *in* Africa. And in doing so it could simultaneously present itself as an emerging model city, not just for the continent but for the world at large.

Cape Town's "road to nowhere," 2021 © Photo: Simbi Nkula

Unequivocally, accolades like the World Design Capital, the European Capital of Culture, or the UNESCO Creative City status offer cities a prolific platform to market themselves—often as much to the outside world as to their own resident populations. This confluence of extrospective branding and introspective politics of persuasion is often a delicate balancing act for local governance networks involved in bringing these projects to life. In assuming the title of Africa's first WDC, the city not only had to persuade the world of its design acumen, it also had to convince its residents of why they should care about design in the first place. Thankfully, it lies in the nature of "world-conjuring projects"[4] like the WDC to offer ample opportunity for telling a good (hi)story.

In the case of Cape Town, this meant reframing South Africa's history of settler colonialism and state-sanctioned racism as "an era of *designed inequality and control.*"[5] In its bid book, the city also sought to show how certain design practices were enlisted to support the nefarious workings of the apartheid state: "*Graphic design* was used to separate people by embedding apartheid legislation into visual representations across the City [...]. Education systems were *designed* around racial policies based on keeping black people inferior [...]. The media was tightly controlled, with blatant propaganda on television and film *designed* to sow division and instil fear [and] *industrial design* was largely geared towards creating a self-sustaining 'state' as well as to protecting the country against the threat of an uprising."[6] In this reading, forced removals and racialized segregation are cast as bad designs. And in turn, the compelling argument continued, it was about time to rehabilitate design from its role as a handmaiden of apartheid and put it (back) into the service of development for all. Through this undeniably emotive narrative, the bid proponents were able to push the envelope of the WDC way beyond that of a mundane city promotion project. Instead, cast as a "vehicle for reconstruction,"[7] the award is elevated to nothing less than a collective moral imperative for the city to *design* its way out of apartheid's sociomaterial legacy, and through this incredible feat become a model for other cities to follow.

From a governance perspective, the paradox of creativity is that it is meant to be simultaneously mobilized and controlled, set free and reined in. This paradox also lay at the heart of Cape Town's design city ambitions. Fortunately, though, while the notion of creativity is neither necessarily conscious nor rational, making it somewhat ungovernable, these are essential preconditions for design in its quest for linking the desirable with the possible. Like art, design offers aesthetic enchantment while, like science and technology, it is simultaneously heralded as "the pre-eminent solution to all the complex and difficult conundrums of modern life."[8] In other words, what makes design so compelling is, firstly, the proposition that it can make beauty and utility mutually attainable, and secondly, that it is a process imbued with notions of scientific rigor and objectivity. With regard to Cape Town's WDC bid, the extensive references to design as a "methodology," a "tool," and a way of "thinking" are important signifiers for this technocratic understanding of design as both purposeful and developmental. By the same token, by putting itself into the service of development, design is able to shrug off its air of exclusivity, (white) hipsterism, and commodity fetishism. As Cape Town's WDC ambitions show, this normative conjunction of design as development and development by design offers ample possibility for mobilizing a range of discursive politics and material urban practices.

In 2014 South Africa not only celebrated the twenty-year anniversary of its first free democratic elections, but Cape Town also assumed its year-long place in the global spotlight as the continent's first World Design Capital. Was this the great connector, the game-changer that Capetonians, inhabitants of one of the world's most unequal cities, so desperately longed for? For a variety of reasons—ranging from budget constraints and political infighting to the fact that most projects did not manage to go beyond symbolic redesigns and thus lacked real redistributive outcomes—the short answer is no. Still, Cape Town's aspirational politics have not remained without consequence, and the promises of *development by design* continue to percolate in the minds of city officials who have to deal with a city in perpetual crisis. In the past five years alone, Cape Town has not only been the country's worst hotspot for the global Covid-19 pandemic; in 2017 it also made international headlines as the first major city in the world to be running out of water, pushed to the brink by the worst drought in a century. A real sense of urgency thus undergirds the statements of municipal officials, who seek to leverage design for building a more resilient city.

Awards like the World Design Capital afford emerging cities like Cape Town the opportunity to draw new connections between the global and the local. These *worlding* practices are, however, no longer premised on emulating elusive Western forms of urbanism but are rather shaped by the ways in which cities everywhere experiment with home-grown ideas, political systems, and aesthetic forms that continuously cast their city out into the world. In other words, this incessant inter-scalar recomposing is taking place in the vast space between

Hostile urban design intervention below the unfinished highway, Cape Town, 2021
© Photo: Simbi Nkula

idiosyncratic local compromises and global narratives of urban transformation. Research seeking to understand contemporary city-making, particularly in cities of the so-called Global South, thus needs to turn to "the mix of speculative fiction and speculative fact in worlding exercises as practitioners aim to build something they believe is for the better."[9] Cape Town's stint as the first African WDC certainly operated as a field of both speculation and translation, one that sought to make abstract, modernist ideas of design locally intelligible by re-articulating them through a lens of development and reconnection, if not necessarily restitution. Furthermore, bidding for the award offered Cape Town the opportunity to think about its location, however briefly, and promote itself as a model city in its own right.

And the unfinished highway? There are probably few other pieces of infrastructure that embody the city's complex aspirational politics—often violent, at times endearing—better than this road to nowhere. After "Future Foreshore," one of this road recognized World Design Capital projects, had tabled an initial round of ideas for the neutered road infrastructure through a student design competition, talk of any potential redevelopment slowly subsided as other pressing issues took precedence. In the meantime, makeshift shelters whose tarps used to hug the pylons in the southeasterly gusts have been replaced by a tightly-knit carpet of granite shards, which protect the city's revamped BRT bus depot and aggressively reject soft, human bodies with their hostile design. Bar a few tents clinging on in the margins, the majority of the displaced have now moved to the top of the flyover, where they, on occasion, vie for space with American, German, or French film crews, for whom it presents the ideal setting for shooting anything from fashion spreads to explosive car chases, presenting yet another way in which Cape Town is cast out into the world.

[1] Awarded biennially by the International Design Association (formerly known as ICSID), the World Design Capital is a city promotion project that seeks to honor accomplishments made by cities in the field of design.

[2] Robert A. Beauregard, "City of Superlatives," *City and Community* 2, no. 3 (2003): 183–199, https://doi.org/10.1111/1540-6040.00049.

[3] Grace Musila and Meg Samuelson, "Viewing the Continent from Its Tip," accessed July 26, 2021, https://www.iol.co.za/capeargus/viewing-the-continent-from-its-tip-1096948.

[4] Aihwa Ong, "Introduction Worlding Cities, or the Art of Being Global," in Ananya Roy and Aihwa Ong (eds.), *Worlding Cities: Asian Experiments and the Art of Being Global: Studies in Urban and Social Change* (Malden, MA: Wiley-Blackwell, 2011), 1–26.

[5] City of Cape Town, *Live Design. Transform Life: World Design Capital 2014 – a Bid by the City of Cape Town,* with the assistance of Cape Town Partnership and Creative Cape Town (Cape Town: 2011).

[6] Ibid. (emphasis added).

[7] Ibid.

[8] Juris Milestone, "Design as Power: Paul Virilio and the Governmentality of Design Expertise," *Culture, Theory and Critique* 48, no. 2 (2007): 175–198, https://doi.org/10.1080/14735780701723264.

[9] Ong (see note 4).

The Urban beyond North and South

Learning across Geographies

by Laura Nkula-Wenz and Kenny Cupers

How can we learn about cities across geographies? In a world shaped by radically unequal patterns of mobility, access, and privilege, this is one of the central questions for contemporary urbanists.

Our historical conjuncture compels us to unsettle the inherited categories by which the infinite multiplicity of urban life is reduced to conventional interpretations, and to develop relational understandings of urbanism in a global condition of deepening crises. To move in and beyond such epistemic divides as the "Global South" or the "Global North," or "Africa" and "Europe," we need not only to critically interrogate these inherited frameworks but also to critically examine and remake our research practices. But how can we concretely develop new research practices in an urban world that is at the same time so digitally interconnected and materially interdependent, while still being shaped by radically incommensurate ways of being? How do we learn not just about cities "elsewhere," but about the many "elsewheres" that shape urban life in an increasingly unequal world?

In response to these questions, our work draws from two different but related strands of work—Southern urbanism and postcolonial approaches to the city and the built environment. Over the past decade, a Southern turn has profoundly reshaped debates in urban studies and, more broadly, the social sciences. As the world has now been declared predominantly "urbanized," with the highest growth taking place in expansive metropolitan agglomerations such as Shanghai, Mumbai, Nairobi, and São Paulo, scholars have called for new ways of understanding the urban through these cities. Rooted in North Atlantic experiences, conventional approaches have long tended to confine city life in the Southern Hemisphere to a narrow focus on a perceived lack of development, modernization, or other divergences from seemingly universal but in fact parochially Western ideals and standards. Starting from everyday urban experiences in cities of the Global South as the basis for rewiring urban studies, Southern approaches challenge this way of knowing and representing the city. They share a commitment to addressing the social, material, and epistemic inequalities shaping everyday life in Southern cities. While key proponents of this debate cover a wide geographical and disciplinary range, their arguments coalesce around a few key markers. The first is a commitment to carefully crafted, context-sensitive, and engaged forms of urban scholarship, immersed in the specific challenges and inspirations of Southern cities. The second is a call for creative ways to build comparisons across cities to expand our knowledge base, and to create bodies of work that embrace the complexities of urbanism in ordinary, distinctive, and regional forms.[1,2,3] This Southern turn invites us to revisit and revise our vocabularies and theories. This means both expanding the meaning of existing words, and creating new concepts rooted in Southern urban governmentalities.[4,5]

A second approach on which our pedagogy builds is found in the need to account for epistemic asymmetries, imperial legacies, and colonial relations of power that shape contemporary urban life. To think cities from elsewhere does not mean just comparing cities, but also understanding the differential entanglements that shape them in material and immaterial ways. Key to this aim has been scholarship in the historical social sciences and the urban humanities that displaces the Enlightenment or the Industrial Revolution from the heart of modernity. The Latin American-based collective "coloniality/modernity" offers a powerful critique of such Eurocentric narratives.[6] Instead, it grounds global modernity in the Atlantic system of colonization and plantation slavery that gave rise to modern Europe and forms the bedrock of today's racialized social order. Achille Mbembe's conceptualization of the postcolony has also opened up new ways for us to think about the intimate geopolitics that shape contemporary cities. Such approaches help us understand how global perspectives themselves are grounded in colonial ways of knowing and mapping the world, and take on a planetary perspective that pushes back against the tendency of urban theorists to reduce the impact of colonialism to the territory of "former colonies." In our attempt to explore the ramifications of capitalism without reproducing its expansionist and extractive impulses in our own work, we rely on theoretical work that helps us understand the production of difference—subjective, racialized, and geographic—as constitutive of capitalism.[7,8,9] Such perspectives contribute to rewiring urban studies by studying built and lived environments beyond the city as methodological container for individual or comparative study. This foregrounds architecture, infrastructure, and landscape not as "authored" artifacts, but as the media through which modes of production, extraction, and dispossession are organized and through which ways of life are contested and negotiated across localities. It is a politically and materially attuned perspective of the long, heterogeneous, and still-marginalized histories of anti-colonial struggle and thought in the city that allows us to explore the contemporary politics of urban development in Southern cities from the perspective of these traditions.

Our pedagogy has developed not only from these different intellectual journeys, but also from two concrete locations: Basel and Cape Town. Working together from and across these locations has confronted us in intimate, jarring, and enriching ways with our different layers of privilege that continue to be reshaped by asymmetries of power.

Being located at the University of Cape Town means living and researching in a city with some of the highest levels of social and spatial inequality and segregation in the world. It also means sitting amidst one of the epicenters of the global struggle for decolonizing higher education. In 2015 student protests erupted, demanding the removal of a statue depicting the arch-colonialist Cecil John Rhodes, which was prominently placed on the main steps of UCT's Upper Campus overlooking the city. A student-led social movement initially formed around the hashtag #RhodesMustFall, spreading to other campuses internationally. In South Africa the movement quickly broadened its scope to also tackle legacies of colonialism, institutional racism, the situation of outsourced service workers on campus, and—particularly after the statue was successfully removed—the ongoing exclusion of Black students through the prohibitively high fees charged for accessing higher education. These interlinked dynamics continue to inform our pedagogy, built around South African contemporary debates, rooted in the ways the past legacies of slavery, colonialism, and apartheid persist in the city, and the innovative forms of mobilization, practice, and intervention that engage and attempt to remake these realities. Our studio work is built on collaboration with nongovernmental and community-based organizations, important partnerships for knowledge coproduction which situate our research in housing and livelihood struggles across the city. Through these partnerships we immerse our students in diverse forms of participatory research: in public debates, in practices driven by the state and by citizens, and in critical forms of mobilization that reshape our thinking and enroll it in struggles for decolonization, racial justice, and transformation.

Questions of decolonization have also been at the center of our Basel-based studio teaching, starting from an interest in the intellectual, urban, and infrastructural legacies of African liberation movements and their geopolitical and political-economic effects. When ports, highways, dams, or railways figure in Africa-focused research, they tend to appear as merely technical problems of development: either they are described in terms of lack, or they are treated as almost magical solutions that reduce poverty and resolve conflict. Focusing primarily on Accra, the studio proposed a different way of understanding the relationship between material infrastructure and everyday urban realities, by taking account of its historical complexity, lived experience, and the multivalent dreams and struggles it generates. Exploring the stakes of these large-scale visions of development, which infrastructure continues to carry across the continent and beyond, our pedagogy asked how infrastructural legacies shape the future of African urbanism.

Engaging with urban practitioners, designers, and researchers in Accra in collaboration with the University of Ghana's Institute of African Studies, the studio centered on overcoming normative assumptions that undergird much urban research on cities of the Global South. It guided students to explore how colonial frameworks as well as historical and ongoing anticolonial and liberation struggles shape African urban and rural transformation. These afterlives inhabit Africa's current infrastructure boom, prompting us to ask what we can learn about this ongoing urban change from studying the continent's intellectual and material inheritances. Understanding these struggles for sovereignty and equality, as well as their contradictory outcomes, helps us to account for the continued challenges of development and neocolonialism today.

At the same time, the studio also brought up crucial ethical and political questions about doing research on urban Africa from our removed and privileged position in Basel. As the Ghanaian writer and filmmaker Kodwo Eshun, inspired by C. L. R James's study of the Ghanaian struggle for decolonization, put it, we needed to address the fact that "a study of revolution that does not set in motion a process of revolutionary questioning of its researcher is not worth undertaking." Studying decolonization requires a deeper questioning of our own premises and positionality—so that ultimately, the researcher becomes the student who is taught by their research. Students took this forward by asking how studio-based urban research could participate in breaking down the epistemic and political-economic divides that shape urban research across geographies.

In June 2020, in response to the global Black Lives Matter movement during the Covid-19 pandemic, Critical Urbanisms students and Basel-based faculty worked together on strengthening our commitments to racial justice. The students subsequently spearheaded the process of transforming our pedagogy and our institutional ways of working within the university. They established the Racial Justice Student Collective, which is now working beyond the university to address not only structural racism in Swiss higher education, but also police violence, racial profiling, and institutional racism more broadly. By linking up with activist organizations across Switzerland and beyond, they have developed new grounds for local engagements that extend well beyond the classroom. This movement for institutional change also prompted further transformation of our pedagogy and strengthened our research focus on the coloniality of infrastructure. Infrastructure offers a lens for dissecting global inequality and the production of urban privilege and marginality. From our Basel-based location, this focus will inform our research-led pedagogy over the following years to center on Swiss coloniality, which ranges from the environmental and urban impact of Swiss-based corporations abroad to the violent logic and racial structures of its migration management.

Basel and Cape Town continue to prompt different ways of thinking about the legacies of empire, structural racism, claims to housing and urban rights, and the politics of public space—questions that are central to critical urbanism today. In the process of discovering, accounting for, and interpreting these differences in our pedagogy across Basel and Cape Town, we have come to see these cities not as radically different or incomparable, but rather as interconnected. Sharing experience is what offered us an opportunity to learn from one another—how we are formed not just in disciplinary terms but also by our locations and the communities to which we are accountable. Ultimately, our pedagogical journey is one of decompartmentalizing the "South"— to see it not as a location, but as a relationship of space, power, and knowledge, as Ananya Roy has suggested.

In this process of developing a pedagogy across geographies and building a sustained partnership across two institutions rooted in such radically different everyday contexts, an ethos has emerged along three axes. The first is that to rewire urban studies from the ground up—developing a master pedagogy without a predetermined canon or professional boundary such as from planning or architecture—*long-term collaboration* is essential. This means unsettling some of the inherited conventions, values, and approaches of our own disciplines. It also meant doing the harder work of questioning the assumptions that underlie our own values and convictions about what good work is—in both academic and ethical senses. Furthermore, it means *accounting for the context* in which knowledge is produced and its effects on the world—not as easy relativism, but rather as a way of accounting for the world-making effects of knowledge production. And finally, it means *learning to pivot*, to think from the border of other fields, and to translate from one context or intellectual framework to another.

Our cross-continental pedagogy resulting from this process reflects this ethos. We provide our students with the opportunity to engage with pertinent urban issues—questions of infrastructure and housing provision, food insecurity, or informal economies—not merely as intellectual problems that can be understood from a removed intellectual angle. Rather, students take on these topics as real-life challenges that shape how different people can or cannot inhabit the city and exercise their rights. This means continuing to address the layers of privilege carried by both faculty and students, with which we must continuously contend and which we must unpick to realize our commitment to ethical knowledge production. Finally, and in close connection to the previous two points, our pedagogy aims to foster an honest appreciation for different sets of knowledge, gathered through careful and respectful listening, and reflected on in a commitment to turn easy assumptions into difficult questions.

The contributions to this section have taken our pedagogical principles of moving forward beyond North/South divides in many ways, either through their choice of theoretical frameworks, research sites, and methods, or through their attention to the creation of new vocabularies. Rosca van Rooyen writes about the work it takes to ground Basel students in Cape Town. Aline Suter addresses the connections of Accra and Europe through the circulation of e-waste. Ernest Sewordor reflects on the project of teaching and learning between Basel and Accra. And the Racial Justice Student Collective reports on its activist work within and beyond the university. The following essays are derived from longer-term research. Lea Nienhoff engages experiences of "Madjermans," Mozambican guest workers, and the remnants of their presence in the former GDR. By engaging critically with the term "Transfronteridad," Evan Natasha Escamilla explores the lives of commuters across the Mexico-US borderlands. Myriam Perret and Maren Larsen question the role of global borders in the contemporary urbanization of Singapore. Giulia Scotto explores the Motel Agip of Dar es Salaam as an Italian product of corporate oil and its legacies. In "Worlding Goma," Maren Larsen challenges divisions of North/South, camp and city, opening up the city's elsewhere through her engagement with UN peacekeeping camps in north-eastern DRC.

Taken together, these pieces suggest some new directions toward developing a mode of urban inquiry that approaches cities from the perspective of situated geographies and their attendant intellectual debates, while also accounting for the multiple scales and interconnections that shape cities globally. They demonstrate that rethinking urbanism beyond North/South divides is not, therefore, simply a matter of shifting geographical perspective, but is rather about crafting a new politics of urban knowledge production.

---

[1] Ananya Roy, "The 21st-Century Metropolis: New Geographies of Theory," *Regional Studies* 43, no. 6 (2009).

[2] Jennifer Robinson, *Ordinary Cities: Between Modernity and Development*, Questioning Cities series (London: Routledge, 2006).

[3] Teresa P. R. Caldeira, "Peripheral Urbanization: Autoconstruction, Transversal Logics, and Politics in Cities of the Global South," *Environment and Planning D: Society and Space* 35, no. 1 (2017).

[4] Gautam Bhan, "Notes on a Southern Urban Practice," *Environment and Urbanization* 31, no. 2 (2019).

[5] Achille Mbembe and Sarah Nuttall, "Writing the World from an African Metropolis," *Public Culture* 16, no. 3 (2004).

[6] Walter D. Mignolo, *The Darker Side of Western Modernity: Global Futures, Decolonial Options*, Latin America Otherwise series (Durham, NC: Duke University Press, 2011).

[7] Gargi Bhattacharyya, *Rethinking Racial Capitalism: Questions of Reproduction and Survival* (London: Rowman & Littlefield, 2018).

[8] Anna Tsing, "Supply Chains and the Human Condition," *Rethinking Marxism* 21, no. 2 (2009).

[9] Denise Ferreira Da Silva, *Toward a Global Idea of Race*, Borderlines 27 (Minneapolis: University of Minnesota Press, 2007).

INTO OUR HOMES

Neighborhood visits have been an effective approach in creating access for students to understand the intricacies of Cape Town as a deeply divided city through the complex lived experiences of its residents, who frequently have to straddle these divides. In small groups of two or three, students are paired with a facilitator who takes them on a day-long visit into their respective neighborhood. The facilitators are themselves postgraduate students at the African Centre for Cities, and this "peer approach" helps ease the burden of exoticization and "othering" that such visits undeniably bear. Each facilitator is free to craft their own itinerary around their day-to-day experience of the city. In practice, this means that some take minibus taxis while others ride the train; some visit Somali-owned migrant businesses or stroll through a public park, while others are taken to private homes to hear all about a mother's community work and enjoy a typical South African "braai." This does not mean that hard social issues are swept under the rug; quite the contrary. Through this embodied and deeply interpersonal experience, everyday challenges such as inequality, gender-based violence, and gang-related crime become more immediate, more relatable. In addition, and speaking from my own experience of facilitating these visits to my neighborhood of Bellville South, these encounters allow people from my community to take an active role in how they want to be seen and heard, ensuring that they are being understood, respected, and acknowledged, and that their lives matter. These are the moments that make humanity beautiful, when you choose to learn from those completely different to you, who are often seen as too incompetent to teach you anything. These visits encourage students to respectfully listen and learn from those resiliently living daily in oppressive systems and places, ultimately making them more empathic and better scholars. **By Rosca van Rooyen**

Learning from local Rasta's "Sak Manne" about indigenous Khoi and San medicinal herbs and vegetables, Bellville Station, 2019
© Photo: Rosca van Rooyen

Lunch with Joy Warries (WOWMovement NPO) in Rosca's family home, Bellville South, 2020 © Photo: Rosca van Rooyen

Agbogbloshie market, Accra, 2018 © Photo: Aline Suter

TOXIC CONNECTIONS

Western media persistently portray Agbogbloshie, a large electronic waste site in the center of Accra, as a sign of a dystopian and dysfunctional Africa. While local residents suffer from the extreme pollution caused by burning e-waste on-site, this portrayal obfuscates how Agbogbloshie is shaped by a global recycling industry. Waste workers, mostly vulnerable rural migrants from northern Ghana, process electronic waste from all over the world in order to extract valuable raw materials. Today, over 80,000 people live in Agbogbloshie and its adjacent neighborhoods. Their livelihoods are threatened by shifting global e-waste policies (including the Basel Convention) as well as local land politics. Forced evictions and resettlements have been part of the history of Agbogbloshie and its adjacent neighborhoods since the colonial era. Moving beyond stigmatization, however, allows for a different Agbogbloshie to emerge. Waste, after all, might not be the correct term, as it refers to the end state of a product. Instead of a dump, Agbogbloshie is rather a site of urban mining. The city is a giant resource deposit, which can be scoured for unused and broken materials that are then transformed into something valuable and functional. A great range of different local and global actors are operating in Agbogbloshie's urban mining. "International materials" are brought to the country by middlemen, often part of the Ghanaian diaspora, while local collectors supply the workers on-site in Agbogbloshie with material from the area. Their work is governed by national and international NGOs and the chairman of the Scrap Yard Dealers Association. Altogether, their activities generate between 105 and 268 million US dollars annually and sustain the livelihood of at least 200,000 people nationwide. Agbogbloshie is both a microcosm and a global node of material circulation. Even though its workers continue to be stigmatized by local government and international media, they are in fact essential entrepreneurs of a thriving urban and international economy. **By Aline Suter**

Agbogbloshie market, Accra, 2018 © Photo: Aline Suter

Agbogbloshie market, Accra, 2018 © Map: Aline Suter

LEARNING BETWEEN BASEL AND ACCRA

Twice since 2018, our first-year master's students traveled to Accra as part of the "Highway Africa" research studio, together with PhD students and instructors. Building on the first, the second research trip started with a one-day symposium themed "Infrastructural Legacies and Future of the African City," organized in collaboration with the Institute of African Studies, University of Ghana, Legon. The symposium offered both faculty and graduate students from Basel and Accra enriching opportunities to exchange, understand, and reevaluate the historical dimensions of Accra while critically imagining its future. It brought together actors and thinkers from multiple backgrounds across the North/South divide and featured ongoing research from the West African sub-region, engaging questions of development, infrastructure, decolonization, and postcolonial state formation through the lens of the city. Our main focus was to understand how African decolonization and the historical transition to formal independence continued to shape contemporary urbanism, including market building, mega-infrastructure, and land reclamation projects in Accra and across West Africa. The symposium fundamentally shaped students' research experiences. For many of them, trained in Western academic institutions, this was their first time in an African city. The symposium, and the resultant further exchange with local researchers, pushed students to question their assumptions about African urbanism as being chaotic, unplanned, or without history. It shaped both their creative adaptation to fluid encounters and the challenges in the unfamiliar context in which they pursued their research. As such, the short fieldwork trip became a crucial step toward independent research. **By Ernest Sewordor**

Poster of a symposium in Accra, part of the Highway Africa research studio, 2019 © Giulia Scotto

ADDRESSING STRUCTURAL RACISM

The Racial Justice Student Collective is a group of Black people, indigenous people, people of color, and white allies, committed to addressing systemic racism within and outside Swiss universities, and to supporting racial justice organizations across Switzerland. Taking our inspiration from the need to decolonize the academy, we are guided by perspectives that insist on acknowledging and dismantling systemic racism embedded within all institutions, and deconstructing Western universities' role in the colonial projects whose violence continues to underpin systemic racism today. The RJSC is organized by and for students, and grew out of an anti-racism initiative in June 2020 within the Critical Urbanisms M.A. program at the University of Basel. Critical Urbanisms' faculty and students published this joint set of commitments to addressing racism, in particular anti-Black racism, within the *Fachbereich*.

Racial Justice Student Collective Action Days at the Rote Fabrik in Zurich, June 11–13, 2021
© Photo: Leandra Choffat and Naomi Samake

On June 11–13, 2021, the Racial Justice Student Collective held a first series of action days—online and in Zurich. The aim of this weekend was to meld theory and practice, connect activists and scholars, and mobilize new racial justice activists. While speakers have participated from various geographies—South Africa, India, Palestine, the US, Germany, and Switzerland—the primary focus was on the Swiss context. Through panel discussions on issues such as "A Decolonial, Antiracist Movement in Switzerland," "Learning to Unlearn: Structural and Institutional Racism in Swiss Education," "Decolonize the University: Mobilizing in, Around and Beyond the University," and "Creating Alternative Spaces of Care, Joy and Resistance," and workshops on topics like "Black Trans Lives Matter," "Acknowledging Racism in Switzerland," "Coping with White Academia," "Community Organizing," "Access to the University," and "Activating White Accomplices," the action days have centered around people who, despite everything, claim and create their own spaces. All our actions aim to activate important conversations and concrete actions toward justice.

By the Racial Justice Student Collective

Racial Justice Student Collective Action Days at the Rote Fabrik in Zurich, June 11–13, 2021
© Photo: Leandra Choffat and Naomi Samake

Logo for the Racial Justice Student Collective Action Days at the Rote Fabrik in Zurich, June 11–13, 2021. © Ana Santos
To learn more about the RJSC, the action days program, and to register, visit: https://rjsc.space.

Madjermans
By Lea Nienhoff

More than thirty years ago, in November 1989, the fall of the Berlin Wall marked the symbolic end of the Cold War. The "iron curtain," imprinted on the political world map since the end of World War II, was lifted—and maps had to be redrawn. The dissolution of the Communist bloc was perceived as a "spatial revolution"; streets, towns, and countries were renamed; the world's geographies were shifting. The Cold War world as a space, differentiated and closed, seemed to be replaced by an unbounded, open, and more global space.

Around 15,300 Mozambican contract workers celebrated the fall of the Wall on the screens and streets of their homes in Rüdersdorf, Suhl, Plauen, Dresden, Berlin, and other places all over East Germany. The subsequent reunification of the German states, however, initiated a process of transformation that excluded migrants. Racist violence had broken loose. The slogan "We are the people!" which was first chanted by GDR citizens who had the courage to demonstrate for democracy and freedom in an authoritarian state, transformed into an affirmation of an imagined Germanness, and was chanted in violent riots against asylum seekers and contract workers. By 1990 the "peaceful revolution" had not brought greater freedom for Mozambican workers in the GDR, but instead new anxieties and constraints. Most workers decided to return to Mozambique.[1]

When the Eastern Bloc disintegrated, it was not only hegemonic powers that collapsed, but also the close cooperation that the so-called brother countries had built up across the North-South divide. Those political alliances had shaped processes of decolonization and yet reinstated forms of exploitation. The agreement of temporary work migration from Mozambique to East Germany was settled in 1979. Though announced as an education program that would prepare a young workforce to realize Mozambican industrial development, only a small number of workers actually received the training they were expecting. The high-minded phrases of GDR state officials on international solidarity and their fight against neocolonialism was countered by the fact that Mozambicans' work was exploited in the mines and factories of East Germany.

Despite their rhetoric, socialist regimes built on longstanding colonial practices. The collective accommodation in company dormitories was strategically used to control Mozambican workers' activities, and one cannot fail to find similarities between East German company dormitories and South African labor compounds. The individual contract worker had no say in his or her allocation of a workplace. They could choose neither the location nor the profession or task they were assigned. When arriving at a new place, the workers were handed a company ID and a dormitory ID. At the same instant, their passports were handed over from Mozambican authorities to the company and locked in a safe until the end of the worker's contract. From that moment onward and for the four years that followed, the workers would "belong" to the company and therewith to the accommodation that was provided for them.

The history of migrant worker compounds and dormitories spans beyond colonialism, to socialist and postcolonial states, as well as to the present. Cities bear the inheritances of such spaces. By 1989, more than 90,000 workers from Cuba, Angola, China, and Vietnam, as well as Mozambique, lived in East German company dormitories. While most former company dormitories have been razed to the ground or left abandoned, the memories and lives of contract workers continue to be shaped by them. Here they fought for their autonomy and lived parts of their youth; here they created transnational networks and formulated dreams of development and demands for justice. Young migrants' perspectives on their new homes and East German society were shaped by socialist education and the struggle for independence in their home countries. They did not only inhabit the geographical and temporal space of the Eastern Bloc; they took part in its production. The stories of Mozambican workers' forms of appropriation and resistance in East German company dormitories and beyond belong to the urban history of the "East."[2]

Gathering of former contract workers in the "Park of the Madjerman"—the park that became the center of their protests, Maputo, Mozambique, early 2000s © Photo: Lázaro Magalhães A. Booova

In the back of factory premises, often beyond residential areas, accommodations catered room for groups of around thirty to 200 Mozambicans. Rooms were shared and assigned to workers without their say, providing a maximum of 5 m² for each person and bed. Men and women were strictly separated. Visitors were registered and had to leave the dormitory by 10:00 p.m. at the latest. Contract workers themselves had a night curfew; any exceptions had to be authorized.

East German supervisors, Mozambican group leaders, and company directors were instructed to regulate workers' activities and report noncompliance with the rules to higher authorities. These were the formal contours of the space in which Mozambican contract workers lived. The inhabitants, however, gave it their own definition of place. They transformed the space and expanded their room for maneuver by circumventing the rules and resisting control. They transformed the poor and degrading environment of the dormitories into a home—and sometimes even into a place of dignity, safety, and youthfulness.

Mozambican workers soon developed a sense of injustice that undergirded noncompliance to the rules. In an interview with David, he reports how workers felt about dormitory rules: "The dormitory rules were inhumane, because we were already grown-ups. When you say, 'You won't go out after 10:00 p.m.!' then I am military, not worker." In the periodic reports written by German dormitory leaders, many strategies of the workers to circumvent the night curfew and limit the possibilities of control are documented. Climbing through windows, "losing" one's company ID, or dismantling door locks were some of these strategies. When Mozambican workers realized how much East German companies were dependent on their workforce, they started confronting dormitory rules more openly. After the girlfriend of a contract worker had received a three-month dormitory ban, it was "detected" that the girlfriend did nonetheless reside in the dormitory. She was requested to leave the dormitory, to which her boyfriend responded that "it is his apartment and that the supervisors have nothing to say there."[3] The dormitory authorities did not intervene further.

Company dormitories "arrested" the workers in segregated spaces. The system of control formed around them was grounded in racialized politics that inhibited workers' independence and their integration into East German society. Banning the possibility of bringing someone home or of sleeping over elsewhere was an attempt to restrain contract workers' sexual activities and romantic relationships. However, through their achievements as workers and the sense of community they had created among one another, Mozambican workers managed to empower themselves and to confront authorities with the "inhumane" character of the dormitory rules. While migrant workers began to claim company dormitories as "their" place, they remained excluded from other spaces and were exposed to racial discrimination outside the dormitory—in the bars, streets, and companies of East Germany.

Mozambican contract workers saw their own lives as part of a general history of colonial exploitation. Their migration to East Germany was often motivated by aiming to continue the struggle against it through socialist education and work training. Those who became contract workers had experienced colonial rule in their childhood. In the so-called colonial state directed from Lisbon, African men were constantly pushed into its extractive machinery. Many fathers, grandfathers, and uncles of Mozambican contract workers had worked in the mines and sugar plantations of South Africa. But unlike their fathers, the postindependence generation of contract workers placed their migration not primarily in the context of an inevitable economic choice, but at the same time in the context of a young nation's hope for more equality and justice—of the socialist revolution spearheaded by Samora Machel.[4] When newly arrived Mozambicans were confronted with the living conditions of migrants in East Germany, they were disillusioned. One worker recounts his first thoughts: "These were the kinds of buildings in which they had put the mineworkers in South Africa. If someone had asked us that day who would like to return straight away, I would have gone back."[5]

Against the rhetoric of international solidarity and the GDR's paternalistic perspective on foreign workers, my research aimed to foreground the experiences and perspectives of Mozambican contract workers themselves. Their stories chart a transnational geography "from below" that is different to our common understanding of the Eastern Bloc and the GDR. Both no longer exist as a territorial space, but they have created "mental maps" that have remained. In the memories and lives of former contract workers in Mozambique, East Germany continues to exist. It is the place in which they learned a profession, and made friends with other workers from Poland, Cuba, or Angola, as well as with German colleagues; it is the place of their best soccer matches, and of their first love. At once, it is the space in which their work was exploited over many years.

The workers' living conditions were dehumanizing, but they managed to make themselves a home and find open niches of freedom amidst all that. Many of those who returned to Mozambique after the German reunification identify themselves today as "Madjermans"—"the Germans."[6] The network that contract workers had created in East

Workers sitting in front of their dormitory during the official visit of the Minister of Labour of Mozambique, Suhl-Heinrichs, Germany, August 22, 1981 © Photo: Helmut Spisla

Germany traveled to Mozambique and tightened through the struggle for outstanding wages and the difficult reintegration. Mozambican contract workers have been bereft of a large part of their wages earned in the GDR as well as of their retirement provision. Those who regularly meet in Jardim dos Madjermanes (Park of the Madjermans) in the center of Maputo continue to protest for compensation and the acknowledgement of their demands. They ask the government: "Who were we? State slaves or workers?" And Lázaro, a member of the group, further says: "Who am I? Where am I from? I am Madjerman. We are Germans in Mozambique and in Germany we are foreigners."[7]

When the border dividing Eastern and Western Europe fell, other less visible borders remained. Madjermans are marginalized in their own society. With no money to afford flight tickets and obtain visas, looking for work in Germany or visiting friends are out of reach for most former contract workers. Today's borders are of a different kind, yet they divide the world in parts while it is inherently interconnected.

[1] About 12,300 workers left Germany and returned to Mozambique in 1990. See: Andreas Müggenburg, "Die ausländischen Vertragsarbeiter in der ehemaligen DDR: Darstellung und Dokumentation," in *Die Beauftragte der Bundesregierung für die Belange der Ausländer* (Berlin: Universitäts-Druckerei Bonn, 1996), 18.

[2] Therein the study aims to follow a larger research agenda to question the idea of the "East" as a cohesive white cultural community and to rewrite its history from migrants' perspectives. See Marcia C. Schenck, "Constructing and Deconstructing the 'Black East': A Helpful Research Agenda?" *Stichproben: Wiener Zeitschrift für kritische Afrikastudien* 34, no. 18 (2018): 135–152; Quinn Slobodian (ed.), *Comrades of Color: East Germany in the Cold War World* (New York: Berghahn Books, 2015).

[3] BArch DQ 3/635, Part 2, "Vorkommnisse im Arbeiterwohnheim und im Betrieb," 30.08.1982.

[4] Marcia C. Schenck, "From Luanda and Maputo to Berlin: Uncovering Angolan and Mozambican Migrants' Motives to Move to the German Democratic Republic (1979–1990)," *African Economic History* 44, no. 1 (2016): 202–234.

[5] Landolf Scherzer, *Die Fremden* (Berlin: Aufbau Verlag, 2002), 63.

[6] The term appears as a self-assertive label of the group as well as a deprecating label imposed on them from outside. I use the spelling "Madjerman," which is related to its expression in Shangaan. Another common spelling is "Madgerman."

[7] Quote from an interview by the author. Lázaro quoted the speech he held as one of the representatives of the Madjermans at the international conference "Respekt und Anerkennung" on Mozambican contract work in the GDR, that took place in February 2019 in Magdeburg.

Transfronteridad
By Evan Natasha Escamilla

Borders are ordinarily thought of as solid political and often cultural divides. What is lost in this representation is the fluidity of certain bodies and goods. Transborder commuters—those who regularly traverse international borders—disrupt our notion of borders, how we cross them, and what it means to be from the "South" or the "North." For the North American transborder commuter crossing between Mexico and the US, border crossings are a mundane quotidian act. Transborder commuters leave their homes, arrive at the border, sometimes on foot but usually by car or public transportation, wait in usually long lines to reach the secured border checkpoints that indicate one is leaving Mexico and entering the US, and then continue to their destination—as with an "ordinary" commute. The difference here is the space of negotiation.

View of the traffic from one of the pedestrian bridges on the Tijuana side, 2019 © Photo: Evan Natasha Escamilla

Transborder commuters in Tijuana and San Diego often lay claim to either dual citizenship or residency permits for the US, and therefore need not limit themselves to the boundaries of one nation-state. Via their routinized border negotiations, some develop what is known in the Tijuana-San Diego region as "transfronteridad," thereby complicating the dominant understanding of a North/South divide.

Transfronteridad, a term that has commonly been utilized only in reference to the Mexico-US borderlands, particularly those of Tijuana-San Diego, stems from an understanding that borders do not create clean breaks capable of stopping the natural flows of people, goods, and practices. Rather, they give rise to borderlands, flexible territories incorporating two or more nation-states along with the dominant ideological formations and contestations of both.[1] "The fiction of cultures as discrete, objectlike phenomena occupying discrete spaces becomes implausible for those who inhabit the borderlands."[2] Habitual border negotiations produce individuals with consciousness deeply entrenched in the various local cultural and political dynamics of both sides. Transfronteridad is created from an elevated level of dependence of people on the relations and activities they ordinarily perform on both sides of the Mexico-US border.[3] Transborder commuters and families in the

Transborder commuters wait at the San Ysidro border between Tijuana and San Diego to cross by car. Stands line the side of the road here and, at this point, the average wait time is still around 30 minutes in the standard lane, 2019
© Photo: Evan Natasha Escamilla

Tijuana-San Diego region regularly utilize the borders to move from home to work and back, to maintain connections to family members on both sides, and for leisure purposes. Transfronteridad therefore acknowledges the meaning attached to each aspect of transborder commuting and transborder living in terms of the consequences, both positive and negative, intended and unintended, of this lifestyle for individuals and their families. It is an identity, a mindset, a shared language, an understanding, and an overall comfort level in a space that incorporates two nation-states and their joint borderland.

Transfronteridad challenges the dominant South/North binary that is folded into the stereotypical images of Mexico-US relations because it blurs the line between them. The deep, impervious black line that, in both mental and physical maps, once represented the unbending,

Food vendors keep the commuters fed as they progress toward the front of the line. Food carts circulate through the rows of traffic and stationary vendors have people taking and delivering orders to the waiting vehicles, 2019 © Photo: Evan Natasha Escamilla

indisputable point where the nation-state of Mexico ends and that of the US begins, is replaced by a softer dashed line in practice. The dashed line is an indication of the still real border complex, the delays, the documents, the prying questions, and so on. But it can no longer be thought of as a point where flows of people and cultures simply come to a stop. The dashed line becomes representative of the families, the products, and the patterns that flow freely inside the borderlands—in this case, the confluence of Tijuana and San Diego.

The borderlands, I thus argue, are not a binary space. In other words, the space that is Tijuana belongs on the same mental map that represents San Diego, and the most practical way to grasp these newfound flows is through a better understanding of transfronteridad and how it motivates people to maintain complex relations in and with the borderlands.

Transfronteridad is cultivated and propagated by "transfronterizos"—those who have internalized and reflected on what it means to be part of two societies characterized by their vast inequalities. Transfronterizos are individuals who are aware that their space of daily negotiation is different than that of those around them. According to

Estefanía, "Transfronteridad is more than a feeling or a question of money. It is the dynamics that the geographic space permits."[4] The concept of transfronteridad is, in itself, intriguing; however, it was not until meeting Raúl, a transborder commuter since 1954, that I made the full connection between transfronterizos and their transfronteridad. He explained: "A transfronterizo interests themselves in what is happening on the other side and is affected by both sides. A real transfronterizo has to know the history and culture of both sides and everything in between. [...] If you're an authentic transfronterizo it enriches your life."[5] Therefore, transfronteridad is not achieved simply through access; there are prerequisites, including living close to the border, and being able to speak both languages and lead a bicultural lifestyle. Transfronteridad is created and maintained by the way a transfronterizo regularly claims and uses their access, in this case to Tijuana and San Diego. In other words, a transfronterizo makes a "home" on two sides of a nation-state border.

For many families living in the Mexico-US borderlands, both to the south and to the north, language is a principal mechanism of creating transfronteridad. Families living in this region may choose to prioritize English in the home and send their children to schools that do the same. From a young age, children are bussed across the border each day to attend primary to high school. Raúl commented that the children with whom he grew up were sometimes not permitted to speak Spanish at home. For some parents, this is a mechanism to aid assimilation of the next generation, both for children based in Tijuana and in San Diego. The ability to speak English without an accent is thought of as a way to mitigate discrimination. It also develops into a tool of identity. For some transfronterizos, the constant traversing of the borders and the routinized interactions in San Diego have the unintended effect of chipping away at their sense of belonging within the spaces in both Tijuana and San Diego.

Although I argue here that the borderlands are connected and join people and spaces, they are also capable of acting, as intended, in ways that divide. For transfronterizos, it is sometimes the delicate balance of their fragmented identities that is affected. For many transfronterizos, their level of perceived transfronteridad may fluctuate over time. Raúl, for example, described the fluctuations he felt in his transfronteridad as periods of development. There were significant events in his education and career that mandated either more or fewer interactions in the borderlands, and each of those events was the start of a new period. Three periods stood out to him: his Americanization period, his Mexicanization period, and his re-Americanization period.

Raúl's first period of development was his Americanization period, which began when he first started to cultivate his transfronteridad. For ten years he crossed the border each day to attend school in the US. From a young age he developed his language skills—Spanish at home and English in school—and interacted with primarily American and Mexican-American children; and for the first time he became aware that in San Diego there are different celebrations, holiday traditions, meal customs, attitudes toward food, cleaning rituals, etc., than those

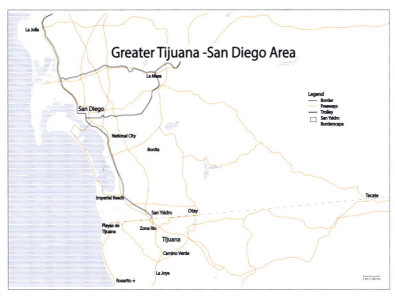

The dashed line is a visual representation of how the border complex impedes flows but does not stop them. Bodies, goods and cultural practices are able to move through the dashed line on the map, just as in real life, 2019 © Map: Evan Natasha Escamilla

commonly experienced in Tijuana.[6] The urban practices and personal interactions Raúl experienced in San Diego and Tijuana melded together to form his newfound lifeworld as a transfronterizo.

The second period he calls his Mexicanization period. This was his first extended stretch in the interior of Mexico, and it began with the initiation of his studies at one of the many universities in Mexico City. He developed a different understanding of the country from that with which he had grown up. Each aspect of daily life in Tijuana is undeniably influenced, both directly and indirectly, by the neighboring San Diego. This influence is visible in the taxes, available products, border traffic, commerce borne by the border traffic, tourism, etc. Therefore, Raúl's time at university in Mexico City affected his transfronteridad by clearly illustrating to him the differences in his daily experiences, as a child growing up in the borderlands, compared to a child growing up in the interior of the country. Raúl and other transfronterizos occupy a liminal space in which they feel they belong. Once outside of the borderlands, in the interior of either the US or Mexico, they are perceived as anomalies. The American holidays celebrated in Tijuana are not recognized in Mexico City, and there are perceptible changes in the language—due in large part to reduced English influence in the interior. It may even be claimed that quotidian life moves at a different speed outside of the borderlands.

Finally, Raúl's third period of development, his re-Americanization period, began when he moved back to Tijuana and commenced his postgraduate education in San Diego. In order to be able to further his education in the US, despite having already completed courses at a prestigious university in Mexico, he was required to retake a number of undergraduate courses at a San Diego community college. This is one example of the delicate cohesion that transfronterizos disrupt when they stop utilizing their borderland access. In essence, what is not constantly and fastidiously maintained is forfeited. By choosing to attend a university in Mexico City before applying to a postgraduate program in San Diego, Raúl inadvertently further fragmented his transfronteridad and, with it, the fragile grasp he had on the borderland space. Upon returning from Mexico City, he went through a period of reintegration and, alongside his community college courses in San Diego, reestablished his transfronterizo access through regular use. This shows how transfronteridad is reliant on connections and habitual negotiations in the borderlands.

By reframing the way in which we think of borders and borderlands, we may reframe how we understand the South and the North, Mexico and the US. By attempting to understand how and why transfronterizos choose to nurture their transfronteridad, we begin to see that it is our taken-for-granted notion of North/South that is warped. The deep divide we have created between North and South has limited the way we perceive these interconnected regions and, therefore, has limited the way we utilize, develop, and speak about them. By framing and discussing Tijuana and San Diego together rather than apart, their respective urban flows, routines, and behaviors begin to meld into one another, forming the picture of a shared borderland where transfronteridad thrives.

[1] For more on borderlands see Oscar J. Martínez, *Border People: Life and Society in the U.S.-Mexico Borderlands* (Tucson: University of Arizona Press, 1994).

[2] Akhil Gupta and James Ferguson, "Beyond 'Culture': Space, Identity, and the Politics of Difference," *Cultural Anthropology* 7, no. 1 (1992): 6–23, here 7.

[3] Norma Iglesias-Prieto, "Nuevos Agentes Sociales, Nuevos Espacios Urbanos y Las Posibilidades De Cambio. Las Artes Visuales en Tijuana," *Berkeley Planning Journal* 21, no. 1 (2008).

[4] Estefanía (transborder commuter). Unpublished interview with Evan Natasha Escamilla, July 3, 2018. For those working in San Diego and living in Tijuana, the salaries are higher and the expenses lower than if the individual or family lived and worked without regularly traversing the nation-state border.

[5] Raúl (transborder commuter). Unpublished interview with Evan Natasha Escamilla, July 20, 2018.

[6] In the context of this paper, Mexican Americans are those who were born and live in the US but have a Mexican background. This should not be confused with transfronterizos, who have a tighter grasp on the customs of both sides of the borderlands. Mexican Americans are Mexican by ancestry, not by practice.

Urbanization beyond Borders
By Myriam Perret

On the ferry boat in the middle of the Straits of Malacca, the bottleneck of one of the main global cargo trading routes, I find myself in between two opposing and seemingly detached worlds. On one side there is the world-renowned financial hub and city-state of Singapore, marked by a rigid system of social control. On the other side is a landscape marked by factories for the electronics industry, neighbored by clusters of shacks known colloquially as *"ruma liar"* or "wild housing." The patchwork urban configuration comprises affordable shops, street food vendors on every corner, places rumored to host gambling and

Opposing worlds in the Straits of Malacca; international container ships and local fishing boats, megacity Singapore and mangrove islands, 2012 © Photo: Myriam Perret

prostitution, and the occasional vacant high-end housing project waiting for upper-middle-class tenants who may never come. Approaching the coast, one can see traditional stilt constructions that have been occupied and extended by Sumatran and Javanese migrants. The original mangrove forests have had to give way to major shipyards that repair the cargo ships coming from the Straits of Malacca. After navigating through the field of cargo ships that share the coastal waters with indigenous fishing boats, we see a sign announcing that we've entered the Batam Free Trade Zone. If Singapore can be thought of as a Southern outpost of world-class capitalism, Batam is not as detached as the sea-crossing suggests, but in many ways acts as a frontier of that capitalism's expansion.

An understanding of the Special Economic Zone (SEZ) and the space of Singapore-Batam can benefit from Brett Neilson and Sandro Mezzadra's recent thinking about borders as method, as an epistemological angle, and as "sites in which the turbulence and conflictual intensity of global capitalist dynamics are particularly apparent."[1] In particular, the French term *partage* is well-suited to speak of the Straits of Malacca through which our ferry boat initially passed and which separates and connects Singapore and Batam. It is precisely this quality of the term *partage*, combining the sense of both division and connection (a linguistic duality also used by Rada Ivekovic), that leaves us at a loss to find an acceptable English equivalent to describe this border condition.

The challenge for the development of territories like the Singapore-Batam SEZ seems to lie exactly in the space between share and divide, attraction and opposition. Free Trade Zones are the spatial result of structurally rooted inequality and abuse, related to the described freedom of interpretation of belonging. In a reality where goods, money, and information experience a borderless, worldwide diffusion, human capital suffers from a tendency toward exclusion, segregation, and injustice. This dichotomy between inclusion and exclusion of the world market is symbolized by the label "Made in Singapore" on products shipped out of Batam—a sign of dominance and profit.

The two ports at either end of my ferry ride and the Singapore-Batam relationship more broadly illustrate economic interdependencies and social imbalances that compel us to reinterrogate the existence and functioning of various borders. On the one hand, the Straits of Malacca underline the political border between Singapore and

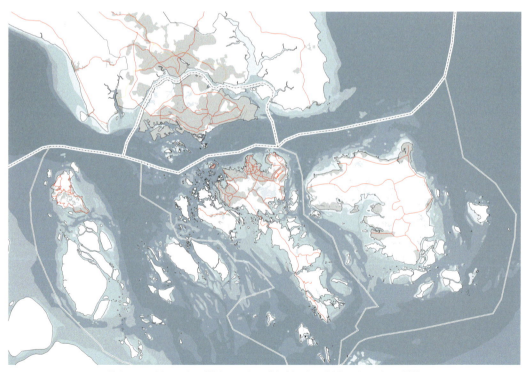

Dichotomy of the straits of Malacca; the political borders dividing the territory, 2012
© Map: Myriam Perret, Chair Prof. Milica Topalovic

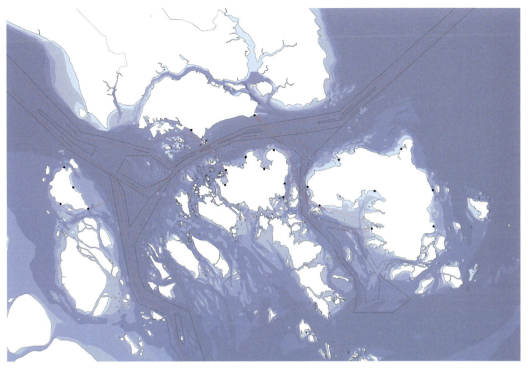

Dichotomy of the straits of Malacca; the sea as connecting surface triggering economic and urban development, 2012
© Map: Myriam Perret, Chair Prof. Milica Topalovic

Indonesia. On the other hand, this same cargo route is the connecting surface and trigger for economic and urban development on its northern and southern shores. While their political boundaries separate them, their economic entanglement binds them to a unified functional territory. Mezzadra and Neilson assert that "symbolic, linguistic, cultural, and urban boundaries are no longer articulated in fixed ways by the geopolitical border. Rather, they overlap, connect, and disconnect in often unpredictable ways, contributing to shaping new forms of domination and exploitation."[2] Below, we delve into the instability of various borders within the shared and divided space of Singapore-Batam.

This contemporary Singapore-Batam space emerged most markedly in the mid- to late-twentieth century. Singapore's resource scarcity at the end of the 1960s coincided with Indonesia's aspirations for growth, materialized in its opening to foreign investment. While Indonesia had to offer land and human capital to support the city-state's growing economic model, Singapore could offer itself as a gateway to the world market. This marked the beginning of a mutual relationship. In order to trigger the foreign investment they sought, the Indonesian national authority designated Batam as a Special Economic Zone in 1971.

Special Economic Zones (SEZs) can be described as geographical areas where goods may be received, stored, handled, manufactured, or reconfigured, and re-exported under specific customs regulations where they are generally not subject to customs duty. Described in

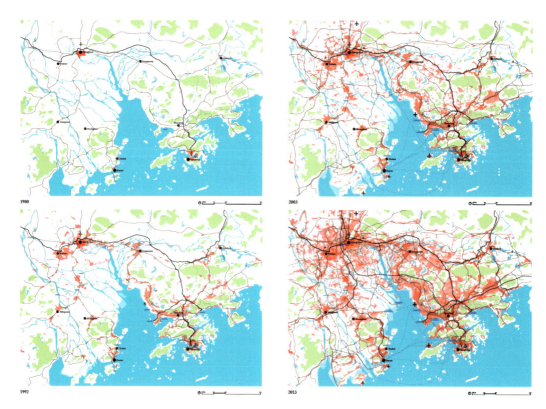

Explosive urbanization of the Pearl River Delta related to the Open Door Policy under Deng Xiaoping, 2014
© Map: Marco Cristuzzi, teaching assistant Myriam Perret, Chair Prof. Kees Christiaanse

detail by Keller Easterling, SEZs form islands of exception and immunity.[3] They are most commonly associated with China, which has the most SEZs of any country, and has been the most successful in advancing its economic goals through their establishment. Yet, as Mezzadra and Neilson describe, "the forms of accumulation they enable spur processes of spatial and social reorganization that extend well beyond their borders, making these sites paradigmatic for any serious political examination of our global predicament."[4]

Batam's development spurred by its SEZ designation is far from being singular. Perhaps the best-known example of transborder development related to SEZs is Hong-Kong's hinterland Shenzhen. It has been analyzed in *Great Leap Forward / Harvard Design School Project on the City* under the direction of Rem Koolhaas.[5] Parallel to the example of Batam, Shenzhen grew out of a small fishing and agricultural village. In the course of the Open Door Policy under Deng Xiaoping, Shenzen was designated as a Free Trade Zone in 1979. Being one of three strategic economic zones, Communist China declared that the Pearl River Delta was designated to boost China's economy. Designed to become China's "window to the world," Shenzhen underwent an unprecedented foreign-investment-driven urbanization. Also at the center of this development was industrialization, focusing on assembling electronic devices such as cell phones, whose sales market was booming all over the planet. Shenzhen and all the other cities, towns, and villages around the Pearl River Delta experienced such boundless growth that they transformed into one continuous yet disconnected and land-consuming urban fabric, forming a metropolitan region of an estimated 120 million people.

The initial assembling and storing activities are being continuously replaced by employment in the tertiary sector, outsourcing production to other Chinese provinces and abroad. Consequently, new SEZs are springing up, especially on the African continent, with the Konza Technology City in Kenya, Touchroad Djibouti Special Economic Zone, and many others.

The economic successes of SEZ arrangements, however, bring with them a slew of social and environmental consequences. SEZs are triggers for immunity, exclusion, and inequality. Cheap industrial production is realized at high human, cultural, and environmental costs. In hope of finding a better life, and to support their families in their home villages, the flux of the rural population to new industrial towns is significant. Even if they succeed in finding a job in the industry, these populations are hardly able to meet their needs. The negligence of labor protection and the prohibition of labor unions in SEZs often result in precarious working and living conditions. Low wages, long working hours, year-to-year contracts, and a poor social security system coalesce to create insecure livelihoods. Losing a job in a factory leaves a migrant laborer with few alternatives other than to return to their villages or enter the informal economy. SEZs lead not only to precarious social conditions, but also to inefficient and incoherent land use, altering the world's surface in an unsustainable and irreversible manner. Environmental protection measures in such zones are largely absent.

The strategic location at the Straits of Malacca, coupled with the legal framework of Free Trade Zones, makes Batam a fertile breeding ground for Singaporean and international companies. The SEZ, through its exceptional rules, becomes a sort of no-man's-land belonging neither to Singapore nor to Indonesia. Profiting from cheap land and labor, foreign firms are attracted to establish their production and assembly sites in Batam. Since its SEZ designation, over twenty industrial parks have been built, focusing mainly on assembly. As a result, Batam has experienced the fastest urbanization process in Indonesia to date, attracting migrants coming from different Indonesian islands like Sumatra and Java. In only thirty years, the quiet island inhabited by fishermen grew to a city with over 1.5 million inhabitants. Furthermore, the island is Indonesia's primary port of entry in terms of the number of arrivals (mainly related to business).

Industrial workers in Batamindo industrial estate, Batam, 2012 © Photo: Myriam Perret

The assembly of electronic devices, which are used all over the world, is a central part of the economic activity in Batam. Parts of electronic chips used in computers and cameras are processed here in a demanding work environment. This sector is predominantly staffed by

Mangrove forest and indigenous stilt constructions are destroyed to make way for container ship yards, 2012 © Photo: Myriam Perret

young women, as factory heads assume that women are less likely to complain and rebel, and are more skilled in the meticulous and precise work that is demanded in this sector. They are therefore the preferred group of employees, as, for instance, in the Batamindo Industrial Park.

The majority of workers in Batam (as in many other SEZs) live in dormitories on the industrial site where they share a room with other workers. The lack of housing and public services outside of the industrial parks restricts the freedom with which workers can conduct their lives. The provision of housing and services within the estate is additionally intended to assure laborers' commitment to their work. Yet in the labor regime of the SEZ factory, personal and professional progress is seldom realized. Despite initial promises, foreign companies often hire for management positions from foreign and global labor markets rather than promote workers from Batam.

Conflicting needs between economic attractiveness and social demands challenge authorities to plan and manage urban development in the Batam SEZ. While emphasis is placed on building large infrastructures to facilitate the movement of goods from industrial sites to the ports, the planning of worker housing independent from the industrial sites is neglected by the responsible authority. As a consequence of the unmet needs of the migrant population, informal housing and economies evolve spontaneously in close proximity to the industrial sites. Meanwhile, the government is facilitating speculative developer housing projects for the upper-middle class, producing vacant gated communities. Large stretches of ecologically valuable mangrove forests have been destroyed to make space for not only shipyards but also such high-end housing developments. Indigenous habitats and maritime ecosystems are threatened by the altered coastal landscape.

Governmental entities and town planners, to a large extent, still imagine Batam to rise as the twin city of Singapore. This urban imaginary coincides with how Easterling describes the development of newer SEZs in other parts of the world as "the germ of a city-building epidemic that reproduces glittering mimics of Dubai, Singapore and Hong Kong" all over the world.[6] She calls for architects and planners to propose spatial alternatives, where new economies and urban developments are interwoven with existing structures. Planning with a fixed imaginary neglects site-specific resources and qualities, which surely differ between Batam and Singapore. Recognizing these differences along with the entanglements between the two territories could be an alternative path to harnessing the centrality of the zone in the global economy and the value generated therein.

Batam is far from being the most striking example of a Free Trade Zone. But the proximity between the opposing realities of life in Singapore and life in Batam highlights, flagrantly, the challenges of a globalized and industrialized economic system, and is representative of more abstract and complex systems of planetary urbanization. Despite

Informal settlements spring in proximity to industrial estates,
due to lacking affordable housing offers, Batam, 2012
© Photo: Myriam Perret

their differences, Singapore and Batam are deeply connected, forming new, albeit unequal, capitalist territories beyond national borders. Through critical mapping, seemingly disconnected worlds can be represented as one territory, attempting to raise awareness of those relations of shared responsibility.

These two apparently disconnected cities must actually be understood as one urban and economic territory with strong interdependencies. While the proximity between Singapore and Batam or Hong Kong and Shenzhen reveals the flagrant disparity between two players of the same game, most of the time those worlds are poles apart, held together by maintaining their strong mutual dependence. As the products assembled in Batam are produced by international companies and exported to a large number of countries all over the world, how can responsibility of the conditions in such places be shared? How can Indonesia and Singapore, as well the consumers of these "Made in Singapore" products, take action for a more just and equal system? In Europe, only recently have various pieces of legislation (such as France's Duty of Vigilance Law and Switzerland's Responsible Business Initiative) raised awareness and sparked debate about holding corporations accountable for their actions abroad. We must not only find more livable and sustainable solutions for productive territories like Singapore-Batam, but also reflect more deeply on how our consumption patterns uphold an economic model with real spatial consequences, such as those felt within the borderland of the Straits of Malacca.

[1] Sandro Mezzadra and Brett Neilson, *Border as Method, or, the Multiplication of Labor* (Durham, NC: Duke University Press, 2013), 4.
[2] Ibid., vii.
[3] Keller Easterling, *Extrastatecraft: The Power of Infrastructure Space* (London: Verso, 2014).
[4] Mezzadra and Neilson (see note 1), 208–209.
[5] Chuihua Judy Chung, Jeffrey Inaba, Rem Koolhaas, and Sze Tsung Leong, *Project on the City I: Great Leap Forward* (New York: Taschen, 2001).
[6] Easterling (see note 3), 26.

The author would like to thank Maren Larsen for her extraordinary copyediting assistance.

Postcolonial Logistics
By Giulia Scotto

Postcard of the Motel Agip of Dar es Salaam, Tanzania, ca. 1960s
© Photo: Alice Quine, personal collection

"The design of the motel was made for the Italian 'autostrada' and placed in the middle of Dar (es Salaam) but it worked, it had everything."[1]

This is how Mr. M., former manager of the Agip Motel in Dar es Salaam, describes the facility he and his family operated for over thirty years between 1964 and 1999—the year of its closure. The motel was built by Agip Tanzania, a joint venture between the Italian national hydrocarbon agency ENI (Ente Nazionale Idrocarburi) and the Tanzanian Government in 1964, the year of the birth of independent Tanzania (as the Union of Tanganyika and Zanzibar). Together with its adjacent gas station, the structure formed part of ENI's expanding oil logistic network—the *"disegno Africano"*[2]—an incremental assemblage of people and infrastructure designed for the extraction, refining, circulation, and consumption of crude oil.

The Agip Motel constitutes one chapter of an ongoing research on ENI's *disegno* that, through the theoretical framework of postcolonial logistics,[3] brings together the critical scholarship on logistics and postcolonial studies, thus allowing a multilayered understanding of the Agip Motel as the materialization of ENI's corporate imperialism overlapping with the Tanzanian state's agenda, and as a lived space embodying multiple, situated, and evolving meanings.

During the 1960s, the science of logistics, originally associated with military operations such as the planning of defense systems, troops dislocation, and supply, became a planning technique of commodity production across space. Logistics transformed not only the logic of capitalist production, but also the ways in which corporations like ENI "imagine, calculate, plan, and build spaces of production and of distribution" for the expansion of markets and the maximization of profit.[4] But logistics is also a category of analysis developed by critical geographers in the last decades to unveil the violence and hidden power structures of capitalist globalization. Through the inquiry of supply chains' flows and struggles, these scholars aim at understanding logistics' irrationalities and uneven geographical consequences.[5]

The term "postcolonial" in postcolonial logistics underlines the ambition of enriching the discussion about modern capitalism through a postcolonial lens able to underline the role of cultural discourses within processes of accumulation and exploitation.[6] This conceptual operation prevents us from elevating capitalism to "the context of context," and to understand logistics' logic as "both indispensable and insufficient" to grasp the complexity of reality.[7] The need to tell history from a plurality of places and experiences, to decenter official Eurocentric "narratives," and to acknowledge the central role of "the margin" in defining global modernity emerged clearly from the work of postcolonial scholars.[8] This means that we need to understand ENI's material infrastructures as the materializations of corporate capital imperialism and, at the same time, query the situated meanings these infrastructures acquire in their specific contexts for the people who experience them, live them, and transform them beyond ENI's intention and control.

Postcolonial logistics, then, allows us to think beyond the North/South divide and to place at the center what has been told as the margin. Our new center—the Agip Motel, Dar es Salaam, Tanzania, the final segment of ENI's distribution network—is not only the manifestation of local agencies and specificity, but also the result of their intertwining with global networks of capitalism and imaginaries of elsewhere. Therefore, its multiple histories, far from being marginal, are key to better understanding ENI's neocolonial imperialism and its spatial and social consequences.

ENI's "*Disegno Africano*"
ENI, the Italian national hydrocarbon agency, was established in 1953 by the Italian government to support Italy's industrial development through the production and supply of fossil fuels. ENI's initial attempts to find oil within Italy were partially successful but not sufficient to satisfy the demand resulting from the rapid industrialization of the Po Plain. Frustrated by the meager discoveries on the Italian territory and by the constraints on crude oil import conditions imposed by the international oil cartel of the so-called Seven Sisters, in 1955 ENI's president Enrico Mattei launched what would later be defined as the "*grande disegno africano*," which can be translated as the "big African project" or "scheme." Through its African expansion, ENI expected to discover rich oil deposits and establish new and rapidly growing markets for Agip's (the commercial branch of the group) refined products.

Despite Italy's colonial past, through a questionable anti-colonial propaganda, ENI managed to established itself as a seemingly neutral actor and, within ten years, it entered the oil market of twenty-five newly founded African countries—including the former Italian colonies and many independent countries of the Sub-Saharan region. The expansion of ENI's supply chain to the African continent took advantage of the shifting geopolitical situation that, with few exceptions, saw the end of direct colonial rule and the formation of new nation-states pursuing economic self-reliance through development. Playing the ambiguous role of the profit-oriented oil multinational and of the caring national agency, ENI offered aid and technical support to newly independent countries who, with this new alliance, sought to emancipate themselves from former colonial powers.

Tanzania was one of the more than twenty-five countries where ENI was active in different sectors, from hydrocarbon extraction to marketing. Here, in partnership with the Tanzanian government, the oil company and its subsidiaries built a refinery, a processing plant for lubricants and bottled gas, a pipeline shipping oil to neighboring Zambia, a distribution network of over seventy gas and service stations, and the Agip Motel of Dar es Salaam. Through their material presence, these infrastructures strategically operated at the intersection between military and marketing outposts, granting Agip a diffuse and long-lasting presence capable of enduring future political transformation.

Simultaneously, this more-or-less visible network of nodes and pipes materialized the intersecting interests of ENI's imperial "disegno" and Tanzania's rural-socialist nation-building project. Indeed, the facilities built by ENI, always in partnership with the local government, were expected to enhance circulation for both trade and tourism and to increase land accessibility and productivity. From industrial plants to gas stations, these infrastructures were welcomed by the Tanzanian elite as the materialization of modernization and nation-building discourses and, simultaneously, as the expression of Tanzania's ability to emancipate itself from its colonial past and attract foreign investors and tourists.

Logistic Spaces
As ENI expanded its supply chain network outside of Italy, its engineering office envisioned new ways of planning and building spaces of distribution and consumption. The "*servizio edile*" (construction service) started developing a series of architectural prototypes to be implemented, with few adjustments, in different contexts. The prototyping was aimed at minimizing unpredictable accidents caused by, for instance, unskilled workers or extreme atmospheric conditions, thus ensuring quality, uniformity, and cost efficiency. The Agip Motel of Dar es Salaam was a specimen of the "Motel 59" prototype.

In Italy, based on recent marketing studies on branding recognizability, ENI built a chain of over thirty motor hotels. Located on the periphery of urban areas or along the newly built highways, these innovative structures offered relatively cheap accommodation to the growing number of Italian motorists. Depicted as a fundamental service to drivers and tourists, motels were part of Agip's strategy aiming at keeping people "on the road" in order to increase mobility and gasoline consumption.

Also in Tanzania, following the invitation of the local government willing to develop the tourist sector in cooperation with foreign investors, Agip Tanzania envisioned a chain of motels; however, the motel in Dar es Salaam was the only one built. Located in one of the most prominent locations of the capital city, close to tourist attractions, the port, and the seat of government, the structure hosted, together with the motel and a complete service station, a showroom for Fiat (the Italian car manufacturer), thus materializing the symbiotic relationship of Italian companies and institutions abroad. The showroom operated as a platform for the motel itself and as an elevated parking lot. The parking level, reachable through a concrete spiral car ramp, hosted the lobby and the motel's restaurant, while the fifty-seven rooms were distributed among three extra floors. Above them, a roof garden offered a spectacular view of the Azania Front Lutheran Church and the Dar es Salaam Gulf.

From the comparison with other Motel 59s, it emerges that the Dar es Salaam specimen was not just "copy-pasted," nor only slightly adjusted; its design was drastically adapted to the urban and postcolonial context. While the car showroom on the ground floor was directly accessible from street level, the motel entrance and the restaurant, elevated and not visible from the road, could only be accessed through the car ramp or a narrow staircase. The showroom platform had a specific design feature adopted by Agip exclusively in the Motel 59 of Dar es Salaam. Unlike the motels built along the Italian roads, where the lobbies, bars, and restaurants functioned as extensions of public space, the peculiar section of the Tanzanian motel created a clear visual and spatial discontinuity between the public street level and the semipublic space of the parking and the entrance. The motel platform, already present in early versions of Tanzanian design, was not a recurring element in Dar es Salaam's colonial architecture, where racial segregation was achieved at the urban scale through zoning and access control, nor was it a typical feature of its contemporary projects. Through its peculiar section and access design aimed at motorists' comfort and safety, the Agip Motel became an architectural segregating device, where exclusion and inclusion were defined by design and logistics imperatives of selective circulation.

<u>Not a Standard Motel</u>
The management of the motel was not standard either. The Agip Motel was not operated directly by ENI or by Agip Tanzania itself, but by a Greek-Tanzanian family who contributed greatly to defining its style and clientele. Agip Tanzania, who owned the building, provided the furniture and other branded accessories but left the M. family to run the

Left: Motel Agip Verona (Italy); right: Motel Agip Marsala (Italy)
© Photo: ENI Historical Archive

business. The M. family was a family of Greek settlers who moved to German East Africa at the beginning of the twentieth century to work in railway construction. Here they acquired land and started managing sisal plantations and mining sites. Like many other Tanzanians of Greek origins, they entered the hotelier business and, for three generations, their lives have been intertwined with the history and destiny of the motel. In the more than thirty years of administration, the M. family further transformed the Motel 59 prototype in order to improve its comfort and match the requirements of its guests.[9]

Thanks to the M. family management, the Agip Motel became a home away from home for the white settler community of Tanzania, and, similar to other sites of the "colonial topography"[10] like hotels, plantations, and mines, it provided a space where white settlers redefined and preserved their identity as a separate social group long after independence. In the motel's renowned restaurant and cocktail bar, Tanzanians born of European descent could experience "fine European cuisine" and earn their position inside (or outside) of Tanzanian society. The clientele of the motel also included members of the new local elite, mainly civil servants and pubic officials who worked in the administration quarter—the former colonial white sector—a few hundred meters away from the motel. Government workers used to drive to "The Agip" restaurant for business lunches and meetings. Here, they could meet foreign employees of NGOs, international organizations, and other multinational companies, who stayed there as motel guests. By hosting these encounters, the motel became a selective contact zone where the postcolonial elite could meet the outside world and negotiate the conditions of their presence in Tanzania.

The car-oriented architecture of the structure, together with its prestige and prohibitive prices, defined the clientele of the motel along class lines. For the local elite who could afford to drive up the concrete ramp of the motel, the Agip restaurant, with its direct view of the parking, offered a stage to perform their new privileges.

Despite the fact that few Tanzanians could afford cars, in the 1960s most of them experienced a certain degree of mobility that, after many years of racial segregation, was perceived as a sign of the newly achieved independence. Similarly, the growing presence of cars and related infrastructures along Tanzania's roads was seen as "proof that national independence had delivered tangible goods."[11] Agip roadside facilities (including the Agip Motel of Dar es Salaam) with their car-oriented design and functionalist aesthetic operated—beyond class divide—"on the level of fantasy and desire," stimulating a "sense of awe and fascination" that constituted "an important part of their political effect."[12]

Motel Agip Gela (Italy), ca. 1960s
© Photo: ENI Historical Archive

Unlike most tourist facilities in Tanzania, during the nationalization campaign of the socialist regime, the Agip Motel maintained its status as a privately managed enclave and, in the years of economic crisis and austerity that followed, it became one of the few places in Dar es Salaam where imported goods were made available to a restricted clientele. The privileged condition of alternative sovereignty of the motel—a space owned by an oil multinational and managed by white Tanzanians with the consent of the state—underlines once more how, in the postcolonial era, some social groups maintained "almost" colonial privileges and others gained new positions of power thanks to their ability to control the flows of goods and capital between the national territory and the outside world.

The Everyday of Logistics
Inquiring local specificity, everyday life experiences, and geopolitical and historical constellations within and beyond ENI, this account of Agip Motel aims at complicating our understanding of its supply chain capitalism. Redrawing the *"disegno Africano"* departing from Agip Motel of Dar es Salaam exposes a series of inconsistencies within ENI's

and the socialist Tanzanian state's narratives, and provides a new lens for viewing their operations. Shifting the focus from the core of the empire to its margins and collecting the voices of multiple actors reveals the fundamental role of ENI's African expansion in the shaping of its modus operandi, and shows how its seemingly neutral infrastructures served as quasi-military tools to expand its market and acquire control over growing territories.

As Derrida famously noted, "to dare say welcome is perhaps to insinuate that one is at home,"[13] which is also a way of emphasizing the host's ownership of the space that is shared. Offering monetized hospitality in a foreign country, both Agip and the M. family implicitly gained a position of power vis-à-vis both their guests and the locals and, in selectively welcoming their guests, they not only affirmed their ownership of the hosting right in a foreign land, but also their right to belong.[14]

Examining the motel's design features, aesthetics, and performances, we have seen how, through the creation of logistics spaces, the multinational oil company co-participated with the Tanzanian state in shaping Tanzanian postcolonial spatial and social relations. As a node of ENI's networked geography shaped by flows, bordering, and containment,[15] we have seen how the motel has the capacity to "disrupt and fabricate space, territories, and lives"[16] and differentiate "groups' rights [...] on the basis of their relationship to systems of supply."[17]

[1] Interview with Mr. M., August 2019, Dar es Salaam, Tanzania. I explain the history of Motel Agip of Dar es Salaam in more depth in "Provincializing ENI's Disegno Africano: Agip Tanzania and the Agip Motel in Dar es Salaam," in Vikramaditya Prakash, Maristella Casciato, and Daniel E. Coslett (eds.), *Global Modernism and the Postcolonial: New Perspectives on Architecture* (New York: Routledge, forthcoming 2022).

[2] Giuseppe Accorinti, *Quando Mattei era l'impresa energetica io c'ero* (Matelica: Hacca, 2008), 3.

[3] Part of my ongoing PhD in Urban Studies at the University of Basel.

[4] Deborah Cowen, *The Deadly Life of Logistics: Mapping Violence in Global Trade* (Minneapolis: University of Minnesota Press, 2014).

[5] Charmaine Chua et al., "Introduction: Turbulent Circulation: Building a Critical Engagement with Logistics," *Environment and Planning D: Society and Space*, August 6, 2018. https://doi.org/10.1177/0263775818783101.

[6] Sandro Mezzadra, *La condizione postcoloniale: storia e politica nel presente globale*, Culture 36 (Verona: Ombre corte, 2008).

[7] Rajyashree N. Reddy, "The Urban under Erasure: Towards a Postcolonial Critique of Planetary Urbanization," *Environment and Planning D: Society and Space* 36, no. 3 (June 2018): 529–539, https://doi.org/10.1177/0263775817744220.

[8] Miguel Mellino, *La critica postcoloniale: decolonizzazione, capitalismo e cosmopolitismo nei postcolonial studies* 31, Meltemi.edu. (Roma: Meltemi, 2005).

[9] These and many other pieces of information are derived from a series of interviews I conducted with Mr. M. between August 2019 and May 2020. Other interviews were conducted with Motel Agip's employees and guests.

[10] J. M. Coetzee, *White Writing: On the Culture of Letters in South Africa* (New Haven: Yale University Press, 1988).

[11] Laura Fair, "Drive-In Socialism: Debating Modernities and Development in Dar es Salaam, Tanzania," *The American Historical Review* 118, no. 4 (2013): 1077–1104.

[12] Brian Larkin, "The Politics and Poetics of Infrastructure," *Annual Review of Anthropology* 42, no. 1 (2013): 327–343, https://doi.org/10.1146/annurev-anthro-092412-155522.

[13] Jacques Derrida, *Adieu to Emmanuel Levinas* (Stanford: Stanford University Press, 1999), 15–16.

[14] Ruth Craggs, "Towards a Political Geography of Hotels: Southern Rhodesia, 1958–1962," *Political Geography* 31 (May 1, 2012): 215–224, https://doi.org/10.1016/j.polgeo.2012.02.002.

[15] Cowen (see note 4), 19.

[16] S. Mezzadra, and B. Neilson, "Operations of Capital," *South Atlantic Quarterly* 114, no. 1 (January 1, 2015): 1–9, https://doi.org/10.1215/00382876-2831246.

[17] Cowen (see note 4), 5.

Worlding Goma
By Maren Larsen

Buenos días!
Buenos días.
Sudáfrica!
Sudáfrica.

The officers in the front line set the pace and encourage the younger *Kaibiles*[1] with call-and-response chants as we jog together around the perimeter of the camp cluster at 5:45 a.m.

Good morning South Africa. Good morning Malawi. Good morning Tanzania.

These men live next to other foreign armies deployed as United Nations (UN) peacekeepers here in Mubambiro, 20 km west of Goma in the eastern Democratic Republic of the Congo, and each contingent is acknowledged as we jog around and through their adjacent camps. Good morning India. Good morning Bangladesh.

We are jogging fast enough that the sound of our sneakers corresponds to the downbeat of the chant, until an uphill climb past an armed Indian soldier in the sentinel tower slows our pace. The last stretch of the jog brings us back to the main gate—a fence painted blue and white, flanked by gabions topped with concertina wire. I'm weary as we pass a painted stone monument just before the gate. It reads, "I will respect my enemy's skill but I will fight it with all of my strength and energy until he's completely destroyed. Welcome to Kaibil Home."

Good morning Guatemala.

The force I am staying with and the collection of armies we symbolically greet on this early morning jog are a reflection of shifting geopolitical priorities since the end of the Cold War. Such historical shifts have resulted in a retreat of the West in UN peacekeeping missions and an overwhelming reliance on "Southern" soldiers to fill the ranks. Deploying troops from the Global South to participate in peacekeeping missions such as MONUSCO[2] acts as a continuation of imperial and colonial patterns and logics of military deployment, argues Philip Cunliffe. For the UN, contingent troops from these countries offer the advantages of cost efficiency, lessened political costs of interventions (due to troop-contributing countries being less powerful states), and legitimation of large deployments that might otherwise look too analogous to neocolonial occupation.[3]

Beginning an analysis of Goma from a particular context like that of the peacekeeping camp immediately calls into question the boundaries between the provincial and the cosmopolitan in ways that escape the accusation that postcolonial urban theory from the South advocates for a provincialization of knowledge.[4] For instance, with an understanding of urbanity as it emerges from the socio-spatial outcome of UN interventionism, internal armed conflicts, troop contributions from the Global

South, and financing from the Global North, situated in urban and rural settings from Cyprus to South Sudan, to which "province" would one even turn with this new knowledge? From which (or from whose) empirical reality should it be said to be grounded? While camping helps me understand the ways in which foreign peacekeepers as well as Goma's residents make their city into social, cultural, and architectural spaces, the form of the camp and the practice of camping should be a lens available to illuminate a multitude of urban conditions, as it emerges neither from Euro-American-centric universality nor from Global South exceptionalism.

By starting from the camp as an unsettled settlement typology, an urban theory of camping enters into the types of theory building proposed by Teresa Caldeira in exploring modes of making sociospatial forms.[5] The anthropology of becoming equally demands resistance to binaries and an emphasis on the processual and in-between by "choosing to look at how lives, rationalities, social fields, and power relations are inflected in one another and in the enclosures, impasses, thresholds, and breakthroughs that are the materials of lifeworld and subject construction."[6] By imbuing camping with the theoretical bridging power of worlding, we surpass the persistent dichotomies through which we approach and increasingly understand the urban with analytics of urban practice that is, in itself, a simultaneously global and situated phenomenon.

Camp entrance Mubambiro, Goma, February 2019 © Photo: Maren Larsen

The lives of peacekeepers in and around Goma are anchored by their temporary accommodation in what have become increasingly enduring camps over the past twenty years of mission presence in the DRC. The interiors of the camps are polyvalent, multilayered spaces in which a myriad of infrastructures and activities come together to sustain the lives of soldiers who live in them, while simultaneously protecting local civilian populations through their presencing and operational assignments beyond the camp. For contingent troops, camp bases function as spaces of shelter, security, and maintenance of camp-bound infrastructures related to rations, ablutions, communications, water treatment, waste management, electricity generation, laundry, and even television. They store and defend operational equipment such as trucks, SUVs, weapons, ammunition, and armored vehicles. Camps accommodate soccer fields, badminton courts, volleyball nets, libraries, gyms, mess areas, bars, and shops for officers and troops to engage in physical exercise and recreation. They are beautified with landscaping, monuments, posters, paintings, and memorials to lift morale. These camps become canvases upon which peacekeepers project a visual and material appearance between being at home and being in the world.

Sandbags are piled up to form an emergency security post. CORIMEC prefab accommodation units are painted with images associated with troops' home country and host country. Signposts direct visitors to different places in the camp. A camera sits atop the signpost monitoring the entrance gate and reception, Goma, December 2018 © Photo: Maren Larsen

The appearance of the world in a peacekeeping camp emerges through the visual images created and projected in that space, as well as the practice-based ways in which peacekeepers make themselves visible to worlds beyond their own camp. These worlds are necessarily multiple and reveal ideas about a world that is simultaneously here (in Goma) and elsewhere. Foreign peacekeepers gain a sense of being-in-the-world through the appearance of local and specific objects in their camps, like replica wooden *tchukudus*, souvenir plaques made by in-camp woodcarvers, and paintings and models of the Nyiragongo volcano just north of town. For many troops from large armies (which are often the countries contributing the most troops to UN peacekeeping), being a blue helmet in Goma is the first and only time their job as a soldier will take them across the world (barring international conflict and warfare), and on behalf of the world. As such, for many peacekeepers in and around Goma, their experience of the city in which their camp is situated becomes synonymous with their experience of the world. Similarly, through practices of exchanging mementos among foreign armies, hosting and attending one another's medal parades, and attending national performances across contingents, peacekeepers collectively inscribe themselves with a more global identity as members of a multinational peacekeeping force. Officers see Goma and its camps as the best places in which to be exposed to what many peacekeepers vaguely refer to as the "international environment," a concept unbound from specificity of a place like "here."

The visuality and practice of being-in-the-world are key components of making camps into social, architectural, and cultural spaces in their own right. The visual culture of peacekeeping draws on local images of urban life as well as global images that help create a sense of peace, unity, and achievement. Making camp in this way, as the appearance of the world as simultaneously here and elsewhere, also constitutes and shapes the making of the city of Goma.

Peacekeepers and urban dwellers alike are not simply acted upon by these multiple and imaginary worlds, but play an active role in their construction. Looking at urban toponymy—or the way that people in Goma give names to places in the city—reveals the tendency to write the city of Goma into a geography of world references that are equally here and elsewhere. Goma is the world, or is at least at its center, according to local T-shirts claiming that *"Si le monde était un pays Goma serait sa capitale"* ("If the world were a country, Goma would be its capital"). The city also contains places that use names from other parts of the world to evoke an attractive sense of cosmopolitanism that could potentially lure clients, such as Shop Manhattan, Kiosk and Restaurant La Shengen, Maison Decors California, or Ibiza Garden Bar. Another ubiquitous type of place label refers to rural home spaces, attracting clients with less busy, bucolic images of a

Quartier Ndosho, Goma, July 2019 © Photo: Maren Larsen

place removed from the world of the city, as denoted by the bar Planète Village, for example, or the Resto-Bar Mon Village. Other places are given specific village names, such as the Ihusi brand of hotels and gas stations, or the Ishovu Cyber Café, named after an island in Lake Kivu. If home is back in the village, then what kind of a world is Goma?

Names, and the images and feelings that various commercial spaces use to get people in the door, reference not only the cosmopolitanism of being elsewhere, but also the realities of what it means to be here, in Goma. Popular naming like Chechnya for a particularly rough neighborhood, Siege de Kabul (Kabul Headquarters) for a barbershop/

Quartier Kahembe, Goma, July 2019 © Photo: Maren Larsen

phone charge point, or Bunker Café for a small counter selling *maziwa* and *chapati* all seem to acknowledge the hardships and insecurity faced in the city at large. Imagined and referenced worlds elsewhere are not always aspirational or normatively better. The materiality and mere presence of peacekeeping forces reinforce both the anxieties of protracted insecurity and the freedoms afforded by being in a heavily "protected" city. Popular toponymy in the city thus constantly acknowledges the complexities of being-in-the-world in Goma.

Goma is written into the world through a peacekeeping presence and place referencing that are both aspirational and acknowledging of a world in crisis and Goma's place in that world. An overwhelmingly Southern peacekeeping force in a city that is at once seeking to center

Quartier Kahembe, Goma, July 2019 © Photo: Maren Larsen

itself in the world and escape it elicits a new style of worlding occurring in intra-, inter-, and extra-camp connections.[7] Peacekeeping camps in Goma instantiate several visions of multiple worlds in formation while influencing the way their neighbors in the city conceptualize the world of which their city is a part, and their city's place in it.

[1] Guatemalan Special Forces.
[2] Acronym of the UN Peacekeeping Mission in DRC based on the French name Mission de l'Organisation des Nations Unies pour la Stabilisation en République Démocratique du Congo.
[3] Philip Cunliffe, *Legions of Peace: UN Peacekeepers from the Global South* (London: Hurst, 2013), 121.
[4] Michael Storper and Allen J. Scott, "Current Debates in Urban Theory: A Critical Assessment," *Urban Studies* 53, no. 6 (May 2016): 1114–1136, https://doi.org/10.1177/0042098016634002.
[5] Teresa Caldeira, "Peripheral Urbanization: Autoconstruction, Transversal Logics, and Politics in Cities of the Global South," *Environment and Planning D: Society and Space* 35, no. 1 (February 2017): 3–20, https://doi.org/10.1177/0263775816658479.
[6] João Biehl and Peter Locke, *Unfinished; The Anthropology of Becoming* (Durham: Duke University Press, 2017), 28.
[7] Ananya Roy and Aihwa Ong (eds.), *Worlding Cities: Asian Experiments and the Art of Being Global: Studies in Urban and Social Change* (Malden, MA: Wiley-Blackwell, 2011).

The Presence of the Past

Imagining Alternative Futures

by Emilio Distretti and Kenny Cupers

How do we deal with the complex ways in which the past continues to shape the urban present? How can the injustices of the past possibly be repaired in contemporary urban life? How can urbanists, architects, and geographers not just account for conflicts and injustices, but work with them productively to build better cities?

Planners and their constituents are usually urged to address the pressing concerns of the present in developing plans for the future. Yet the way those concerns are framed and lived by the many different communities that make up the city is also shaped by material remains, monuments, memories, and hauntings of the past. Indeed, cities register historical layering, and contain the many different and contested histories of the people who inhabit and travel through them across time. They are patchworks of traces, clues, and memories of past and present struggles that furiously entangle and overlap with desires, imaginations, and future prospects. In the city, the past cannot really be musealized, the present is never contingent, and the future remains always open for change.

Among the many debates that can be drawn on to tackle these questions, we are inspired by cross-disciplinary approaches from postcolonial theory, critical geography, and heritage studies, and the methods of architectural and urban history. David Harvey famously proposes that "the past serves to underline the importance of understanding how people situate themselves with respect to the future."[1] In this respect, the validation of narratives, identities, and belongingness, as Stuart Hall points out, informs the struggle for the "postcolonial metropolis," for the inclusion of the margins in the center, the outside in the inside.[2] Despite the demarcations, surveillance, seams, and boundaries described by Ann Stoler as the negative spaces created by centuries of imperial and colonial dispositions,[3] the urban is where, Sara Ahmed suggests, public life is forced to come to terms with the ghosts from the past.[4] Precisely at the threshold of these tensions, our work develops an urban pedagogy that recovers and interrogates these spaces, margins, and traces—and thereby reorients and expands aspirations for the making of a just city.

Since the globalizing moment of 1492, the invention of a European modernity through the slave trade, and various colonial and imperial regimes, the urban has represented hierarchical nodes of global connection and disconnection across geographies. Around them, empires have grown and developed by placing and displacing, centering or decentering humans and things, across and along North/South divides. The national liberation struggles and postcolonial mobilities following the formal end of empires afford novel interpretations of our global urban moment. This form of the urban is an entanglement between the global and the local, where colonial hierarchies such as center/periphery, here/there, and North/South are refracted and transformed. As Robbie Shilliam and Olivia Rutazibwa have explained, this process had a twofold outcome: Through ongoing displacement, migrations, and diasporas, there is a South in the North; at the same time, with the rise of local elites and attendant forms of capital-intensive urban development after colonialism, a North exists in the South.[5] By articulating these entangled histories, transcultural processes, and geopolitical legacies, cities can be better understood as dynamic nodes of trans-spatial and transtemporal networks. Cities act as symbols of colonial rule, conduits of contestation, and spaces of counterimagination, where lived experience does not conform to Western narratives of imposed "modernity" and "modernization." By engaging with these contradictions, critical urbanists can forge new historical narratives of continuity and discontinuity that can mobilize the past for new projects.

International and intersectional struggles for racial and economic justice and equality have confronted us in the past decades with the ways in which the past is not a given, but rather the outcome of those very struggles, as people assert their lives beyond and against racialized, classed, sexualized, and gendered hierarchies, divisions, and segregations. As part of a pedagogy that recognizes and aims to contribute to these struggles, we encourage students to engage their traces and testimonies. This means reorienting the narratives about the past in order to come to terms with the *longue durée* of colonialism and empire, which shape novel patterns of coloniality and anti-colonial struggles in the lives of cities in both the Southern and Northern hemispheres. Inspired by postcolonial critique attempting to center urban theory in the "South," this section of the book thus develops different gazes that consider the (post)colonial in relation to historical urban shifts, from the age of European imperialism to geographies of ongoing anti-colonial struggle. Here we reframe and displace dominant notions of urban heritage and urban development that still operate along the lines of colonial and modernist divisions between modern/nonmodern, urban/rural, and human/natural. By contesting such paradigms and narratives we aim to address not only the colonial afterlives of the urban present, but also to engender ideas for an alternative future and inspire new trajectories for urban theory and practice.

Our pedagogy encourages students to regard cities as sites for "awakening." In Walter Benjamin's view, "awakening" stands at the inception of every historical presentation.[6] Here, the emergence of "individualities" and "difference" manifests in the spatial dimension as a form of awakening/remembering, where people experience, generate, and activate "space" as historical experiences. According to this hermeneutic approach it is possible to read different and distinct historical experiences with and through the city. This awakening is evident in the emergence of singularities, fragments, and anecdotes that refer to individually and collectively lived struggles that shape relational and transgenerational experiences, determining lasting temporal effects. This method of looking at and experiencing the urban echoes an archaeological praxis, inspired by Agamben's idea of archaeology which "in historical investigation has to do not with origins but with the moment of a phenomenon's arising and must therefore engage anew the sources and tradition." Agamben continues: "The moment of arising [...] has the form of the past in the future, that is, a future anterior. [...] The point of archaeology is to gain access to the present for the first time, beyond memory and forgetting or, rather, at the threshold of their indifference."[7] Likewise, we see the urban as an "excavation site," as the main stage where we can detect arising phenomena from the past, describing the present and projecting the future, thereby disclosing realities of significant epistemological value.

Building on these approaches, the city forms the core of our pedagogy, as we encourage students to attend to the **multiple temporalities of the urban** through a range of research methods, and to provide them with conceptual tools and research skills to study the city as a sociomaterial complex. To understand the urban from the vantage point of critical urbanism means using the city as both a documentary form and a *medium* for establishing relations between past, present, and future. In so doing, we do not look at "urbanization" only as an economic, social, and political process, but also as a transformation in "brick and mortar." As they focus on understanding urbanization as a dynamic process, humanities and social science researchers often regard the built environment as little more than a passive reflection or manifestation of abstract forces. Yet the city effectively exerts power through its material constitution and transformation. The city shapes and is shaped by the production, circulation, and consumption of materials and things—from gold to waste, from oranges to cell phones. Buildings and streets shape not only meaning and experience but also social identities and cultural differences. And the city's physical form and transformation over time guide the agency of its residents—however fickle and unpredictable.

Within this approach we follow theorizations of history as retrospective knowledge production shaped by footprints, where the urban is the space where "traces" are in constant reshuffle. In this sense, the city appears as a site of selective public and/or private memories, a physical collection of records shaped by various power dynamics, and a metaphor for holding knowledge. It is in these three senses that the archive is central to the mediated production of urban space. Historians tend to approach these existing archives as repositories of "primary sources," yet the materiality and media of the city itself can also be used as evidence in urban research. We begin with the premise that archives are not a collection of neutral records of events, but shape difference and "otherness" with regard to gender, class, ethnicity, sexuality, and ability. Such critical perspective on existing archives prompts new imaginations of the **city as archive**, and thus new approaches to urban research as the *production* of archives. Starting from the bureaucratic violence of government archives and the painful absences in the colonial archive, together with our students we imagine alternative ways of curating urban knowledge. Engaged forms of research can therefore lead to producing new archives that speak through the voices of a range of marginalized or otherwise silenced interlocutors. Beyond the production of oral histories of the city, we can also ask how material properties, **textual records**, and human testimonies speak differently about the city, its locality, and its global entanglements: from street signs to buildings, from dust to data, the city is an open archive offering an entry into its polymorphous political worlds.

But the city is not simply a mediator of reality. In this sense, we also insist on looking at cities through their textual dimensions. Acting as a recipient of various semiotic flows for the definition of political and cultural identities, cities are considered here through their symbolic and functional components in defining the boundaries of the social, political, and economic dimensions of human life. Through the textual dimension of architecture and infrastructure, we consider the ways in which urban traces wed the city to discordant semiotic flows that produce identity markers, generating overlapping textual realities and conflicting narratives and fluctuant chains of interpretation. This entails recognizing not only the continuity of mechanisms and technologies of power between past and present, but also the way in which historically constructed identities are produced and negotiated *in*, *with*, and *through* the urban.

Therefore, the following "voices" and essays explore how historical inheritances and colonial afterlives influence contemporary challenges, and the ways in which such legacies still shape the lives and minds of people and their ecologies. This section of the book starts with an intervention of Hanna Baumann presenting local reinterpretations of the "modern" in today's city of Tema (Ghana). Alexander Crawford illustrates the legacies of European urbanization in Bobo-Dioulasso, the second largest city in Burkina Faso. Carla Cruz explains how a running competition in Cape Town has become a collective act of memory-making of the histories of slavery and apartheid.

Kenny Cupers interrogates the role played by infrastructure in shaping a global modernity, whose roots in colonial history continue to shape new mechanisms of control and power, but also movements of resistance and contestation. In his piece, Emilio Distretti asks "what is to be done" with colonial architectural heritage, and elaborates on new possibilities for critical approaches and decolonial options for preservation of this heritage. Moving to questioning the relation between the urban and the natural world, Janine Eberle explores transformations in nature, constantly shaped and reshaped to its political ends, and discusses the case of the Edith Stephens Wetland Park in Cape Town and its role in South Africa's post-apartheid landscape. Manuel Herz explores the multiple lives of colonial modernist architecture in independent Kenya, Zambia, and Ivory Coast as examples of entangled histories of decolonization. The section closes with an evocative piece by Ernest Sewordor, who, through a fictional trialogue, offers an epistemic reorganization of the archival material from the colonial archives in Kew, London, and the Public Record and Archives Administration Department in Accra.

---

[1] David Harvey, "Heritage Pasts and Heritage Presents: Temporality, Meaning, and the Scope of Heritage Studies," *International Journal of Heritage Studies* 7, no. 4 (2001): 319-338.

[2] Stuart Hall, "Whose Heritage? Un-Settling 'The Heritage,' Re-imagining the Post-Nation," in Jo Littler and Roshi Naidoo (eds.), *The Politics of Heritage: The Legacies of Race* (London: Routledge, 2004).

[3] Ann Laura Stoler, "Reason Aside: Reflections on Enlightenment and Empire," in Graham Huggan (ed.), *The Oxford Handbook of Postcolonial Studies* (Oxford: Oxford University Press, 2015).

[4] Sara Ahmed, *Strange Encounters: Embodied Others in Post-Coloniality* (London: Routledge, 2000).

[5] Olivia Rutazibwa and Robbie Shilliam (eds.), *Routledge Handbook of Postcolonial Politics* (London: Routledge, 2018).

[6] Walter Benjamin, *The Arcades Project*, trans. Howard Eiland and Kevin McLaughlin (Cambridge, MA: Harvard University Press, 1999).

[7] Giorgio Agamben, *The Signature of All Things: On Method* (New York: Zone Books, 2009), 105.

LIVING MODERNITIES

The city of Tema was planned and built at a turning point in Ghana's postcolonial history: under the leadership of President Kwame Nkrumah, who led the country through decolonization, Tema came to symbolize Ghana's independence and a project of social transformation that would sever the ties with its colonial legacies. Nkrumah appointed the Greek architect Constantinos A. Doxiadis to arrange a master plan that would provide new homes for workers coming from all over Ghana. Following the rationalities and principles of the spirit of African modernism, the plan aimed at the transformation of "traditional" Ghanaian lifestyles by creating a city life grounded on industrial work and "modern" family life. The plan presented a design of a row house with an external back yard to accommodate the workers and their families. But by imposing the nuclear family model on Ghanaian society, the plan imported a model of Western-style domesticity, where the man is the breadwinner and the woman is confined to the house. De facto, it reinforced a typical colonial stereotype that stigmatizes the local extended family model as unfit for a modern society.

Today, however, the reality in Tema looks quite different. The story of Barbara's family is a clear example of how, despite the premises, things have changed. Among the first residents in Tema, Barbara's family grew over time beyond its nuclear size. The back yard of the house, initially intended for gardening and drying laundry, is now fully covered with concrete. In need of more living space, the family built extra rooms and a roof terrace, using the free space between the rooms as the kitchen area. Other inhabitants have done the same; families in the neighborhood have expanded their houses and set up small shops, bars, or hairdressers, offering services and goods to the community.

Today, the remodeling and reuse of the houses is proof that, despite the modernist premises of the city, residents shape their living environments according to the needs of the community that inhabits it, substituting the planned modernity of Doxiadis with an alternative sense of the modern—a lived one. **By Hanna Baumann**

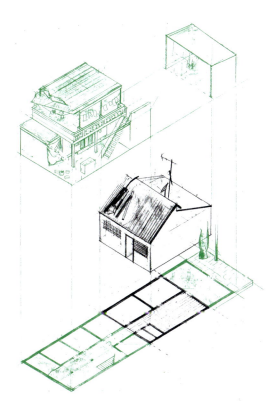

Drawing of Barbara's family home with extensions, 2019
© Plan: Hanna Baumann

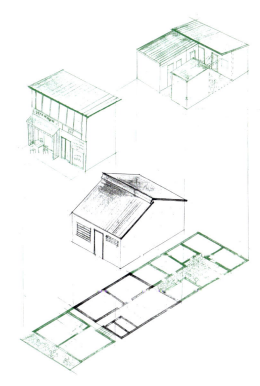

Drawing of Kojo's family home with extensions, 2019
© Plan: Hanna Baumann

THE VALUE OF (A) BRICK

"Using clay bricks to build homes, instead of cement bricks, doesn't have much to do with the question 'of being or not being modern,'" explain Ousmane and Mohamed, two residents in the district of Dogona in Bobo-Dioulasso, Burkina Faso's second-largest city. "Many people here," Ousmane continues, "prefer building with cement bricks due to their durability and the sense of permanence which is regarded as more suitable. But it is very expensive." For these reasons, it is very common for local residents to adopt a hybrid building technique that blends clay with cement. In so doing, residents use their financial resources strategically to secure affordable and comfortable living. "But because of the use of clay," Mohammed concludes, "it is still very hard to wash off the stigma of being traditional." The stigmatization of clay as a "traditional" and "nonmodern" building technique has a clear colonial origin, from the time of the French occupation. As in many postcolonial cities and countries, the colonial, civilizational, and modernist divide between traditional and modern still occupies and influences local ways of living and being. Bobo-Dioulasso is no different, as it still bears witness to the legacies of European planimetries and urbanization: subdivisions of spaces between formal and informal spaces and housing, and aesthetics canons that date back to the French occupation. To undo these legacies, the challenge is about how to break the chains of colonialist narratives, which for centuries have shaped the connection between comfortable living (grounded on secure and safe buildings, efficient infrastructures, sanitation, electricity, etc.) and the modern. Breaking this narrative means reclaiming the right to security, safety, and comfort from a non-Western perspective, and claiming space as being otherwise modern.

Cement bricks stockpiled for private use, Bobo-Dioulasso, 2019
© Photo: Alexander Crawford

In this direction, Dogona is indeed a good example of the ways the residents are making an urban identity grounded on affordability and the fulfillment of their housing needs. Originally an independent village attracting Burkina Faso's internal rural migration, since 1991 Dogona has been incorporated as part of the developing city. Since then, building techniques have been transforming, combining older and newer strategies. Specifically, the interchangeable use of clay and cement as building materials proves creativity and dynamism that refuse and go beyond the modernist divide between nonmodern and modern styles of living. **By Alexander Crawford**

A clay brick structure encased by the construction of a cement one, Bobo-Dioulasso, 2019 © Photo: Alexander Crawford

All the races begin in front of the City Hall, official photo of the Slave Route Challenge Facebook page, Cape Town, March 2019

ROUTES OF REMEMBRANCE

The Slave Route Challenge is a running competition that started in Cape Town in 2011. Taking runners and walkers throughout the slave route, the race entangles South Africa's histories of slavery and apartheid. Running through the city became both a collective ritual and an exercise of memory-making, where runners flock the city, "unveiling" the landmarks of slavery and the country's long history of institutional racism. The itinerary of the route shows how many streets designated for the race mark historical sites that link to histories of struggles dating back to the times of the slave trade in the Cape. The Slave Route Challenge is therefore a political practice against collective forgetfulness and amnesia, keeping alive the memory of centuries of racist violence and an enduring resistance to it. The race is also an occasion for the city's different communities to come together and perform, through a run, a relational memorial day.

But the race is not solely a matter of making heritage that looks at alternative ways to speak about the past. It made running a spatial practice that addresses questions of ongoing racial and economic inequalities in the city. For decades, running has been a sport of limited access, as it was a white-dominated sport. During apartheid, Black and colored people simply could not run freely; their access was restricted by segregation. Today, in the post-apartheid city, running inevitably changed. The race has made it a collective disruptive practice: it is an act of place-making that connects to the responsibility to remember the right to the city. **By Carla Cruz**

Running through the Castle of Good Hope, official photo of the Slave Route Challenge Facebook page, Cape Town, March 2019

Runners heading up the cobbled streets of Bo Kaap, official photo of the Slave Route Challenge Facebook page, Cape Town, March 2019

On the Coloniality of Infrastructure
By Kenny Cupers

Imagine a giant, thirty-five-kilometer-wide dam crossing the Strait of Gibraltar. Now imagine a similar dam at the Dardanelles, the much narrower strait that divides the Aegean Sea from the Sea of Marmara and ultimately the Black Sea. These two feats of engineering allow engineers to hydrologically close off the Mediterranean Sea. With the Mediterranean basin no longer supplied with fresh water and continually evaporating, its water level gradually falls. Imagine the dams

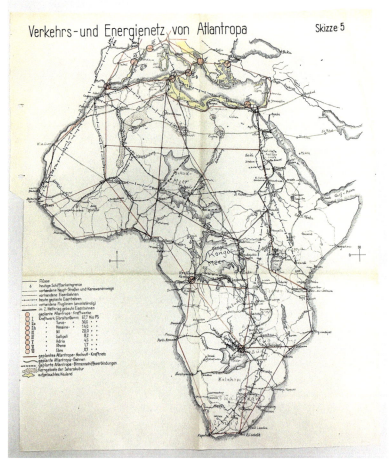

Traffic and Energy Network for Atlantropa, 1949
© Herman Sörgel, Deutsches Museum, Munich

remain closed until the water sinks a hundred meters lower—a timespan of approximately a hundred years. Vast, fertile tracts of land, previously covered with ocean, are now cultivated, and port towns are transformed into continental cities. Modern transportation and communication lines connect Spain with Morocco, Sicily with Tunisia, as Africa and Europe form a single continent. This vision of a continental merger is what Herman Sörgel spent most of his life working toward. From 1927 until his death in 1952, the German architect worked tirelessly to design and promote the project he called Atlantropa, so named to suggest the founding of a single continent along the Atlantic Ocean.[1]

The Mediterranean has not evaporated, but in the course of the twentieth century Europe and Africa changed in ways that make Sörgel's Atlantropa look more like a premonition than a racist fantasy. In the international press at the time, the project was rarely described as a lunatic's dream, perhaps because it so truthfully conveyed the dominant political rationality. Following the destruction wrought by World War I, European elites feared civilizational decline, especially with growing American and Russian hegemony. To ensure European dominance in that rapidly changing world, Europe and Africa needed to be "integrated." The project, which became known as "Eurafrica," aimed to bring about a new world order by merging two continents on fundamentally unequal terms, entrenching colonial control in Africa in order to perpetuate Europe's privilege. Eurafrica was a proposal for a more advanced, coordinated form of colonialism in Africa, the conquest of which European powers had already begun to coordinate since the Berlin conference of 1884–1885. Even though it is almost entirely written out of the official histories of the European Union, the project of Eurafrica was central to the history of European integration.[2] During the 1950s, leading European politicians still espoused the idea that "it is in Africa that Europe will be made."[3] Uniting Europe around infrastructural governance would finally allow it to achieve its so-called civilizing mission in Africa, now reframed as development. Older traditions of racism were folded into a new economy of dependency, shaped by global Cold War competition. In this context, Atlantropa continued to provide the infrastructural imaginary of Eurafrican colonization, in which vast swaths of the continent, including the Sahara, would be turned into resource hinterlands. Just as the Eurafrican project was undergirded by the racialized expropriation of life and land, Atlantropa projected an infrastructure of white supremacy.

Atlantropa, 1932 © Herman Sörgel, Deutsches Museum, Munich

Coudenhove-Kalergi's Paneuropa project (as represented by the *Schweizer Illustrierte Zeitung*, 1932)

Despite the limits of these colonial fantasies, and, more importantly, the end of formal colonial rule, the power relations through which these infrastructures were imagined and built continue to shape the present. And it is infrastructure which attests to their endurance—even as Africa enters a new age of global financial investments dominated by China. Pipes in the Mediterranean Sea continue to bring African gas to Europe, and many of the private extraction companies nurtured by former colonial powers live on today. Their business model continues to rely on mineral extraction from Africa, now for supposedly "cleaner" electronic products and energy systems. Not unlike in the colonial past, the infrastructure that connects Africa with Europe and the rest of the world facilitates the mobility of things and people for the benefit of the Global North. Similarly, that same infrastructural network restricts African mobility and regionalization. Once facilitating European settlers moving southward, infrastructure is now built to contain unwanted mobility northward. European infrastructure and development aid for Africa is increasingly being targeted to counter the movements of the undesired—without touching the global extraction economies that have their roots in colonial rule. This unwanted migration is the reversal of colonial-era flows of European settlers to the African continent. Where African *land* was once presented as the magical solution for Europe's demography, African *people* are now cast by some as Europe's existential threat.

Europe is waging an exceptionally lethal war against migration, facilitated by a growing range of infrastructures, from border walls to databases, drones to ships, and reception centers to deportation hubs. Since the Mediterranean migrant crisis in 2015, such so-called migration management has risen to the top of the EU policy agenda. Key to this agenda is the "hotspot approach."[4] This infrastructural approach to migration refers both to a location that is experiencing an overwhelming number of migrant arrivals, and to the specific infrastructural apparatus which the EU mobilizes in response to such an emergency. Infrastructure here shifts what was initially an emergency measure into a permanent exception—like the Greek hotspots which have transformed into de facto concentration camps. These camps are the starkest illustrations of the colonial logic inhabiting European infrastructure, recalling colonial mechanisms that valued life and dictated death along racialized lines. Despite strong denunciation by human rights advocates, the EU has thus far continued to promote the hotspot approach as a policy of migration management.

The EU hotspots: colonial traditions of European infrastructure? Lesvos, Greece, 2019 © Photo: Thomas Schirmer

Yet the hotspots are only the most visible element of an imperial border apparatus spreading across continents. Outsourcing and externalizing its border work to African and Middle Eastern states, the EU's infrastructural power far exceeds its territorial jurisdiction. If we wish to understand Europe as an infrastructural condition that produces its own forms of political collectivity, we need to begin by asking how colonial logics continue to striate the political subjectivities engendered by infrastructure.[5] As infrastructure not only shapes specific publics but contributes to the reinforcement of citizenship regimes, too, it also shapes the global inequalities that are historically produced by these regimes.

What does it mean to speak about the coloniality of infrastructure in this context? It is obvious that our current networks and systems of transportation, communication, and energy have roots in colonialism. Railways, ports, and telegraph lines have indeed long been studied as so-called tools of empire, facilitating the extraction and movement of things for imperial centers while curtailing the freedom and mobility of colonized peoples on an unprecedented scale. Yet as colonial relations of power exist as a constitutive part of the global modernity we are living today, the coloniality of infrastructure is more than just a matter of colonial remnants. The accelerated forms of colonialism and the consequent "becoming black" of our world today, as Achille Mbembe recently suggested, call on us to understand the persistent promise of infrastructure today—to deliver progress, modernization, and development—as entangled with colonial ways of doing, knowing, and being.[6] These ways are palpable in the built and social fabric of cities, in the networks that feed and connect them, and in the infrastructure and development projects shaping their future. Infrastructure shapes territories and governs the movements and processes within and across them; but it does more than just facilitating inclusion in modern citizenship. Infrastructure also excludes, contains, and subjugates, as much as it includes, moves, or liberates. Key to this differentiating power of infrastructure is race—a mental construct and category of human difference spurred by colonialism. The notion of coloniality, therefore, does not serve to rehash debates about historical continuity, but rather to engender a new way of understanding and reimagining the presence of the past, and with it, the power and promise of infrastructure.

Such an inquiry suggests alternatives to the continual rearticulation of Afro-pessimism, by recognizing that the effects of infrastructure are often multiple, paradoxical, or inconsistent. If infrastructure had been targeted in anti-colonial struggles (for example the sabotaging of railways), it nevertheless continued to play a key role in struggles for independence. During the 1950s, dams, highways, and electricity networks became the unquestioned material basis of postindependence nation-building and development, and some even mobilized hopes of Pan-African integration and international solidarity. Infrastructural visions of connecting continents continued to remain central even in this process, now to overcome centuries of European colonialism.

Infrastructure would, finally, connect Africa with itself: it would spur inter-African economic and social development, and the formation of a new African collectivity, overturning the extractive logic of colonial railways that usually ran from inland to port. Infrastructure was in effect meant to be an instrument through which ordinary Africans would first and foremost become economic producers as well as consumers.

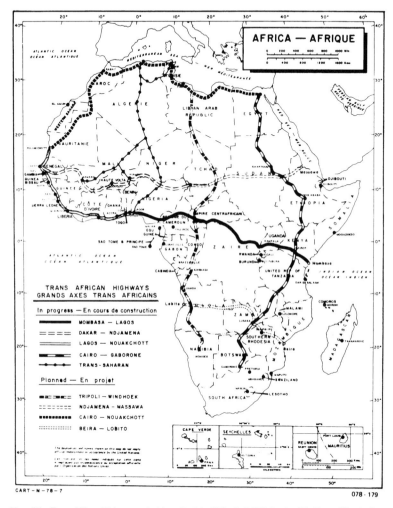

Map of the Trans-African Highway project from the late 1970s, in Rolf Hofmeier, "Die Transafrikastraßen: Stand der Planung und Realisierung," *Africa Spectrum* 14, no. 1 (1979): 31–51, here 35.

Paradigmatic of these hopes was the construction of a transcontinental highway network covering the African continent. Despite the decolonial rhetoric of Pan-African development, the project for a Trans-African Highway network was shaped by a web of governmental and corporate initiatives that still very much reproduced late-colonial norms and ideas. Large-scale infrastructure required technical expertise and development aid which in effect further entrenched Africa's unequal relationship with the Global North. This is the dialectical nature of infrastructure, whose hopes of liberation and dangers of subjugation are reflected in individual experience as much as in the fate of nations.[7]

It is only during that era of state-led decolonization that the term "infrastructure" emerged in its modern, encompassing sense, to denote all sorts of public works and technical systems. The emergence of infrastructure, at that time, coincided with a global development complex and with a new form of governing the future, based on calculative practices applied to the economy as a new factual object. Across Cold War boundaries, elites conceptualized infrastructure as the technical (and therefore seemingly neutral) basis for economic and social development, even though it perpetuated imperial forms of territorialization and control.

Attending to the coloniality of infrastructure allows us to decenter this dominant economic and political rationality, and to foreground other practices of world-making—not least those engendered by the anti-colonial struggles and alternative visions that preceded, undergirded, and transcended state-led decolonization. This suggests we should extend our analytical perspective from colonial afterlives to the multiple ways in which infrastructure is inherited from the past—not only through material artifacts and physical configurations, but also through spatial imaginaries, affective relations, and shared memories. Saidiya Hartman's work on inheritance, as being "chosen as much as passed on," can inspire us to explore how multiple inheritances shape infrastructural lifeworlds and connections.

Modernist architecture of a now-disused rest stop along the Trans-African highway near Tsavo, with the new Chinese-built Standard Gauge Railway in the background @ Photo: Cupers, 2017

Such inheritances may be immaterial, as in the way a colonial railway conveys romantic memories of travel for some or resilience against the traumas of subjugation for others. They may be projective, fueling individual aspirations of prosperity, mobility, or belonging. Or they may signify "roads not taken," propelling dreams of another, radically different future. Inheritance can also be forged from material artifacts. As new, not rarely monumental infrastructures of postcolonial nation-building have risen, colonial-era infrastructures have crumbled. Yet with the rise of modern heritage preservation, colonial architecture and urbanism are often reappropriated as touristic opportunities; they also, however, become instrumental to new cultural or political claims and designs. It may be seductive to conceptualize infrastructure as the oppressive instrument of racial capitalism in order to explain how development projects sold as lifting Africa onto the global stage are often the same ones that perpetuate expropriation and dispossession. Yet recognizing the coloniality of infrastructure also means departing from the idea of a single, shared globality, and therefore attending to other worlds, ways of being, and inheritances.

As African countries are attempting to learn the lessons from East Asia in order to become middle-income economies, researchers should consider the possibility that they do not just reiterate the political strategies of the European colonial era. Even though many low-income countries have little bargaining power in today's global financial environment, their infrastructure projects speak of an African future. To gauge the possibility that the current infrastructure boom makes hard on such promises, we need to account for what people do *with* and *through* infrastructure—not only in the livelihoods they forge, but also in the lives they project by means of its promises. It is in this way that we may see the spatial imaginations and political struggles at work in infrastructure, and understand their effects on mobility and belonging—in ways that challenge not only the purview of nation-states but also the established categories of "Europe" and "Africa." Approaching infrastructure from this perspective offers a way of seeing how the effects of infrastructure are not only circumscribed by, but may also transform colonial hierarchies of power.

[1] Wolfgang Voigt, *Atlantropa: Weltenbauen am Mittelmeer, Ein Architektentraum der Moderne* (Munich: Dölling und Galitz, 1998); Alexander Gall, *Das Atlantropa-Projekt: die Geschichte einer gescheiterten Vision: Herman Sörgel und die Absenkung des Mittelmeers* (Frankfurt a.M.: Campus, 1998).

[2] Peo Hansen and Stefan Jonsson, *Eurafrica: The Untold History of European Integration and Colonialism* (London: Bloomsbury, 2014), 13.

[3] Jean-Michel de Lattre, "Les grands ensembles africains," *Politique étrangère* 20, no. 5 (1955): 543.

[4] See the report "Infrastructure Space and the Future of Migration Management," a research project led by Bilgin Ayata, co-coordinated by Kenny Cupers, and funded by the Swiss Network of International Studies (2018–2020).

[5] On the making of infrastructural publics, see *Limn*, Issue 7 (2016): Public Infrastructures/Infrastructural Public, ed. Stephen J. Collier, James Christopher Mizes, and Antina von Schnitzler. See also Sven Opitz and Ute Tellmann, "Europe as Infrastructure: Networking the Operative Community," *The South Atlantic Quarterly* 114, no. 1 (January 2015).

[6] Achille Mbembe, *Brutalisme* (Paris: La Découverte, 2020).

[7] See Kenny Cupers and Prita Meier, "Infrastructure Between Statehood and Subjecthood: The Trans-African Highway," *Journal of the Society of Architectural Historians* 79, no. 1 (2020): 61–81.

Notes on Heritage (Re-)Making
By Emilio Distretti

The question around the role of colonial architectural heritage has always been a thorn in the side of state and identity formations and transformations, in both formerly colonized and colonizing societies and spaces. On the one hand, in the postcolony, the dilemma has been framed around different solutions: either the appropriation of colonial official buildings as sites for newly independent governments, for practices of memorialization, or as abandoned to collective forgetfulness. On the other hand, in the "ex-metropole," the question around buildings, institutions, and monuments is transmitted and articulated through the paradoxical coexistence of amnesia of the colonial past with the hyper-visibility of urban designs of colonial origin. This dual direction, rather than creating a contrast, opened up the question of whether it makes sense to inquire into the "loss of meaning" of colonial architecture.

What do these buildings really represent and mean today? While the question of meaning has become central to many other debates since postmodernism impacted upon architectural and spatial theories and practices, in postcolonial worlds we see the relics of colonialism having been normalized within cityscapes. Here, the concepts of "deviation," "dissociation," "discontinuity," "dispersion," and "rupture," that with postmodern theory have contested the idea of an architectural knowledge as embedded into power, authority, and violence, clash until this very day with the problem posed by the immanence of colonial structures in a postcolonial world.

In fact, it is true that such immanence cannot be simply dismissed as an innocent remnant of the past. On the contrary, colonial architectural heritage still pervades our cultural and mental spaces as long as what Anibal Quijano has defined the "coloniality of power" endures: namely, when the principles of colonial rule—after its conclusion—have survived the rule itself. In fact, as an integral part of a capitalist and patriarchal domination, colonialism did not vanish when historical colonialism ended. Furthermore, colonial legacies continue to actively shape the present in manifold ways: the recentering of far-right politics in the Global North, global migration and the incapacity of Europe to cope with the *longue durée* of fascism and colonialism, collective amnesia and melancholia about the colonial past, resurgent ethno-nationalisms, and the claims that the white West has the "right" to preserve its hegemonic status.

In response to this regressive path, a multitude of voices, practices, and movements have gathered under an unconditional claim: if coloniality is still on, so is decolonization. In this way, struggles for decolonization in the former colonial world persist beyond their historic manifestation (temporal and spatial) and beyond campaigns for posthumous justice and reparations for past crimes: decolonization is perceived as an unfinished project of ongoing experiences of resistance against capitalism and patriarchy and the persistence of Western-centric epistemologies and knowledge. Moreover, practices and theories of decolonization continue permeating the Northern Hemisphere, where people with a migratory, refugee, and slavery background (and their allies) live and strive.

In a world that until this very day experiences the survival of the principles and rationalities of colonialism—from institutional racism shaped around economic inequality, class divides and the racializa-

The first edition of the Difficult Heritage Summer School at Borgo Rizza, Carlentini, Sicily, 2021 © Photo: Emilio Distretti. The Difficult Heritage Summer School inaugurates a space for critical knowledge and pedagogy. It takes place in Borgo Rizza, a rural settlement originally built by Italy's Fascist regime in the Sicilian countryside, to investigate the afterlife of colonial Fascist architecture. As an attempt to redraw the contours of colonial architectural heritage and the narratives built around it, the participants discuss—as a collective— questions of access, decolonial reuse and entitlement over that painful and violent heritage. The Difficult Heritage Summer School is a collaboration between DAAS-Decolonizing Architecture Advanced Course (Stockholm), Critical Urbanisms (Basel) and the municipality and local community of Carlentini.

tion of borders, ongoing settler colonial projects across the globe, and policies of illegalization of non-white migrants and citizens that foster their invisibility, de-humanization, and disappearance from the social, political, and class spectrum—what is the place of its old sanctuaries and temples? What can be our understanding of colonial architectural heritage in the present reality? What values does it stand for today, and what image of society does it aim to represent?

As a way to answer these questions, a critical reflection on the question of heritage is necessary. David Harvey has offered an important historical analysis of the development of heritage practices.[1]

He points out that every society has a relationship with the past, in the way we tell one another about it, in what we remember and what we forget. In such terms, "heritage" is understood as a social process, a political product, a performance of public memory where the question of the present is the one that really matters. Most importantly, since antiquity the production of heritage connects to the reuse and reinterpretation of spaces, sites, and physical remains that occur as the result of political and cultural transitions. Heritage is therefore the expression of a tension enacted by reuse and reappropriation.

The idea of heritage as a tension *therefore* breaks with an idea of heritage as the outcome of harmonious and linear historical continuities. Heritage is not a given, as it bears antagonism, conflict, and negotiations, together with outstanding ethical and political burdens. To explain the conflict and violence that can lie at the roots of these questions, Andrew Herscher interestingly points at heritage as a product of modernity.[2] He does so by looking at the devastation of architectural heritage in the context of the 1990s civil war and ethnic cleansing in former Yugoslavia. There, the heritage of the "other" was the target for destruction. Referring to the relation between heritage-making as inextricably tied to destruction, Herscher relates the fabrication of heritage to a very typical modern and modernist feature that is the need to self-impose via the identification of "nonhistorical counterparts" that are excluded and expelled from society as nonmodern and empty of value. If we borrow this framework of analysis and read it against the violence and destruction caused across centuries of colonial and imperial dominations and in the (post)colonial present, we recognize that the inner civilizational and selective feature of "heritage" is a product of European Modernity. At the time of empires and colonialism, architecture—in its traditional role as the "right hand" of sovereignty—provided material configurations to modern and modernist ideologies by putting facts on the ground and implementing disciplinary regimes in the colonized populations: southward transfer of infrastructure technology (roads, railways, bridges, and ports), as well as the imposition of new trading networks (the introduction of trading and extraction systems that erased local economies), the polarization between "White Towns" and "Black Towns," the allocation of governmental buildings, courts, schools, and prisons together with urban zoning reflected a Western modernity based on the principles of dispossession, violence, and segregation.

The superimpositions and presence of these built forms and structures must be read in relation to the progressive eradication and exploitation of forms of native life, indigenous labor, knowledge, culture, and ecologies in the colonized world, but also in relation to the parallel proliferation in the "metropoles" in the Northern Hemisphere of more ministerial buildings, offices, private businesses, banks, stock markets, and museums, reflecting practically and symbolically the global spread of colonialism's tentacles. This defines what Samia Henni has correctly addressed as the ramification of coloniality via architectural forms, histories, and theories. [3]

In the present day, where the legacies of this past are more tangible than ever, it is timely and appropriate to wonder about the present and the future of this colonial architectural heritage. What should be done with those buildings and many other physical remnants that bear witness to an enduring history of violence and injustice?

As suggested by Harvey, understanding heritage means rethinking it in terms of reuse and reappropriation. These questions have gained an important role in relation to the work of Giorgio Agamben and his notion of "profanation." Agamben borrows the term "profanation" from a theologian lexicon and transforms it into a political operation that "deactivates the apparatuses of power and returns to common use the spaces that power had seized." The notion of profanation posed against repression and intertwined with architecture is then a way to "return the practice itself to the everyday users of those spaces," addressing the necessity to break the tie that binds architecture (as knowledge and practice) to power (political and economic). In the last decade the concept of profanation has become a leading principle of new modes of politics embedded to architectural analysis, practice, art, and activism (see for instance the work of DAAR—Decolonizing Art and Architecture Residency in Palestine), where the concept of decolonization merges with processes of "deactivation of control and security devices."[4] Hence, to profane something is a positive act for the simple reason that it liberates things and practices for communal usage: "The creation of a new use is possible only by deactivating an old use, rendering it inoperative."[5]

Along these lines, it would be important to rethink our interpretation of heritage, both as a concept and as a practice. In terms of reuse, heritage is therefore not bound to the aesthetic and symbolic realms, nor does it passively document interchangeable and shifting paradigms. On the contrary, it must be read in its interrelation to the question of justice, as a matter of rights and entitlement: after centuries of spoliation and enduring injustice for the crimes of colonialism, who has the right over the remnants of that past—over colonial architecture? Can the heirs of the colonized claim some sort of ownership over those symbols that centuries ago had been originally designed and erected in both hemispheres to rule and dispossess them?

These challenging questions aim at increasing public awareness of the afterlives of those architectural relics, and produce alternative narratives that can tell these histories through anti-colonial optics and lenses. But action should not be limited only to the sphere of the narrative. From a conservationist perspective, we might note that many of those buildings and infrastructures are also very old, and while still standing are in dire need of fixing. Should we destroy them or protect them? Beyond any dilemma that risks perpetuating "universal" narratives and practices around heritage, I suggest that any act of physical and material repair of colonial architectural heritage should necessarily understand the repair as an attempt to heal from the colonial wound, which—as Christina Sharpe has suggested—should entail and open to "reimagine and transform spaces for and practices of an ethics of care (as in repair, maintenance and attention) an ethics of seeing, and of being in the wake as consciousness." The struggle against the racist, violent, gendered, civilizational principles and rationalities that constitute the foundation of colonial architecture will therefore need collective processes of imagination in order to facilitate the proliferation of new critical and decolonial approaches of preservation of this heritage, whose ultimate task, let's not forget, is to turn this very architecture against itself.

[1] David Harvey, "Heritage Pasts and Heritage Presents: Temporality, Meaning, and the Scope of Heritage Studies," *International Journal of Heritage Studies* 7, no. 4 (2001): 319–338.

[2] Andrew Herscher, "Counter-Heritage and Violence," *Future Anterior* 3, no. 2 (2006): 25–33.

[3] Samia Henni, "Colonial Ramifications," *E-Flux architecture, History and Theory* (2018), https://www.e-flux.com/architecture/history-theory/225180/colonial-ramifications/.

[4] DAAR, *The Book of Profanation* (January 2009), http://www.decolonizing.ps/books/profanation.pdf.

[5] Giorgio Agamben, *Profanations* (New York: Zone Books, 2007), 87.

[6] Christina Sharpe, *In the Wake: On Blackness and Being* (Durham, NC: Duke University Press, 2016), 131.

(Post-)Apartheid Nature
By Janine Eberle

In this time of climate change, environmentalism, and nature conservation, projects are commonly seen as a silver lining in public debates about sustainable development strategies, and ultimately even about the future of the human race. Given the high expectations and hopes placed in environmentalism, it is important to critically analyze the categories and normative implications inherent in this discourse. Our modes of knowledge production in nature conservation—just as in any other field—depend on social conventions and institutionalized hierarchies. The contingent character of knowledge as a social product means that it has to be up for debate whether the ways in which we learn and teach about nature, conceptualize our relationship with the planet, and produce power structures through environmentalism are reasonable and comply with our visions of how we want humanity to shape the world.

The natural world can also be considered as a social construct. Its image, perception, and conservation are also the products of historical and social changes, that enable an imagination of the nature/society relation beyond modern separations and dichotomies. In this text, I will read and discuss the question of nature conservation: as a colonial construct, and as the result of a modern approach that looks at nature as an exploitable world that can be turned into "value" and "property." Specifically, I look at the case of the Edith Stephens Wetland Park in Cape Town to explore the question of the protection of natural landscapes in (post)colonial and (post-)apartheid South Africa. Due to historical imbalances and the need to redress damages from colonial times and apartheid, the South African constitution enshrined the legal requirement of participation in many public issues to work away discriminatory legal mechanisms. The ways in which natural spaces, gardens, and urban parks in Cape Town's cityscape still reflect racialized relations of power—issues such as access and entitlement to green spaces and the mobility across them—are also seen as related to the issue of nature conservation as a matter of public land use.

As we highlight efforts of participation within nature conservation, we avoid a categorical distinction between what is natural and what is human. As a consequence, this case study on post-apartheid urban nature conservation allows us to shift the focus away from the operational work and management strategies put in place to conserve a nature space. Instead, it sheds light on the different users of the space and their relationship to one another. These actors comprise, for example, the park's workers and its management, the overarching governmental structure of the City of Cape Town, the local schools that come for day trips, the wood collectors whose livelihood depends on harvesting trees, local residents who dispute their access to the land, security guards who deal with issues of violence and safety around the park, and many more. The reframing of nature conservation from a categorical to a relational understanding is important, because it puts the social context in the foreground and allows us to include voices in the conversation around land which are otherwise silenced. A common reason for certain voices being silenced within the discussion around nature conservation is that these voices are simply not heard, as they do not come from academic or governmental institutions. Their knowledge often derives from their own everyday experiences with land and their traditional uses of nature, which oftentimes does not fit into a scientific category.

At the same time, as we open the discussion to voices which typically do not belong to the narrow circle of experts on nature, we need to critically analyze the voices we typically consider as "expert," and look at how expert opinion shapes our relationship with nature. Feminist geographer Cindi Katz pointed out that one way in which nature is often

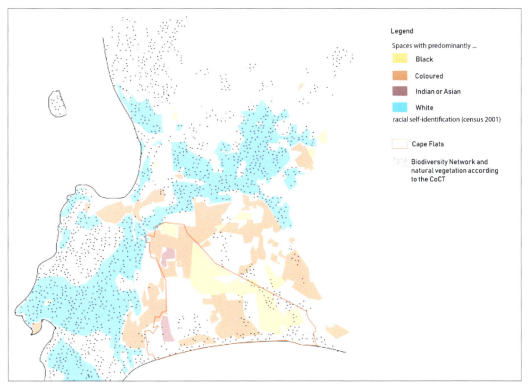

Racial segregation and nature spaces in Cape Town, 2019 © Map: Janine Eberle

conceptualized in environmental debates is as an accumulation strategy.[1] She argues that Enlightenment thinking and social relations of production have, due to capitalism, established an instrumentalist view of nature as a source of value. Nature as a resource has been analyzed by Marxist and eco-feminist writers who exposed parallels between the exploitation of nature and the exploitation of people. In order to use nature as an accumulation strategy, Katz holds that nature has become an investment in the future. In a next step to secure this investment, the commodification and privatization of nature unfolded on a global scale. Katz argues that preservation agendas promoted by corporations, foundations, nongovernmental organizations, and governments are directed at an instrumentalist cause. In other words, nature is seen as a commodity which can be valued and compensated in purely monetary terms. This view of course reduces the possibility of far more complex relationships between humans and nature, which can be spiritual, emotional, and even just infrastructural.

In an attempt to explore alternative ways of relating to nature, I focused on a nature conservation site in Cape Town where users, so-called experts, and nearby residents together invest in a recreational green space in a place where nature conservation is normally considered a luxury problem for the privileged few. In the 1990s, the heritage site of Edith Stephens Wetland Park was established as a nature reserve as a consequence of an extensive public participation process.[2] It was June 2000 when the city finally bought the surrounding conservation-worthy land, which the municipality identified as a key open space in the spatial plan called the Wetton-Lansdowne-Philippi corridor. This land is inhabited by highly threatened vegetation which represents a transition from Cape Dune Strandveld to Cape Flats Sand Fynbos. With this land addition the park reached its current size and was officially named Edith Stephens Nature Reserve.[3] With its expansion and official status as a Nature Reserve, which is part of the City of Cape Town and its Biodiversity Management Branch, the construction and restoration of the park was initiated. Considering the social context of the park, an awareness program of the reserve was developed which took into account the target audience as well as the circumstances of the communities who live closest to the nature reserve. The district in which Edith Stephens is located has the second highest unemployment rate of all districts in Cape Town, a concerning lack of economic activity, and a very high population density. Gang violence, a severe backlog in housing and infrastructural services, as well as a lack of safe, open, and green spaces characterize the harsh living conditions the nearby residents have to cope with. This context can only be understood in connection with the historical injustices brought about by colonial and apartheid urban planning, which established green spaces in the predominantly white city center and restricted nonwhite groups of people in densely populated outer districts where natural spaces were neglected altogether. The "green" was therefore mobilized to enhance and perpetuate racial segregation.

During apartheid, racial categories have been enshrined in a legal apparatus which enabled a racist white settler minority to rule and exploit the native population. As the end of apartheid has introduced legal racial equality but has not yet led to a redistribution of property or land, South Africa remains spatially racialized. As a consequence for its population, means of transportation, housing opportunities, and, as highlighted in this paper, access to nature and green spaces represent Cape Town's racialization of everyday life.

The spaces that the City of Cape Town marks as places of natural vegetation are areas where we see a concentration of predominantly white inhabitants. The space within the boundary of the Cape Flats is one of major concentration of colored and Black groups of people, which does not overlap significantly with natural spaces. This also has to do with the fact that these areas are generally much more densely inhabited than those marked in blue. Areas not marked as populated by any of the racial groups are either fairly mixed or very sparsely inhabited.

It is important to note that the racial categories depicted on the map were constructed by apartheid rule and legally imposed on the South African population in order to control and degrade a Black majority. Crucial for this legal regulation of people was the Population Registration Act (No. 30 of 1950) which legally classified every South African according to race. This made it possible to impose further acts to separate these groups of people by strict spatial segregation (Group Area Act No. 41 of 1950 and Bantu Authorities Act No. 68 of 1951) and by education (Bantu Education Act No. 47 of 1953), to mention only a few examples.[4] With the downfall of apartheid, these acts were invalidated. However, almost fifty years of apartheid not only defined legal restrictions but also ingrained this logic of classification and separation into the minds of people. This is why these categories are still often referred to today when talking about self-identification and cultural differences. Scholars and officials also still refer to these categories in policies and statistics in order to be able to address historical imbalances and discrimination which are still experienced today.

If we acknowledge these restrictions and similar difficulties posed to nature conservation through the social context of every place, it becomes clear that the work done in a nature park needs to deal not only with technical and primarily biological concerns, and that it only functions if it adapts to its historical, political, and social contexts. The analysis done in Edith Stephens is a remarkable example, I argue, showing the way in which the social context of nature conservation defines our understandings of what nature is and what ideal we therefore aim to protect. The thematic analysis of my field notes revealed that participation at Edith Stephens primarily works through *dealing with limitations of the institutional context, negotiating, and coping with danger*—meaning poverty-related crime, environmental degradation, and political instability—and *knowing insiders and outsiders*. A substantial part of the work that needs to be done for the nature reserve to succeed and to provide services to its users is invested into these four tasks. These tasks are all about allowing participation, and they do not reflect the typical work associated with nature conservation. Nature conservation understood within a nature/culture divide is not able to acknowledge these participatory efforts as significant. It is unable to, because to dwell in this divide makes it impossible to pay attention to the social context, in this case specifically the apartheid legacy, as an active and dynamic factor of nature conservation.

In conventional, modern approaches to nature conservation, nature is usually conceptualized as an apolitical realm outside the social world. Realizing that this notion of nature is not god-given, but rather produced in a social discourse, is the first step toward imagining other ways of how nature can be understood.

At Edith Stephens Nature Reserve, the debates around what kind of issue or project is part of the work reflect the blurring of the nature/culture divide. It is clear that without people who arrive at work safely and contribute to the management and the upkeep of the park, and without the park users, this space would not exist. It is also clear that these people are inseparable from the historical, political, and social events happening at this space. This is the case in any nature reserve, but the constraints, obstacles, and discussions that people need to deal with in order to arrive at work safely, invest their time and energy in this space, and thus bring it to life are not always easily visible and need to be acknowledged. Once the typical idea of who nature is for and what cost is justifiable to maintain it is challenged, we recognize that both nature and society are debatable notions. The reason we sometimes do not see the obstacles and restrictions that come with nature conservation is likely due to the fact that we naturalize them. Naturalizing and normalizing circumstances happen easily if we have never been exposed to how different ways of engaging with nature might work. For this we need to train our imaginations and remind ourselves that, even though our world is the way it is, it does not mean it cannot be different.

[1] Cindi Katz, "Whose Nature, Whose Culture? Private Productions of Space and the Preservation of Nature," in Bruce Braun and Noel Castree (eds.), *Remaking Reality: Nature at the Millennium* (London: Routledge, 1998), 46–63.

[2] Luzann Isaacs, "Integrated Reserve Management Plan," City of Cape Town Environmental Resource Management Department (2011), 21.

[3] Ibid., 9.

[4] Sean Field, Renate Meyer, and Felicity Swanson (eds.), *Imagining the City: Memories and Cultures in Cape Town* (Cape Town: HSRC Press, 2007).

A Tale of Three Towers
By Manuel Herz

On September 24, 1973, Kenyan President Jomo Kenyatta and World Bank President Robert McNamara opened the annual meeting of the IMF and World Bank Group in the city center of Nairobi. It was the first time an annual meeting of the two main global financial institutions had taken place on the African continent. Over the next four days, almost 3,000 delegates from 126 nations would crowd the various halls of the just completed Kenyatta International Conference Centre (KICC). Soaring twenty-eight floors into the sky, the KICC was by far the tallest structure in Nairobi, and, at the time of its completion, the tallest skyscraper on the African continent outside of South Africa. With its large convention hall ("The Plenary") and its circular amphitheater space, it was perfectly suited to bring the world to Nairobi, just ten years after Kenya had gained independence. It was a proud symbol for a young country to connect to a global league of nations.

Hotel Ivoire, Abidjan, 2014 © Photo: Iwan Baan

During the late 1950s and early 1960s, most countries of Sub-Saharan Africa gained their independence. Architecture became one of the principal means with which the young nations expressed their national identity. Parliament buildings, central banks, stadiums, conference centers, and universities were constructed, often featuring heroic and daring designs. Modern and futuristic architecture mirrored the aspirations and forward-looking spirit that dominated at the time. A coinciding period of economic boom made elaborate construction methods possible, while the tropical climate allowed for an architecture that blended the inside and outside, and focused on form and the expression of materiality.

At the same time, this architecture also shows the difficulties, contradictions, and dilemmas those countries experienced in their independence process: in most cases, the architects were not local, but came from countries such as Poland, the former Yugoslavia, Scandinavian countries, Israel, and even the former colonial powers. Could the formation

Kenyatta International Conference Centre, Nairobi, 2014 © Photo: Iwan Baan

of a new national identity through architecture therefore be described as a projection from the outside? Or does the international dimension instead represent the aspirations of those countries aiming for a cosmopolitan culture? To what extent do projects such as the KICC act as stepping stones that propel a country forward or rather as vanity projects initiated by authoritarian "Big Man" policies?

Initially, the KICC had not been planned to be the tallest building in independent Africa, nor as a venue for hosting international conferences. In fact, it was originally intended to be the headquarters of the Kenya African National Union or "KANU," being the main—and eventually the only—political party of the postindependence era. In 1967

Jomo Kenyatta approached the Ministry of Works with the task of designing and building a new headquarters for his political party in the central business district of Nairobi. For the project, David Mutiso, Head Architect within the Ministry, recommended one of his staff, Karl Henrik Nøstvik, who had recently arrived from Norway, as his most talented planner.

Nøstvik's design for the building showed a short tower, a rectangular plinth, and a small auditorium, with the tower originally planned with thirteen floors. In the midst of the design process the World Bank and the IMF decided they would host their 1973 annual global meeting in Nairobi, underlining the continent's importance in global consciousness at the time. Nøstvik reworked his design, almost tripling the height of the tower to thirty-two floors, enlarging the plinth, and considerably expanding the auditorium to host major international events. Instead of the KANU Headquarters, it was to become the Kenyatta International Conference Centre. From a building of previously national importance for a political party it developed into a complex of international scope.

Nøstvik developed an architectural language of massing and volume as well as the scale of building elements through brise-soleils, canopies, and atriums. Multiple stairs and ramps negotiate the exterior plaza shaded by cantilevers and exterior galleries made of exposed concrete. Lush greenery seems to be growing off the facades and cantilevers, reaching down into large water ponds and fountains.

The interior of the main plinth consists of multiple cascading stairs and platforms on various levels seemingly crisscrossing one another. A strong sense of robustness pervades an almost Escherian space treated with a beautiful combination of raw exposed concrete and dark-red wood. The amphitheater, the KICC's main assembly hall, is contained within a flower-like building cantilevering daringly above and across the southern wing of the plinth. Light falls over a height of more than twenty meters through a central skylight and reflects across a myriad of wooden leaves and over several levels of balconies and terraced seating, giving the space an aura of majestic importance. It exudes a sense of pride, of a country finally independent, meeting other nations at eye level.

Having attracted the World Bank and the IMF to Nairobi for a conference was significant for the nation's capital. Eventually, though, the building's importance for the nation proved to go much further: with the IMF and World Bank meeting, the United Nations Environment Program (UNEP, one of the UN's main sub-organizations) opened offices in the KICC. The following year, the Kenyan government gifted a large piece of land in the northwest of the capital to the United Nations. Over the years, that UN campus would grow to house the headquarters of the UNEP and UN Habitat, as well as several regional headquarters of UN suborganizations. Nairobi had become one of the four capital cities of the United Nations and from then on would always be mentioned together with New York, Geneva, and Vienna.

Today, the KICC remains the iconic masterpiece that it already symbolized at the time of its completion. The building is cherished by the Kenyan population, which becomes evident by the large number of local tour groups and school classes that come to pay it homage, as well as by its well-maintained condition. Its various meeting halls and conference spaces remain much used, for everything from Sunday services of Pentecostal churches, via a plethora of trade shows, to international meetings such as the UN Conference on Trade and Development, thus still bringing the world to Nairobi.

But the world that Kenya connected to with the KICC was to a certain extent skewed to the Western world and capitalist countries. Even though formally part of the Non-Aligned Movement, representing a supposedly neutral path between the two super powers, during the Cold War period Kenya sought close ties to the UK, the US, and other European countries. Other countries on the continent, such as Zambia, followed a different political and ideological path, which also became visible in their architecture.

Since the 1930s Zambia has been a mining country and one of the main exporters of copper in the world. At the time of its independence in 1964, Zambia was the strongest economy of Sub-Saharan Africa (with the exception of South Africa), with a GDP per capita similar to that of Portugal. After it gained independence, however, the main mines, as well as its banks and insurance companies, were still owned by foreign investors, mainly based in the US, the UK, and South Africa. As Zambia saw itself as having obtained formal independence, but its key economies still controlled by outside interests, its president Kenneth Kaunda decided in 1968 to pursue a policy of nationalization. Ownership of most of the mines, banks, and insurance companies was transferred to the Zambian state. These new state companies—amongst them FINDECO (Financial Development Corporation)—needed new headquarters, and hence new buildings.

With its independence, Zambia also became a member of the Non-Aligned Movement. Unlike Kenya, though, Zambia took a central role in shaping that union, by hosting the third global summit in its capital Lusaka in 1970, and with Kenneth Kaunda becoming its secretary general in the same year. Having angered Britain and the US, unsurprisingly it sought new economic links with countries that were also central to the Non-Aligned Movement—amongst them the former Yugoslavia, one of its founding nations. For the design of the FINDECO headquarters, located along the southern stretch of Cairo Road, Lusaka's main axis in its central business district, two Yugoslavian architects, Dušan Milenkovic and Branimir Ganovic, were appointed.

The FINDECO building consists of a three-story plinth and a tower split into two sections: a fifteen-story main body, and another three floors on top separated from the main body by a gap. The plinth features an elevated shopping zone that is connected to the street level by a number of stairs. The floors of the tower are suspended between the concrete core and steel columns, which themselves are supported by a strong sculptural concrete cantilever below both tower sections, giving the building its iconic form. The facade features windows and ionized aluminum panels that shimmer in a greenish-golden hue. The FINDECO House is one of the most distinct buildings along Cairo Road. It is a vertical icon among the otherwise mostly horizontal fabric of the city. Not only does it mark the southern end of downtown Lusaka, it also marks the policy of nationalization, and the end of Zambia's economic boom period. In the year of the building's completion, 1977, Zambia fell into a major recession from which it has taken the country more than twenty-five years to recover.

While Zambia was building high-rise buildings for its nationalized industries, and Kenya doing the same to attract international conferences and organizations to its capital city, in Abidjan, the economical hub and then capital of the Ivory Coast, a very different kind of tower project was being developed: namely, a hotel. While this program sounds slightly underwhelming compared to the loftier aspirations in Lusaka and Nairobi, it was hardly so. Félix Houphouët-Boigny, Ivory Coast's first president, understood that luxury hotels represent a key ingredient in the process of nation-building. Not only do they open the country to a growing international tourist market, they also afford the possibility

Findeco Tower, Lusaka, 2014 © Photo: Iwan Baan

of hosting business people and important politicians from all over the world, provide the infrastructure to hold international conferences and meetings, and communicate an image of success and glamour to the Western world. Consequently, one of the first projects that Houphouët-Boigny initiated after independence was the construction of one of the most luxurious hotels in all of Western Africa, if not the whole continent—the Hôtel Ivoire.

Houphouët-Boigny commissioned Israeli architect and real-estate developer, Moshe Mayer, who in turn designed the project with the Israeli architects Heinz Fenchel and Thomas Leitersdorf and the Californian architect William Pereira. The hotel is located in the upmarket neighborhood of Cocody, near several embassies, on a site overlooking the lagoon with a view toward Abidjan's central district, Le Plateau. It was developed in three stages. The first phase saw the construction of a two-story plinth building containing a lobby, a restaurant, and other general functions, and resting upon that plinth was a thirteen-story space for approximately 200 rooms. In the late 1960s a twenty-five-story tower was added, offering sweeping views over the whole region and containing an additional 200 rooms as well as meeting and conference spaces on the top floors. In the third phase, a conference center was added to the large open plaza at the foot of the tower. The hotel features a gigantic swimming pool—aptly named "Le Lac" (The Lake)—which is 250 meters in length and covers an area of more than 7,500 square meters. Several bars and restaurants are located along the pool. Furthermore, the hotel complex includes a casino and the country's first ice skating rink, which has, however, been nonoperational for years.

The Hôtel Ivoire indeed fulfilled the president's hopes and became a glamorous destination for tourists, politicians, business people, and stars from the film and music industry. Fancy parties were held, fashion shows and beauty pageants were staged, and musicians from all over the world performed concerts there. Weddings of the rich and famous from West Africa were celebrated in its halls; Hollywood stars and other international celebrities such as Michael Jackson and Mohammed Ali stayed in its suites. Toward the end of the 1980s, the "Ivorian Miracle"—the economic boom that underlay this development—came to an end. In the late 1990s the country descended into a period of internal conflict. Though no longer operating as a hotel, the Hôtel Ivoire, and especially its tower, remained an important actor in the country's dynamics. In the early 2000s it became the base for the militia group Jeunes Patriotes and in 2004 it was taken over by French UN troops, both of which understood the strategic advantage that occupying the tower would lend them in controlling large swathes of the urban fabric of Abidjan. When, on November 9, 2004, Ivoirian demonstrators amassed around the hotel to protest against the presence of French troops in their country, snipers from the French unit positioned in the tower shot and killed as many as twenty demonstrators. Far from being a simple piece of architectural infrastructure, the Hôtel Ivoire itself became an actor and part of the machinery of urban conflict. One cannot escape the tragic irony of the building that was meant to symbolize independence more than any other edifice in the Ivory Coast becoming a tool of urban warfare by the troops of its former colonizers. As another step in its contentious history, in 2011, under the management of Sofitel, the Hôtel Ivoire opened again with much fanfare almost fifty years after its initial inauguration. Since then it has enjoyed a renaissance as one of the prime luxury hotels in West Africa.

The three towers stand *pars pro toto* for a series of architectural projects that attempted to push the young nations forward, and to actively participate in a nation-building process. This process, which is often understood as a linear development, exposes its tensions and contentiousness by looking at these buildings. The towers become an analytic device for reading contradictions within the supposedly linear and teleological process of nation-building. Instead of seeing them merely as a result of an economic or political decision, we can observe how the buildings themselves became actors in this process. The towers can also be seen as a way to understand the very specificities of the years after independence. Kenya, Zambia, and the Ivory Coast—just as any of the other nations of Sub-Saharan Africa—chose very different trajectories in their path of independence. By telling the stories of these three towers, we start to understand the different conflicts, contradictions, and complexities of this process of decolonization, and we understand how different this process was for each of these countries.

Hinterland Trialogue
By Ernest Sewordor

<u>Prologue</u>
A "trialogue" can do many things. It can work as an analytical tool, as a way of conducting research, and as a fictional tool for storytelling.

The Hinterland Trialogue will be all these things together.
It will tell the entangled histories of urban transformations and of brutal colonial extraction at the time of the "Gold Coast" in colonized Ghana. This trialogue aims to animate and stage imagined conversations dwelling on past events, colonial archives, and contemporary academic debates.

These conversations never happened, or maybe they did.
     The following scenes adapt imaginary actors in conversation, around evidence collected from colonial archives in Kew, London, and the Public Record and Archives Administration Department, Accra (the respective national archives of the UK and Ghana). By dusting off archival data, this trialogue reshuffles them to present a political provocation that upends colonial infrastructural imaginaries. It opens with intellectual musings among academics and backtracks into snapshots of historical encounters in British imperial Ghana to sketch the urban and spatial implications of industrial mining enterprises.
     The Brits came and "conquered," but in doing so did they overwrite everything near and far without question?
     This trialogue will project the hinterland as being more than a passive space that is shaped only by external capitalist developments—as exerting its own agency to constitute sociospatial change.

* * *

Trialogue

Neilb and Chrisch, both Ghanaian professors, are seated on the patio of their shared bungalow accommodation, discussing a report in a 1905 issue of The Economist.

Neilb: [Reads from *The Economist*] "The chairman pointed out that when they met a year ago it was anticipated that from January 1st the return of gold from the Obuasi group would be one ounce per ton, but that promise was unfortunately not fulfilled, and in January they only had a yield of practically half that amount. As soon as the board received this result they decided that the time had arrived to send out an independent mining engineer to report on the property." Fascinating!

Chrisch: Indeed! Those were the active colonial days, but they did not always promise all that imperial capitalists imagined as quick gains accompanying violent territorial conquests.

Neilb: You are right. Hear this too [reads again]: "The precautions taken against the robbery of gold had reduced the practice to a minimum, and the government intended to register all the native goldsmiths and make them keep records of their transactions."

Chrisch: Clearly, colonial officials and private investors were in bed together. With the legal backing of the former, the latter left no mining concessions untouched. Hence, many indigenes were dispossessed of their lands while others became laborers in the mines. Mining finance from pockets in London really had dramatic effects in this country.

Neilb: That is without question. Anyway, are we still expecting our guests?

Naanya: Well, the question is whether capitalism succeeded in consuming everything everywhere. It changed a lot here and there, and spurred urbanization too. Yes. But not everything gave way to it easily or became taken.

Neilb: Naanya has arrived on a controversial note. Oh, there comes Roger too.

Roger: What are we discussing today?

Chrisch: Mines. Neilb and I agree that the penetration of mining finance from faraway London, under local colonial administrative supervision, caused much change in mining districts. Imagine this as capitalist urbanization on a global scale. Naanya has a different opinion, though.

Roger: That is a seductive formula, Chrisch. I think it may be an argument that fits better today. We live in an intensely networked global era now, and that makes a more practical context for your point. I am afraid that may not be easily said of the past.

* * *

14.12.1903. Aboard S.S. *Kingstonia* bound for the Gold Coast (now Ghana) is Robbie—traveler, anthropologist-cum-geographer, and novelist. On arrival at Port Cape Coast, she is received by Mr. Cade—an English investor and forerunner at Obuase, one of the colony's richest gold mines.

Cade: A delight to finally meet you, Ms. Robbie!

Robbie: Likewise. I appreciate that you've come all the way from Obuase to meet me.

Alan: My lady, as the District Commissioner of the Central Province, I have been instructed by the Colonial Secretary to facilitate your planned interviews. Mr. Addie here will escort you on your errands to meet chiefs and important commercial interests in the colony.

Robbie: Very well.

Cade: I shall be on my way too; lots to do, you know. Adios.

Robbie: Goodbye, Mr. Cade. Thank you, Mr. Addie; very nice to make your acquaintance, sir.

Addie: I am happy to share with you the immense information gathered from my recent survey of the mining fields in the "bush."

Robbie: Hectic it must have been.

Addie: Oh, yes! But I imagine your sojourn through Great Britain's empire must be equally tasking.

Robbie: For the joy it brings me, the accompanying dangers are worthwhile. I hear there are talks of progress in this colony and the development of mining estates here have brought tremendous economic gains.

Addie: Of course! We are currently experiencing a gold-mining boom, so the colonial government is quite busy enacting laws to protect the industry. If the clueless European concessionaires and the greedy chiefs who will stop at nothing to sell concessions are left to their own devices, chaos will preside over their activities. Speaking of greed, the local business class of Cape Coast has attained notoriety for seducing inexperienced agents of English companies into buying wastelands here and parading them as treasures at home. *London's Standard* newspaper puts it right: "Worthless Concessions!"

Robbie: Is that really the case? I hear rumors of speculative investments, too.

Addie: Well, I have arranged your interviews with the Cape Coast Chamber of Commerce, chiefs, and a company man from Australia. So surely you shall leave here with sufficient answers.

* * *

20.12.1903. Robbie in an interview with a chief of the Western Province, and others.

Addie: [To Robbie] Meet my good friends, Chief Nana Enimil, and Mr. Dawson, an Australian miner. Unfortunately, Mr. Eyison of the chamber is unable to join us today. [To interviewees] I thank you both for your time. As previously discussed with you, here is Ms. Robbie, a famed English writer. As you already know her mission, I am sure you will extend her your generous courtesy.

Dawson: Absolutely. Pleased to meet you, Ms. Robbie.

Enimil: Welcome to our shores, my lady.

Robbie: To begin with, gentlemen, I know this territory takes pride in the abundance of its gold, but I have not quite understood who owns that wealth.

Enimil: Well, you see, at one point the colonial government tried to take a vast amount of native land as "Crown Lands." But that was vehemently opposed. Had succeeded, perhaps there would be no discussion with me. But we fought hard and retained our traditional control over our lands. So we the chiefs represent the people who are, in fact, the landlords.

Robbie: [To Enimil] So if I want to start mining in the colony, to whom do I go first?

Enimil: It is not always a straight path, you know. There is much that goes on here. But initially one has to obtain a concession he is confident will pay, usually from a chief like me or a person with such rights to dispose of a piece of gold-bearing land. Then the paperwork at the Concessions Court begins, and so forth. But as I said, it is not always a straight path.

Robbie: So I heard. Mr. Dawson, I would like to hear how you came to this shore of gold and what your experiences with the people have been like.

Dawson: I first came here three years ago after many years of working in Australian mines to help set up a concession located fifteen miles northeast of the Ankobra River, that is, along the Tarkwa gold-bearing ridge. At the time, speculations were rife about the Wassa properties in the Gold Coast, and as the rush to invest in Australian mines was losing steam, company men like myself were naturally looking for jobs elsewhere. So I found my luck with a company that was looking into the mines here. A good deal was offered, I took it, and here I am. I must say, many who had visited this place before me returned as skeptics since they were convinced the value of mining here was nothing but hot air. I mean, mere speculations.

Robbie: That may have been so; but is mining work not paying significantly now?

Dawson: Oh, do not misunderstand me. The hinterland is opening up as mining towns are established and prosperity is enjoyed by natives and private investors alike. I think everyone gets a fair share of the boom that is now underway.

Enimil: I hesitate to agree to this point.

Robbie: [To Enimil] How so?

Enimil: Think about it this way: chiefs may have the natural right to the land and may have fought well to defend it against colonial aggression. But now, the working of profitable mines is subject to laws that are not made by us, the native people, but rather by the colonial government. Clearly, some interests will be considered above others, no matter how hard one resists what he may consider unfair to the landlords. We take the ground rents, yes. But the government is entitled to a portion of the annual income as tax from the mining companies. Overall, the landlords are at the losing end of financial profits, yet it is their labor and hard toil that mines depend on to extract the gold. Tell me how that is "a fair share" for everyone!

Dawson: This is the argument I struggle to come to terms with!

Enimil: [To Robbie] You see what I mean? Those who benefit the most are in the habit of completely shrugging off genuine concerns about the conditions of those who do the most work.

Robbie: [Sounding uneasy] Finally, people in England complain about inadequate transportation for the mines. What is the truth?

Addie: I will take that. The railway from Sekondi to Tarkwa is making good progress, and it is anticipated that if the seasons are not unfavorable this line will begin to pay. Surveys of certain other routes have been made, including a flying survey for a line to Kumasi.

* * *

African underground miners of the Ashanti Gold Mines, Obuasi, Gold Coast"
INF 10/124 series, The National Archives, UK

It is 1924, and in a meeting of the Legislative Council of the Gold Coast, members consider a bill entitled "Ordinance to Regulate Mining Towns and to Protect Public Health Thereof."

Hodgson (Colonial Secretary): Gentlemen, I will be sitting in for the governor from today until the end of his leave of service in six months' time. First, we shall consider a bill "…to Regulate Mining Towns and to Protect Public Health Thereof." It is the object of this bill to provide, generally, the effectual, legal, and judicial parameters in which mining towns may be regulated, and ensure the protection of the health of surrounding settlements. This has become necessary in view of recent developments, by which I mean the destructive tendencies of mining activities that have burdened our courts even more with litigations, denuded forests, and not least an increase of brothels and prostitution.

Mr. Stephens (Attorney General): I rise to second the bill as moved for a third reading.

Sarbah (unofficial member): In saying a few words, I believe I speak for the African members of this council. I think this bill is timely and is welcomed with open arms especially by the indigenes.

Nana Kow (unofficial member): Before coming here I met my sub-chiefs, who altogether make the natural custodians of the richest mining lands of this colony. They say in one voice: "Never again will we let monetary incentives persuade us to sell our birthright." What they mean, sir, is that for decades many chiefs have been enticed by the promised immediate wealth from mining booms only to be strangled by colonial laws and the predatory practices of European mining firms. Last month, a case involving an alleged brothel madam and a migrant laborer was brought to my court. "What is the matter?" I asked, and was told by the plaintiff of his ordeal of losing his whole month's pay after being intimate with a woman whom the defendant had supposedly arranged for him at a price. This situation, Your Excellency, is one of many similar stories one hears these days from mining towns, and thus poses a serious threat to the moral fabric of our communities.

Addie (government surveyor): Being very familiar with the concerns raised by Mr. Sarbah and Nana Kow, I feel obliged to say that it will be very prudent to restrict the application of the bill to a specific number of mining areas and not impose it on the entire Gold Coast as a general rule. In my view, not all mining towns are bedeviled with such problems, and so it will be unfair to impose it on those communities where it may be needless to apply it.

Nana Kow: Even though I appreciate the spirit in which Mr. Addie makes his point, I beg to differ. Indeed, his view is that the problem applies only to some mining districts, and not all. But I dare say that nothing prevents "strangers"— who mostly cause such problems—from migrating from one place to another. That said, we should make the law so that it accommodates changes that may be foreseeable as small villages grow into large towns.

Hodgson: I associate myself with your point, Nana Kow, and add that it is by this token that the draft law also provides for the health of mining towns. Nonetheless, another practical challenge with the bill is that it may not adequately regulate, with clarity, the overlapping authorities of different entities within mining districts. Mining concessions are often sited near or around native towns, and though the mine is responsible for the health within its concessions, the colonial government takes care of areas outside the mine's boundaries. But it is clear that people move in and out of those spaces for various reasons and in effect blur these dividing lines. It remains unclear to me how this bill takes care of such a situation.

Stephens: Under such conditions as Your Excellency has pointed out, a duplication of responsibilities arises and must be attended to before the bill is passed. This will prevent the undue stress that may be placed on the already stretched number of men in colonial service.

Sarbah: I rise again to state that certain mining companies have become notorious for refusing to provide adequate and proper housing for their laborers. This is a bad example that others are keen to follow. And even though some miners wish to stay in towns near mining concessions by choice, the situation of overcrowding and housing shortage has created a gap from which an enterprise of providing makeshift shacks—often poorly constructed and noncompliant with building regulations—has sprung. Under these circumstances, mining towns are fast becoming chaotic.

In and between Theory and Practice

Engaging the Urban

by Sophie Oldfield and Manuel Herz

As critical urbanists, how can we root our work in complex and shifting dynamics of the city, in a myriad of forms of expertise and debate, in the contentions and consensus that shape cities? In doing so, what urban spaces and forms of change, conflicts, and (in)justices are made visible?

These provocations inspire our approach to working in and between theory and practice in city contexts where distinctions between the two are blurred and dissolved in critical ways. A multiplicity of overlapping actors and spaces, as well as economic, political, social, and cultural forces, challenges us to think theory through practice and practice through theory. These provocations inspire cross-sectoral, diverse methodological and interdisciplinary approaches to the city.

As Gautam Bhan[1] powerfully argues, commonsense knowledge hierarchies need consistent unsettling, especially the idea that "particular modes of practice can be neatly mapped onto particular kinds of practitioners." In other words, activists and slum dwellers, or architects and ordinary residents, are as much urban theorists and policy experts as are academics and municipal planning officials. By engaging with varied city actors and their distinct forms of expertise, we enrich knowledge-making. We embrace the creative and complex ways in which a multiplicity of protagonists and different forms of expertise shape city spaces and processes, forged in diverse ideas and forms of practice and engagement. Dissolving artificial distinctions between theory and practice, this approach disrupts a persistent and misleading caricature that, on the one hand, theory is the realm of the academy, a space for pure thought, for reason and scientific standards; and, on the other, that practice is messy, a mere question of application, of *"techne"* rather than epistemological thought. City complexities immediately challenge this simplified and outmoded division between theory and practice, which too easily becomes a compartmentalization of questions and approaches, led by an expert culture, whereby knowledge remains strictly bound to its own realm, unable to take other disciplines, practices, actors, and spaces into consideration. In contrast, research and pedagogy can and must be grounded in the city, in varied engagements with ordinary citizens and activists, policymakers and politicians, architects, designers, artists, and other practitioners of and in the city.

In and between theory and practice, our approach builds on interdisciplinary traditions and genealogies of research and pedagogy which place engagement with practice at the center of scholarly theory building and learning. A starting point of our pedagogical journey has been the research studio model, a tradition of research-led pedagogy derived from architectural education since the 1960s. "Learning from Las Vegas," for instance, a project by Denise Scott Brown, Robert Venturi, and Steven Izenour, together with students at Yale University in 1968, has become the paradigmatic example for architects' engagement with urban research, followed by Rem Koolhaas's "Project on the City" at Harvard University in the 1990s, and Studio Basel by Herzog & de Meuron, Diener and Meili at the ETH Zurich during the early 2000s. "Forensic architecture" offers another example of studio work, one which draws on techniques of architecture and spatial analysis to investigate human rights violations, institutional and state conflicts, and acts of crime. Interrogating actual conflicts to engage human rights and build technologies of investigation, it connects activist work with a range of cultural institutions, offering a model on which we have built and on which we will draw to further develop our Critical Urbanisms pedagogy in future. In short, we have adapted and transformed these approaches to studio teaching in two ways: First, beyond the disciplinary outlook of architecture, we engage with theories and methods of visual culture and the humanities to attend to multiple ways of knowing the city, from the perspectives of inhabitants, activists, planners, and architects, among others. Second, we have expanded the studio's "learning from" to a "learning by doing" model. This approach opens both pragmatic and critical modes of working, in which the studio becomes a site for interrogating the epistemological and institutional divide between university and city, as well as between theory and practice.

Our collaborative approach in our pedagogy equally builds on long traditions in Southern urban work, immersed in varied concrete development challenges and crises, embedded in state and societal imperatives for development. Conscious of the limitations of academic knowledge in responding to these needs, practices of co-production and collaboration link the academy in productive, yet often unexamined ways to the state, social movements, and community groups. These practices, Sophie Oldfield and Zarina Patel[2] suggest, offer modes of engaged research in relationship with everyday policymaking, as well as social and political struggles. Likewise, our practice has derived from a feminist geographical tradition: an approach to knowledge production, as Richa Nagar[3] notes, that shifts when we collaborate, when we "turn our theoretical goals from a 'northern' (university) academic project to the struggles of those with whom we collaborate."[4] These approaches, Edgar Pieterse argues, "demand contamination; it demands immersion into profoundly fraught and contested spaces of power and control."[5] Finally, theory in collaborative practice, as Geraldine Pratt suggests, is "open to other geographies and histories. It puts the world together differently, erasing some lines on our taken-for-granted maps and bringing other borders into view."[6] In their always-varied rhythms, engaged approaches offer ways to work in and between theory and practice.

In developing our pedagogy, we have found a space in which to experiment with forms of teaching inspired by these traditions. Grounded in both theory and practice, these approaches effectively bring together theoreticians and practitioners, merging theory and practice across disciplines and city contexts. Without theory, practice is unaware of its—often uncomfortable—blind spots and repercussions, while without practice, theory remains too easily dislocated, removed from its responsibilities toward the public. In building in and between theory and practice, we provide various trajectories, bridges across which we connect different spatial spheres, modes of knowledge production, and disciplinary approaches, infusing theory with practice, and vice versa.

First, our curriculum in Critical Urbanisms experiments with varied traditions of **studio work**. We have drawn on diverse studio approaches from architectural and social science traditions, which anchor our pedagogy. These approaches have given students the opportunity in Basel, Cape Town, and Accra, for instance, to move outside of the university classroom, insert themselves into the city, and consider their own positionality and the publics with whom we work. These approaches open up a core question of what Critical Urbanisms is: How do urban activities and practices of everyday life produce different knowledges about the urban? Studio work across our program has taken varied forms, moving across North and South, situating itself in historical questions as well as in contemporary practices, forming in collaboration with experts across the city, from activists, ordinary residents, and nongovernmental organizations, to architects, artists, and designers. Our approach to studio work offers an experimental and interdisciplinary space to play with a wide array of research tools and representational techniques, such as writing, cartography, multimedia representation, and so on.

Second, we have developed a multidimensional approach to city-based fieldwork, its practices and spaces. We **immerse** students intentionally in various city partnerships and city spaces, engaging with different actors in a wide range of contexts, from professional and policy to activist practice, from the center of cities to urban peripheries, from well-resourced city contexts of the North to the resource-strained spaces of the Global South. These contexts confront and shape our knowledge; they define the critical edge in our approaches to engaging the urban. In this work, we are inspired to mix the visual and the narrative, to interplay the two in more complex and multidimensional ways, to play around with forms of storytelling and ways of writing, to experiment with visualizations in concrete and abstract forms. This approach requires that we listen to one another, that we pay attention to how we narrate and write in our various fields, how we seek and shape evidence, the conversations and partners that are critical in these conversations, and how we engage in different city spaces and traditions.

In short, this mix of approaches **makes visible** the ways in which theory and practice are entangled, through creative forms of writing and visual representation, as well as forms of theory building immersed in practice. In this mix, we confront, unsettle, and rediscover our positionalities and privileges. In these approaches we situate ways in which urban activities and practices of everyday life produce a new and different knowledge about the urban.

Our approach to urban studies is not aimed at forging or reducing our work to a singular practice. Instead, we have built on multiple approaches, varied pathways that work across intellectual traditions and disciplines, situated in varied cities and their particular spaces, the contexts in which our partners work. Developing our pedagogies hasn't been easy or straightforward, a simple additive mix of disciplines and approaches. Rather, it has been and continues to be a journey built on conversation, experimentation, and the friction, and occasional conflict, that accompanies building in and across diverse disciplines and contexts. In this mix, we have developed ways of engaging with different relationships of theory and practice. Through this work, students find pathways, an anchor, an approach, a set of questions that resonate. They bridge and build creatively as the next generation of urban scholars, for whom an interdisciplinary and immersed approach forms the way forward.

The richness of this pedagogical work, its varied narratives and visual forms, its immersion in city tensions, are evident in the voices and visuals which follow this introduction. Carla Cruz makes visible figures of the runner, while Florence Siegenthaler accounts for running as a city practice, a collective way of navigating Cape Town both in the day and at night. Oliva Andereggen engages Rasta mobilities, practices of collecting and selling herbs, as an insurgent and eco-led way of producing and practicing the city. The individual essays that follow these texts situate varied ways in which our research embraces theory and practice. Manuel Herz shows how collaborative work with Sahrawi refugees, which culminated in the Pavilion of the Western Sahara, can act as an insurgent reworking of the Venice Biennale. Basil Studer's work makes homelessness visible as an otherwise concealed phenomenon in

Basel, and uses photovoice as an immersive participatory research tool. Florence Siegenthaler engages with tourism as a space of practice that is cosmopolitan, reworking in subtle ways the divides of segregation that characterize the City of Cape Town. Shourideh C. Molavi reflects on the politics of knowledge production and the relationship between the academy and the public in the face of varied forms of state violence and lockdown. The section concludes with Sophie Oldfield's reflection on NGO-community-university collaborations in South African cities. In rich and varied ways, the pieces in this section share research built on forms of engagement, in diverse ways of working that work creatively to interweave theory and practice.

---

[1] Gautam Bhan, "Notes on a Southern Urban Practice," *Environment and Urbanization* 31, no. 2 (2019): 640.

[2] Sophie Oldfield and Zarina Patel, "Engaging Geographies: Negotiating Positionality and Building Relevance," *South African Geographical Journal* 98, no. 3 (2016): 505–514.

[3] Richa Nagar, *Muddying the Waters: Coauthoring Feminisms Across Scholarship and Activism* (Urbana: University of Illinois Press, 2014).

[4] Richa Nagar, "Footloose Researchers, 'Traveling' Theories, and the Politics of Transnational Feminist Praxis," *Gender, Place and Culture: A Journal of Feminist Geography* 9, no. 2 (2002): 184.

[5] Edgar Pieterse, "Epistemological Practices of Southern Urbanism," African Centre for Cities Seminar series, University of Cape Town (2014): 23.

[6] Geraldine Pratt, *Families Apart: Migrant Mothers and Conflicts of Labor and Love* (Minneapolis: University of Minnesota Press, 2012), xxxiv.

RASTA MOBILITIES IN CAPE TOWN

Joseph, Gad-Fire, Asher, and Simon identify themselves as Rastas and are part of the makeup of Cape Town. I met them as I walked past them almost every day on my way to university. They sold their herbs and medicines on a busy road only a couple of minutes' walk from where I lived, right in front of a supermarket called Shoprite. The Rastas belong to the different kinds of healers in South

Joseph is preparing a medical herb mixture, Cape Town, 2019
© Photo: Olivia Andereggen

Africa. Medical pluralism is a major debate in South Africa, as people seek treatment from different medical practitioners such as Sangomas, kruiedokters, herb doctors, bush doctors, conventional doctors—the list goes on. As I started talking to them, and throughout the many conversations we had, they often talked about the five bleeding wounds in the Rastafarian belief system. They are: "the hungry must be fed, the naked must be clothed, the sick must be nourished, the elders must be protected, and all the infants must be cared for." The work that the Rastas do, and the lifestyle they live, are deeply embedded in their commitment to the third bleeding wound—the sick must be nourished. They see themselves as healers not only of individuals, but also of themselves, as well as the nation.

The question, then, is how their commitment to healing aligns with mobility and movement. For Crosswell (2010), mobility is not only linked to how and when people move, but also to why, and what meaning is associated with it. Thus, understanding the movement of the four Rastas is also about understanding their belief system as well as their socioeconomic background. The Rastas I spoke with all come from long-standing colored communities in areas that are quite far away from Cape Town's city center. In Cape Town, mobility has a long history of inequality and restriction, Rink argues, so this in particular relates to specific races and classes. These restrictions have been enforced through apartheid, but still linger on in the present. "The experience of mobility in contemporary Cape Town remains firmly entrenched in the racialized spatiality of the past, where a white urban (and coastal) core is contrasted by a vast peripheral edge where the majority black and colored population endure long daily commutes to work" (Rink 2016, 62). Thus, focusing on mobilities in Cape Town reveals power dynamics within the city.

In light of this, my aim was to track down how Joseph, Gad-Fire, Asher, and Simon specifically moved through the city, and thus I brought maps of the city to trace with them their movements and stopping points. This method proved useful to me, as thanks to the map I was able to see how they move, and was reminded about distance, different areas, and modes of transport.

Wild garlic shown by Joseph, Cape Town, 2019
© Photo: Olivia Andereggen

Collectively they travel all over Cape Town, within the built areas, as well as the mountains, beaches, cliffs, and forests in order to gather herbs and medicines to be sold later.

But their quest for herbs and healing brings them beyond the areas of greater Cape Town; they travel much of the country as well. As we drew the map of their movements, I became more aware of their reasons for travel. One of them is the need to have all kinds of medicines ready for the people who come to them for healing. Not all herbs and medicines grow in the Cape Town area, hence the Rastas need to travel to gather and exchange them. During those travels they have established a large network of other Rastas with whom they stay, gather herbs, and learn from. At the same time, as they travel, they also visit communities that do not have easy access to medical practitioners and healers. But for the Rastas, in order to be able to heal, one also has to heal oneself, thus those travels are additionally used to go through spiritual transformations. At times they sleep in the mountain area, and go through specific rituals resulting in inner and outer transformations. Joseph undertook one of these travels, and now no longer wears standard clothing but sack clothing. Therefore, the Rasta bush doctors are also known as "Sackmen" or "Sackmanne."

Joseph, Gad-Fire, Asher, and Simon have consciously decided to devote their lives to healing, and to live a life that is not defined by materialism. Their journey begins in deciding to become a Rasta—this is the first transformation they go through; then, through being a Rasta, their mobilities increase in Cape Town and throughout South Africa. As they move around, the way they travel is influenced by this decision, by their ability to communicate, build relationships, and haggle with different forms of payment. They haggle not only because their funds are limited, but also for the same reason they wear sack clothing, and move around by hiking as their ancestors used to—hence for making connections with people. **By Oliva Anderreggen**

Tim Crosswell, "Black Moves," *Transfer: Interdisciplinary Study of Mobility Studies* (Special Issue: Race and the Politics of Mobility) 6, no. 1 (2016): 12–25; Bradley Rink, "Race and the Micropolitics of Mobility," *Transfer: Interdisciplinary Study of Mobility Studies* (Special Issue: Race and the Politics of Mobility) 6, no. 1 (2016): 62–79.

One of the manu natural grounds where the rastas/sackmanne collect their medicinal herbs in the Western Cape, 2019
© Photo: Olivia Andereggen

RUNNING THE CITY

The canon of feet is punctured by short interjections. "Attention, potholes!" The information is passed on to the last person at the back of the group, like an echo created by different voices as the swarm of bright neon shirts moves around the obstacles and across the streets, into the woods which frame Cape Town's M3 at this busy time of the day.
I participate in this running club to gain both a bodily and intellectual understanding of the ways in which physical movement—articulated as group exercise—shapes and is shaped by the city.

Some few decades have passed since Michel de Certeau has reflected on the practice of "walking in the city" as being "to the urban system what the speech act is to language"[1]—appropriating and implying relations. If we think of walking as both a spatial speech act and a mode of being at home in the city, I propose to think of running as punctuation. I imagine it as an exclamation mark, a claim of the city's space and its time.

Of all the beautiful encounters within the context of the running club, two in particular have stuck with me. I articulate them here as vignettes to illustrate the idea of running the city as punctuation.

Itheko Club runners finishing race together, Cape Town, 2019 © Photo: Sophie Oldfield

Running the City class group at the end of the Ravensmead Race, Cape Town, 2018 © Photo: Sophie Oldfield

I approach Shameena because of her beautiful violet running pants. She bought them to get herself started with running, to have a colorful reminder in her wardrobe that she wants to move her body beyond the daily work commute. Now, years later, the fancy pants have stayed, but her motivation has changed. Why does she run now? "Running produces time," she says. "People always think it costs time. But for me joining the running club has done the opposite: I seize the time I got."

Caroline Peters did not always run. She tells us her story on a windy afternoon in Nantes Park, a place she had to reclaim for herself. Caroline did so by founding her own running club in her neighborhood. She got started with a small group of friends, running through the neighborhood. "We ran all through the roads, because we wanted people to know that we run," she says. And people did, one by one, join her in this endeavor. One day, Caroline took her club to run in Sea Point, along the city's coast, an area formerly segregated as racially white. "Two women had tears in their eyes," she recalls. "It was like their mindsets had to be freed: You can actually run here!"

Placing their bodies consciously in the city's rhythms, Shameena and Caroline—through their different stories, their histories and geographies—formulate "running the city" for me. Shameena uses running to punctuate her everyday life. To be in control of, or to make time. Caroline draws on it to reclaim her neighborhood spaces, to make them safe for women. By founding her own running club, she has also encouraged other black women to assert their right to the cityscapes of Cape Town.

Months after these encounters, I carry these stories with me every time I run, every time I place my own exclamation mark in my hometown Basel. I am making space for my and other bodies to be in this city, to insert our rhythms into it and engage with the ones it offers; right at this time, right in this place. **By Florence Siegenthaler**

[1] Michel De Certeau, *The Practice of Everyday Life* (Berkeley: University of California Press, 1988), 97.

FIGURES OF MOBILITY

"Who am I? I am a runner. I possess my own pace. I am fast. I am slow. I walk, and then I learn how to run. I stop running for weeks, for months, for years… And then I come back, inevitably."

I chose to focus on the figure of the runner. There are three panels that show different forms: a man, a woman, and a child, all in a running stance. If you were able to look a little more closely and read the words that make them up (that is, apart from the shadows), you will have noticed that they're composed of the same set of words. Some statements oppose other statements. This is because the words are not any one person's words, but come from many points of view. My reason for doing that is to demonstrate that the runner can be anyone in the city. The runner comes in different forms.

The words that make up these figures are words I've heard and remembered from my encounters while running the city, and while working on this piece; whether I intended it or not, they have somewhat transformed into a sort of running manifesto. In it there are real reasons, the motivations of real people we've met during the runs, goals I've heard uttered, my own experiences of running in the evenings.

We encounter the runner, this figure of mobility in the city, so distinct from the casual pedestrian or *flâneur* or street dweller. The runner traverses the city differently and takes different routes, creating a completely different dynamic in the shared urban space by adjusting their speed, their direction, even their manners in dealing with vehicles or other people on the street. They can be easily identified.

Figure of Mobility 1, original artwork, 2019 © Carla Cruz

In recent years, running has grown to be a novel way for citizens to build intimate connections in Cape Town, just as it seems to have become an alternative means to reclaim spaces commonly viewed as venues of crime or otherwise charged with remnants of historical conflict. One observable case is the creation of the Nantes Running Club, which transformed the semiotics clouding Nantes Park into something more positive and inclusive, fashioning a vibrant, social language in the area.

To be a runner is an identifiable lifestyle that permeates the city; there are groups of runners across the city every evening, composed of a diversified demographic of people, recognizable by their attire, their stance, and their speed. They inhabit and therefore experience the city differently, attuning themselves to the everyday rhythm of the city. Their routes are not accidental but thought-out, and they run with purpose.

I've been running for eight years. I've been running for four months. I started three weeks ago. I'm starting again. I can finish 5 km. I've joined hundreds of races. I will join my first race. I can do 56 km under four hours. I can do it under six. It takes me ten minutes for each kilometer. One day it will take me three minutes less. I see others run. There are hundreds. Thousands of us. I am a runner. **By Carla Cruz**

Figure of Mobility 3, original artwork, 2019 © Carla Cruz

Figure of Mobility 2, original artwork, 2019 © Carla Cruz

Nation-Weaving
By Manuel Herz

We had landed at the small airport of Tindouf, deep in the southwestern corner of the vast Algerian territory. Stepping out of the plane, the smell of the desert and the dry, scorching heat embraced us. We were picked up by a representative of the Sahrawi refugee organization, and half an hour later were on our way south. Our convoy consisted of three aging Land Rovers bearing Sahrawi license plates, flanked at the very front and back by Algerian military vehicles. After driving approximately twenty kilometers we came to a checkpoint. There, following a brief stop, the military vehicles pulled away, and we continued our journey without Algerian escort. We had now entered the Algerian territory that was under Sahrawi control. After another fifteen kilometers some huts and low-rise buildings started to emerge in the desert landscape: Camp Rabuni. Bypassing it and continuing a few hundred meters east, the cars stopped at our destination. We were standing in front of an unceremonious gate that gave way to a group of one-story buildings. The sign above the gate reads in Arabic and in Spanish: "*Parlamento Saharaui*." The Sahrawi Parliament, located in Algeria, is the only national parliament of a refugee nation.

National Parliament of the Sahrawis in Camp Rabuni, Algeria, 2016
© Photo: Iwan Baan

The Western Sahara is located at the western edge of the African continent. It was colonized by Spain at the end of the nineteenth century. In the early 1970s Spain came under pressure to withdraw from the territory, both from the local population (the Sahrawis had formed the Polisario as a liberation front), and from the United Nations. On his deathbed, Franco made a gentleman's agreement with Morocco and Mauritania for these countries to continue the colonization of the Western Sahara. With the so-called Green March, Morocco occupied the Western Sahara, initially with a civilian population which was quickly followed up with a military invasion by Morocco and Mauritania. With the beginning of a guerrilla war against both countries, most of the Western Saharan population had to flee across the border into Algeria, where it settled in refugee camps, today housing approximately 160,000 Sahrawis. Even though Mauritania was quickly defeated, Morocco occupied more and more territory through the erection of one of the world's most absurd constructions: a 2,500 km long wall or berm running through the desert, that until today separates the three-quarters of the territory held by Morocco from the portion accessible to the Sahrawis. Even though the Sahrawis do not have control over their own country, they proclaimed independence of the Western Sahara on February 27, 1976. Its sovereignty is recognized today by forty-five countries, though its status remains unresolved.

Rabuni

The notion of sovereignty becomes most evident in Camp Rabuni, which serves as the administrative center for the refugees. One's first impression upon entering Rabuni, though, does not initially suggest this significance. The center of Rabuni is marked by a large parking lot-cum-bus stand, which is surrounded by a myriad of car repair shops, improvised petrol stations, and shops selling everything from groceries to clothes to building material—usually all these simultaneously. The service stations look as if, over time, they have accumulated the leftovers and spare parts of so many vehicles and other paraphernalia that they have begun to take on a life of their own. The vehicles, mostly aging Land Rovers from the 1950s and 1960s, have seen so many repairs that they seem like moving—or sometimes immobile—bricolage. The hot, dusty desert wind covers everything in a fine layer of sand.

View over Camp El Aiun, Algeria, 2016 © Photo: Iwan Baan

North of this market area lies a large compound enclosed by a giraffe-patterned wall—the Ministry of Defense of the Sahrawi government. In fact, the urban landscape is dotted with all the ministries that also make up any other national governments of regular nation-states. As with the other constructions in the camps, all these institutions are single-floor compounds, built from cement bricks and covered in cement plaster to withstand the very rare, but then eventually very heavy rains, and the frequent sandstorms. Being all single-floor, the institutions occupy large swaths of ground within the fabric of Rabuni. Their low profile does not allow for grand symbolic gestures, in general being relatively unpretentious and functional in appearance. Nevertheless, a certain unconventionality marks their appearance. Further to the west lies the Ministry of Foreign Affairs, whose cross-shaped floor plan looks like it was lifted directly from the Swiss flag. To the east, we pass the large compound of the National Hospital, located next to the Ministry of Public Health. Just a few hundred meters further is the Ministry of Construction and Development, a building whose symmetrical layout is marked by four main corner rooms, each roofed by prominent domes, giving the overall impression of a wedding cake. Inside, the Minister of Construction shows us a proposed scheme for housing units combined with an education center.

The Sahrawi refugees are the only refugees worldwide who govern themselves and who enact a system of sovereignty in the territory of their camps. With Rabuni, they have built up a spatial manifestation of their own system of administration and political representation. It is here in this camp that a national foreign policy is formulated, the new curricula for schools are put together, decisions for public health are made, cultural policies are devised, and new codes of law are written. Instead of being another example of a "humanitarian space" with the typical presence of a dominant NGO culture, as is often the case in refugee camps, Rabuni gives testimony to the Sahrawi refugees' self-reliance. They set their own rules, from something as seemingly trivial as traffic regulations, to pivotal questions of economic strategies or national defense. With Rabuni, the camps are consciously used by the Sahrawis as a political project. The refugees are not only in charge of their own lives but are also developing expertise and experience in running a country. While still in exile, they are using this time of living in the camps to prepare themselves for the nation yet to come. The time spent in the camps has not been idle or wasted. Rather, it anticipates and prefigures the nation.

Beyond its political dimension, Rabuni also introduces something that we do not typically consider when thinking about refugee camps: everyday life. In the morning, hundreds of ministry employees arrive at work, having traveled the ten or twenty kilometers from the residential camps of Smara, Awserd, El Aiun, and Boujdour either by public bus or one of the private taxis that offer their services for a few dinar. People work in their offices, go for lunch at midday, and in the evening return home, again by bus or taxi. This ordinary routine is significant precisely because it is quotidian and unremarkable. We imagine refugee camps to be places of extremes: places that are constructed to save lives, places that are mainly about providing enough food and water to ensure survival and possibly prevent suffering, and where the refugees are reduced to their pure biological functions. In our imagination, the quality of the everyday has no validity in this place of extremes. The Sahrawi camps show us not only that these mundane activities of everyday life exist in refugee camps, but also how important they are.

Everyday Life
Unlike most other camps internationally, the UNHCR was not involved in setting up the camps and it continues to have little role in their officiation. Today, five residential camps—Boujdour, Smara, El-Aaiun, Awserd, and Dakhla—are home to approximately 160,000 Sahrawi refugees who have been living in Algeria for more than forty years. Climbing one of the few hills in the mostly flat desert landscape, one can see Camp Boujdour stretching out below all the way to the horizon. There is a relatively dense fabric of buildings, huts, and tents, all single-floor buildings, interspersed with larger institutional facilities such as schools and administrations, and denser clusters of shops and small markets. The Sahrawi families have constructed residential compounds for themselves which often consist of a number of huts arranged around a small central open space. The huts, constructed out of adobe bricks, typically perform single functions: one hut for cooking, one for sleeping, one for drinking tea and receiving guests, and so on. Depending on the family size and the financial situation of each family, these compounds can consist of one or two huts, or grow to include up to seven or eight.

Given the long history of the camps, the fact that improvisational architecture such as tents remains in place requires explanation. Primarily, there are functional considerations. In the heat of summer, when temperatures reach above 50°C, the tents provide a comfortable climate during the night, as they cool quickly and allow a breeze to enter. They also reference the nomadic tradition of the Sahrawis, and hence allude to the time before their country was lost to Morocco. But beyond these questions of culture and comfort, another reason for using tents is symbolic: they serve as an architectural signifier of the fact that the Sahrawi refugees have not surrendered to living in exile, but are still struggling for a return to the Western Sahara. The tent—signifying temporariness—employs a building typology to signal that the situation is not settled and expresses through architecture a political demand to return to their home country. Similarly, the question of whether to use clay or cement bricks is not only a technical one of construction method, but one that also alludes to issues of permanence, just like the choice of roofing material, or whether interior decorations are made of textiles, such as tapestries, and are thus movable, or rather of stucco. It shows how every architectural element, every detail, has additional messages and meanings. Architecture is never neutral, never innocent.

The Sahrawi camps are spaces in which inhabitants are in charge of their own lives—at least to the extent possible with the continuing occupation of their home country. It is a space that has given rise to a novel system of administration, and new social structures, where nomadic traditions have transformed into modern concepts of family structures and new identities have been created. In stark contrast to the common conception that these camps are not spaces where politics is permitted, within the Sahrawi camps politics is both facilitated and promoted. Not only is the Sahrawi population encouraged to engage itself in political matters, but the camps themselves are seen and used as political projects in their anticipation of the Sahrawi nation state of the Western Sahara. The Sahrawi camps therefore provide proof of the camp as a form of urban space. At a time when spaces of control and surveillance are multiplying in our cities, where gated communities and corporate compounds withdraw ever more space from public and political interaction, the opposition of the urban condition to camp spaces becomes less and less valid. Maybe the Sahrawi camps represent a spatial quality that is, in fact, more urban than many of our cities.

Interwoven Sovereignty

What makes a state a state? How do we define sovereign statehood? The most widely accepted answer to this question is the Montevideo Convention of 1933, that lists four conditions of statehood: (a) a permanent population; (b) a defined territory; (c) a government; and (d) capacity to enter into relations with the other states. The convention also declares that the "political existence of the State is independent of recognition by the other States." The Montevideo Convention is thus a clear *de jure* definition, in contrast to a *de facto* definition of statehood.

When we look at contemporary case studies, we come to understand the limits of the Montevideo Convention: Syria's population has tragically become impermanent with more than half of its inhabitants having either fled the country or having become internally displaced. Ukraine lost control over a substantial part of its territory with Russia's occupation of the Crimea Peninsula. Belgium did not have an elected government for a period of almost two years in 2010–2011, nor did Somalia for a period of fifteen years during the 1990s and 2000s. In none of these cases, though, would one reasonably argue for the annulment of statehood of Syria, Ukraine, Belgium, or Somalia. And conversely, several territories or countries that have declared independence and that fulfill the conditions of statehood of the Montevideo Conventions, such as Somaliland, but are not recognized by any other state, also show the limitations of the de facto practice of statehood. Statehood is thus not a question of absolute categories, of black and white. Rather, a range of different types and "shades" of sovereignty and statehood exists.

What type of statehood does the Western Sahara represent? The Sahrawis declared independence of the Western Sahara (officially: the Sahrawi Arab Democratic Republic—SADR) on February 27, 1976. It has a constitution, a functioning government with a president, a prime minister, several ministers with distinct portfolios, and a parliament consisting of fifty-three seats. The Western Sahara is a full member of the African Union, and currently forty-five member states of the United Nations recognize its sovereignty. It exchanges ambassadors with most of these nations, and has representatives in several other nations that officially do not recognize the SADR, such as most EU countries, the US, and Russia. Territorially, though, the situation is more complex. The Sahrawis' control of their own country's territory is limited to a thin sliver of the Western Sahara along the Algerian and Mauritanian border. It represents approximately 20–25% of the entire territory of the Western

Sahara. The Sahrawi government, though, has almost full control over the Algerian territory in which the refugee camps are located. While its limits are not demarcated and precisely defined, almost all aspects of political, social, cultural, and economic life are administered by the Sahrawi government. The refugees have Sahrawi identification cards, Sahrawi driving licenses, learn according to Sahrawi curriculums, are

Checkpoint controlling access to Camp Smara, Algeria, 2016 © Photo: Manuel Herz

judged by Sahrawi judges, and are protected by the Sahrawi army. But at the same time, Algerian sovereignty still applies to this region as well. Algerians living in the same region still pay taxes to Algeria, have Algerian driving licenses, Algerian IDs, and are judged by Algerian judges. Hence two sets of sovereignties coexist at the same time, and are woven together across the same territory. The Sahrawi government does not see itself as a government-in-exile, as it does control parts of its territory, and also regularly meets in Tifariti, located in the "liberated territories" of the Western Sahara. What we are witnessing, therefore, is the emergence of a novel type of statehood and sovereignty, one that overlaps and is interwoven with other sovereignties; a sovereignty that is incomplete, but also prefigured, and a statehood that is performed rather than static.

A National Pavilion
When I was invited to present the architectural and urban production of the Sahrawis at the Venice Biennale of Architecture in 2016, it was my immediate intention to use the institution of the National Pavilion, which is so paradigmatic. Hence, I requested the site right in front of the Central Pavilion, as it would be a very powerful statement, to make a National Pavilion for a nation without territory, that is positioned in the center of the Giardini, right at the end of the main boulevard. Here, the

National Pavilion of the Western Sahara in the Giardini of the Venice Biennale, 2016
© Photo: Manuel Herz

architecture of the Biennale pavilion speaks of the demand to claim nation status for a nation of refugees. Paraphrasing Beatriz Colomina, it is temporary architecture that can be the site of true experimentation. This is true for the refugee camps, as perhaps for the pavilion.

The building references the tents in the refugee camps, but it very consciously is not a tent—it is not a tensile structure. Rather, it shifts the typology of the tent into the typology of the pavilion. The design also plays with the ambiguities we find in the camps. It looks like a light textile materiality, but the metallic surface also gives the impression that it might be cast aluminum and very heavy. At the same time, there is a gap that separates the volume from the ground, giving the impression that it might be floating, in spite of its seeming weight. The wind and the sea breeze of Venice give the textile a flowing curvature of folds, but the folds are in fact frozen, and carefully designed and drawn. The textile, seemingly precious, can also sometimes seem like camouflage from a military context. Thus, the building plays with polarities that in fact coexist simultaneously, such as temporary and permanent, modern and traditional, or luxurious and barren—the same coexisting ambiguities we also identify in the architecture of the camps.

Inside, we find an account of the architectural and urban production of space in the camps, told through different media. The content is a collaborative project between the National Union of Sahrawi Women and myself. Its main element is a series of large-scale tapestries that tell the story of the architecture and the urban spaces. One tapestry documents the flight in 1975–1976 through the Western Sahara into Algeria. A second tapestry represents the spaces of everyday life in one of the residential camps, and a third depicts the culture of public architecture such as schools and community centers, that are of extraordinary spatial quality. Together with a group of thirty weavers, we devised the content and the weaving techniques. We were relying on traditional weaving techniques and the iconography practiced by the women, but pushing them into an architectural dimension. Even though the tapestries stand in an artistic tradition of representing spatial and geopolitical discourse through carpets, such as the work of Alighiero Boetti, they stand apart also by the fact that they have been co-produced in the camps by the refugee women. Even the physical materiality of the carpets gives testimony to their specific production, as the wool for example had to be sourced from another settlement 1,200 km away. The historic looms in the camps defined the dimensions of the carpets, and each tapestry was woven by up to ten women simultaneously, showing within itself the individual craft of each weaver. Weaving becomes a technique of giving testimony to the socio-

Interior view of the National Pavilion of the Western Sahara at the Venice Biennale, 2016
© Photo: Iwan Baan

political condition of life in the camps. The carpets are heavy. They are thick and have a beautiful material quality. They are sensuous to the touch and they smell a bit of camel. Besides the tapestries, slide shows and videos provide a portrait of the spaces and buildings in the camps. It was important that this is not an exhibition of emergency architecture or humanitarian architecture. It is architecture with a capital A, that has great spatial qualities, and that can meet any other nation's architecture shown at the Venice Biennale at eye level. The

Weaving process of the carpets in the Sahrawi camps, Algeria, 2016 © Photos: Tchla Pachri

National Pavilion of the Western Sahara acknowledges the contribution of the Sahrawis to the practice and discourse of architecture, and how it is used as a means of prefiguring statehood.

Eventually, we also had the opportunity to produce one additional carpet that was shown at the Museum of Modern Art in New York in the exhibition *Insecurities*, curated by Sean Anderson. This carpet shows the camp Rabuni, the Sahrawi center of administration and capital in the camps. This carpet has subsequently been acquired into the MoMA permanent collection of architecture. Considering the institutional and established character of the MoMA, this could be seen as a paradigm shift, showing the museum turning toward a more urgent and more politically engaged artistic and architectural practice. It was the first time in its history that the MoMA acquired an artistic piece from a refugee collective, and it is the first piece from the African continent in its architectural collection.

Detail of carpet showing the location of the refugee camps, 2016
© Photo: Manuel Herz

Making Homelessness Visible
By Basil Studer

Intro

In Basel, the city parliament and the government have repeatedly stated the need for urban spaces to be inclusive. Public spaces are for everyone's use. However, in practice, there have been difficulties and conflicts in meeting these goals.

When a central area of the city, the Wettsteinplatz and Theodorsgraben-Anlage, a square and the adjacent park positioned next to the night shelter and soup kitchen, were redesigned in 2005, there was a public debate about the appropriation of the space by marginalized people. Some members of the public mentioned that their use of the space made common usage difficult. However, to counter the demolition of the public toilet facilities and the sheltered space in front of them, residents of the neighborhood agreed upon a pavilion specifically to accommodate the needs of the homeless. The Stadtbildkommission, an expert panel dealing with the aesthetics of planning proposals, which is the last step in the authorization of construction, overruled the decision on the basis of its appearance in the overall design.

In recent years there have been multiple occasions when appearance and attractiveness have entered the political discussion as well as urban planning policy. The usage of places has been entangled with their design, while there has been a stronger drive to regulate the usage of public spaces. The aesthetics of public space can therefore be described as being strongly politicized.

This opens the question of how social groups see and assess the aesthetical dimension of urban spaces differently. It also raises the issue of visibility within the urban realm in general. What do we actually observe when we walk through the city, and what do we disregard? To test these questions, I conducted a series of photographic workshops with the clientele of "Schwarzer Peter," a street-worker organization in Basel. The subject of the workshops was urban space in the perception of marginalized people, the group of people commonly referred to in Basel as "Randständige." I provided cameras, and the participants would go on to show their perspectives of the city. The goal was to understand the differences in perspectives, and in the spatial realms by the marginalized people within the urban environment. We also wanted to put together printed books of the collected photographs, for each participant to keep and share with their acquaintances.

Method

Theorists from the Global South politicize urban space and everyday life by recognizing the expertise of ordinary people instead of foregrounding the expertise of professional planners,[1] as well as opening the methodology to the "lifeworlds" of said people by being aware of the aesthetic and functional aspects of everyday practices.[2]

Photography as a methodology therefore seems fitting, as photographs "can convey something of the feel of urban places, space and landscapes [,] can thus capture something of the sensory richness of the city,"[3] and "provide an effective and vivid way for people to show firsthand their perceived strengths and needs."[4]

Participatory photographic methods thereby try to diminish the power differential between the researcher and the research subjects. Many scholars have used the simplest single-use cameras, to ensure the participants are familiar with the technology, and if not, that they can quickly learn it.[5] However, others have noted that some participants are reluctant to ask for explanations if the technology is too simple and one is "supposed" to be capable of handling it.[6]

I chose digital cameras, firstly because they were less expensive overall, secondly because of the immediate results as it eliminated any waiting time developing the films; and, perhaps most importantly, I wanted to show the participants my sincerity and that I was taking the project seriously. I therefore bought cameras that looked professional. I wanted them to have an optical zoom, and a screen that was big enough. The participants should be able to take better pictures with the cameras than with their phones.

Six participants showed up to our first meeting, two of them women, and one of the men being homeless at the time. Initially I intended to conduct the workshop only with homeless people. However, marginality cannot be defined along clear lines of, for example, homelessness and settled living conditions. The stories of the marginality of my participants were interesting, but I did not try to reduce the participants to those stories. In the first workshop we got to know each another, after which everybody took a camera and we took a walk through the neighborhood. After we came back, I asked everybody to choose one of their photographs, give it a title, and show it to the others. This was also why the cameras needed a screen big enough to view the photos.

Then everybody could take a camera for two weeks to take more photos. The day before the next workshop I was at Schwarzer Peter, so the participants could come and tell me which photos they wanted to have printed. Those prints were theirs to keep. The fact that I had a computer and printed the pictures at home was one of these moments where power was distributed unevenly. Oftentimes when showing me photographs, the participants would tell me to choose the images I liked best. As Frith and Harcourt[7] note: "Indeed, participants in photo-elicitation projects may also need reassuring that they do not have to take photos that (they think) the researcher will find 'interesting.'"

The second meeting consisted of everybody showing their photographs to the group, and we discussed them and chose which ones to include in the finished book.

Data
Photographs have to be seen as objects used by people to perform social identities and relations.[8] For example, one of the participants wanted to give some of the photos away as gifts to the people depicted in the images. She took many personal pictures and also wanted to have more copies of the book to give as Christmas presents. Another participant clearly wanted to tell his story of being homeless in Basel, and wanted to represent the caravan community where he used to live; he used the pictures to educate us about his life and as a political message.

Stairway to heaven, Basel, 2019 © Photo: Basil Studer

Belonging
The participants showed deep attachment to the city, especially to the neighborhoods they grew up in and often still lived in. They filled the descriptions of photos from those neighborhoods with rich histories of the buildings and spaces, and often connected them to their youth. When they were in other parts of the city, they tended to focus on aesthetic explanations for their pictures, or they resorted to metaphors.
Historical artifacts and buildings are emotionally loaded. This does not depend purely on an official heritage status given to the buildings. Affect in these cases acts as a kind of intelligence about the world, creating a map of important sites for the participants.
      The participants took photographs of social institutions for the poor and homeless. Of course, they took pictures of Schwarzer Peter, but also of the soup kitchen, for example. Even those participants who do not frequent these institutions performed their socialities as a way to create an affiliation among the "Randständige," while at the same time trying not to lose their social status.

Soup kitchen "Gassenküche," Basel, 2019 © Photo: Basil Studer

These photographs show efforts of place-making through aesthetics. Graffiti and street art—individuals' impact on the urban fabric—were common subjects for the participants. Ali, for example, could express his affective feelings toward his neighborhood as well as a socially accepted disdain for the police through a picture of graffiti. He also expressed his connection to the city through the football club, while at the same time taking panorama pictures of the Rhine. Knowing graffiti slang or pointing to how long a certain "tag" has been present, is a sign of status, of knowledge of the city and the scene.

Participating

Shopping is part of the experience of being an inhabitant of the city, and browsing through the things at a flea market belongs to the joys that Michaël indulges in every week. The picture above allows us to explore "the spectrum of the aesthetic and the functional on the banal mundaneness of everyday practices."[9] The economic factors in the participation of social life in the city emerged in the form of price tags, signs promoting shops, as well as with the free "Kaffee Surprise" standing on the table in the courtyard of a local bakery. "Kaffee Surprise" is an initiative by a local NGO, by which people who cannot afford a cup of coffee can still participate in this normalized part of city life. The normalization of these pleasures has made life more expensive, diminishing the influence of the state. NGOs and private actors jump in to provide these infrastructures and opportunities.

In several instances there was a strong connection between economic possibilities and emotions. The picture of a kiosk "with heart" reaped cheers from everyone in the workshop.

The participants were aware of the consumerist approach to public space, making a reference to a tourist aesthetics in some of the pictures. This aesthetics looks at public space through the lens of visual consumption. We can see that the "selling" of cities, promoting the city to attract tourists and foreign investment, is not only active as a front to the outside but also in the perception of the inhabitants.

"Kaffee Surprise" at a local bakery, Basel, 2019 © Photo: Basil Studer

In the same pictures they pointed to the building, where some city institutions are located, speaking about the unpleasant encounters they had with the agencies. This can be read as what Ghertner[10] calls the start of politics, because "the consolidation of an aesthetic consensus does not resolve the question of how the aesthetic ideal is to be reached or how the city's resources shared."

Here the emotional aspects of citizenship and belonging come into play. While citizenship has been recognized as a status, an entitlement to rights—in our example, the right to social benefits—it is also experienced on the level of feeling.[11] The social becomes enmeshed with personal histories, with the sense of belonging, and creates an emotional response. Participation in a community is therefore based on emotional aspects of belonging.

Kiosk run by a kind-hearted owner, Basel, 2019
© Photo: Basil Studer

Contesting

The caravan commune, where one of the participants used to live, is actively using aesthetics to counter common understandings of property. This commune used to be an open area everybody could enter. Because of partygoers who came following "revitalizing" efforts by the city and the commercialization of the area, its residents had to close off the commune to be able to live in relative peace. They had to resort to conforming to certain aspects of a normalized notion of property to protect their lifestyle. They are aware of the use of aesthetics for commercial purposes and are able to subvert it, listening to punk and drinking beer, while the customers at the food stand drink overpriced champagne.

Conclusions

The aesthetics of urban spaces is a strongly politicized subject, which is supported by my research on many levels. I looked at how the participants experience these entrepreneurial strategies of governance. The pictures they presented to me showed that in large part they replicated a normative view of the city. They were aware of the tourist aesthetics in some of their pictures, and addressed their feeling of alienation toward the administration.

The power structure internal to the group during the discussions played a role in how the presentation and interpretation of the photos took place. While some members of the group made many comments, others stayed mostly silent. The general mood played an important role in what participants focused on while explaining their photographs, rather than their content—the positive or the negative, the beautiful or the political, for example.

The participants used the opportunity of this project to form bonds of community, and shared pictures of places to which they have an emotional connection. They also highlighted the agency of individuals to change the image of public space through graffiti, street art, or even flower pots.

Participants also showed how they use aesthetics to make political statements, protesting for affordable housing and against the commercialization of public space. Through this they were able to expose how the image of marginal culture is incorporated for this commercialization.

Through the participatory approach participants were able to take the research to places I could not have gone to or would not have thought of. They also felt encouraged to look at the city and their favorite places in a different light.

The participatory method enables showing assets instead of just focusing on problems, and it gave participants some power: the emotional power of the photographs together with their own authority to tell their story.

[1] Faranak Miraftab, "Insurgent Planning: Situating Radical Planning in the Global South," *Planning Theory* 8, no. 1 (2009): 32–50.
[2] Edgar Pieterse, "Grasping the Unknowable: Coming to Grips with African Urbanisms," *Social Dynamics* 37, no. 1 (2011): 5–23.
[3] Gillian Rose, *Visual Methodologies: An Introduction to Researching with Visual Materials* (London: Sage, 2016).
[4] Caroline Wang and Mary Ann Burris, "Photovoice: Concept, Methodology, and Use for Participatory Needs Assessment," *Health Education & Behavior* 24, no. 3 (1997): 369–387.
[5] Josh Packard, "'I'm Gonna Show You What It's Really like out Here': The Power and Limitation of Participatory Visual Methods," *Visual Studies* 23, no. 1 (April 2008): 63–77, https://doi.org/10.1080/14725860801908544.
[6] Ailsa Winton, "Using Photography as a Creative, Collaborative Research Tool," *The Qualitative Report* 21, no. 2 (2016): 428–449.
[7] Rose (see note 3), 307.
[8] Ibid.
[9] Pieterse (see note 2), 18.
[10] D. Asher Ghertner, *Rule by Aesthetics: World-Class City Making in Delhi* (New York: Oxford University Press, 2015), 157.
[11] B. E. Wood, "Young People's Emotional Geographies of Citizenship Participation: Spatial and Relational Insights," *Emotion, Space and Society* 9 (2013): 50–58, https://doi.org/10.1016/j.emospa.2013.02.004.

Township Cosmopolitanism
By Florence Siegenthaler

The tourism industry is a key—though often unexamined—actor in the representation of cityscapes. In the South African context, representation and narration of townships has to date been predominantly formatted through the "township tour." Tourist agencies send local guides to pick up visitors at luxury hotels and transport them to selected townships in small buses or cars. There, they venture on short guided neighborhood walks to see and encounter township realities, from challenging housing situations to the creativity of local businesses and the vibe of communal spaces. Working on the "township tour," historian Leslie

View from the car onto the streets of Langa, on one of several guided township tours which can be booked in Cape Town, January 24, 2019 © Photo: Florence Siegenthaler

iKhaya Le Langa is often traversed by tourists on various "township-tours," 2019 © Photo: Florence Siegenthaler

Witz,[1] for instance, describes the tours as stage-managed by tourism businesses, designed explicitly for the explorative perspective of the tourist—what geographer John Urry[2] in his pioneering work tagged as the "tourist gaze," which he critically portrays as a colonial practice.

Does this assessment capture the work of tourism in townships in contemporary Cape Town? I engaged this question through an exploration of tourist practices in Langa, a Capetonian township.[3] Through various encounters in the township spaces we traversed on several "township tours" in early 2019, I realized that in and beyond the narrative of a "poverty safari," local township agents and entrepreneurs were involved in tourism in various ways. In these processes, they represented the township as a multidimensional space. Through digital technologies, such as social media, Uber, and Airbnb, these actors created multiple spheres of engagement. This contemporary practice challenged this one-sided theoretical notion of the "tourist gaze." Through this research on the multidimensional work of tourism in townships, I set out to rework, enrich, and complicate this partial, out-of-date story. It too often leaves out the implications of tourism practices for the urban environment and its sociocultural dimensions. It too easily bypasses the perspective, agency, and engagement of township residents, portraying them and their living spaces as fixed and immobile. And researchers themselves too often remain invisible, third parties, gazing onto, but exempt from, the powers of the "tourist gaze."

I built instead on Ruth Butler's[4] notion of tourism encounters in township spaces as "exhibitions" in which township tours are "unlikely assemblages" of people, materials, media, and objects, curated by local guides. In this framing, Butler opens space for exploring the reciprocity of processes of gazing and "othering," shaped by a multiplicity of actors in the tourism-township sphere. In a similar vein, Meghan Muldoon[5] interrogates "township tourism" through the perspectives of local community members. She experiments with a "reversal" of the gaze by giving local residents cameras to document tourism practices, and from this vantage point engage and critique the place of tourism in the township. Both Butler and Muldoon offer through their work an awareness that local agents are not and should not be treated as passive objects in tourist-linked processes that traverse the township terrain. They offer alternative modes of research that bring the actual practices of tourism-township intersections, especially the tourist gaze, into view more fully. Their work enriches perspectives of tourism studies in township spaces at the same time as they point to a need to diversify rather than merely "reverse" the gaze. These approaches had a considerable impact on my own research, refining and enriching the places in which and the people with whom I anchored my research, rooting my thinking in the ways they narrated the township and its place in the post-apartheid cityscape.

I based my research at "iKhaya Le Langa" (the home of Langa), a space which simultaneously identifies as a tourist destination and a community space in Langa, Cape Town's oldest township. This space brings together a variety of agents from the community of Langa and the tourist industry. Through it, mothers and grandmothers offer Airbnb homestays. Tour operators use Uber, rather than buses, to get around the township. Social media managers promote tourism in the township. And young entrepreneurs work on the establishment of a digital currency to trade with locals and visitors alike. To document their varied engagements with tourism, and the practices and vision that inform their work, I accompanied them. To do so, I drew on a range of approaches, from neighborhood walks and in-depth interviews to Airbnb homestays and group discussion sessions, to engaging with the social media and the digital currency being produced. Through following these practices, I interrogated the imaginaries which underpinned their engagement with technologies and the social and spatial relationships they enacted and envisioned.

During the research and its writing, I was challenged on several occasions to explain why I, of all people, should tell these stories. I grappled with this critical question, with how to position myself in this work in ways that might reflect my presence, the small ways in which I myself became an agent in the conversations about tourism practices that shaped my research. I drew on and built a practice of writing that explores not just "those under investigation"—Langa's tourist-linked agents—but also the roles I played, first as a tourist, then as a researcher, and later, in varied ways, as a participant. I framed my analysis through a set of creative, nonfiction, first-person narratives. While the agents featured in these stories provide multiple ways of transcending the binaries which have tended to inform our theorizing in tourism studies, the narratives I wrote helped me reflect on my own positionality as a white European researcher in a Black township, and to acknowledge the multiple roles I came to fill. In making these positionalities visible, I could illuminate interpersonal connections and relationships that formed and grew which were central to my research and its development.

Tozamile, a local artist and tourist guide in his art studio at iKhaya Le Langa, 2019 © Photo: Florence Siegenthaler

The following is a short narration of my encounter with Siya, who manages the social media content at "iKhaya Le Langa" to promote tourism in this space as well as for emerging entrepreneurs (such as the Airbnb hosts) in Langa. This narrative illustrates the ways in which this mode of writing offers an opportunity to conceptualize tourism practices through Siya's vision and practice, rooted in Langa and in innovative contemporary social media strategies, situated as well in the conversations through which the research unfolded.

#Langa: Reflections on Instagram

"Langa is like a village, it is frowned upon not to greet on the streets," says Siya. And so I do greet, as I had already been taught before: "Molo" when there is one person, "Molweni" when there are several. It is a small thing, and still, my tension fades, as I come to accept myself in the spaces I traverse. Siya was born in 1993, on the verge of South Africa transitioning into a democracy. As we walk past the graffiti-decorated walls witnessing the last art contest, Siya tells me that he would love for tourists to come to Langa for reasons other than confronting apartheid legacies and poverty. "Today, there are all these great things happening here in the Langa township—sports, arts—which people need to see." That is where we are going now: to all the things he would love tourists to see of Langa—to post them on Instagram.

We come to a halt at a vast, bright-blue sports field. Siya is a passionate hockey player, and he regularly posts about his sports activities. "I should post a picture of this, too. Maybe tourists also want to come and see a game. It's where we all come together." As I raise my camera to capture the infrastructures with Table Mountain in the background, I pause. What does Siya think of all the tourists coming here, taking pictures of living spaces, posting them in an often-aestheticized manner? "I think it's good when they post pictures," he says. "I want the whole world to know we're here!" For him, communication technologies can be both a way of being seen and a link between what is and what can be. "You know, when you grow up in a township, you get used to it. So, digital technologies and social media, they play an important role: there is suddenly a possibility to look at Langa through someone else's eyes. And I have found out something about those hashtags. In the beginning, I was a bit put off by them. But they quite like the local Xhosa slang." I look at him curiously. "You know, here in this township, we have our own language that only local people who interact with each other regularly would understand. With the hashtags, I realized that they are like a code for groups. Only people who use them regularly will be able to understand."

Screenshot of a post on iKhaya Le Langa's Instagram account, 2019

Revisiting and writing down these encounters were an important way of reflecting on the roles that the agents I encountered played in and beyond my research, and of ascribing them a place in my work. Short narratives like these also gave me an opportunity to let myself be visible to the reader, in conversation and engaged with Siya, my informant. Siya's story became an important entry point to discuss and challenge the theory of the "gaze." His engagement with social media such as Instagram illustrates how these visual practices in tourism are a multisited endeavor, in his case an opportunity to see the township "through someone else's eyes."

Encounters with local agents like Siya were central to my research. The process of curating these encounters as stories, and then assembling them, invited me to revisit the theoretical base from which I had departed. They allowed me to rethink tourism and its gaze as mutually explorative, as means of producing knowledge and learning. They resonated with recent moves in tourism studies to embrace *cosmopolitanism*, a means to think tourism as a practice that engages sociocultural and spatial "others," in which visual practices are important. For a long time, the understanding of cosmopolitanism, much like that of the gaze, was attributed to those who travel, and seems to have been reduced to a sense of "being at home in the world."[6] Shameem Black, however, beautifully flips this around and situates the cosmopolitan in the hyperlocal and familiar space. She says that cosmopolitanism can also be a way of "recognizing the world through the home."[7] Salazar develops this idea further. He argues that when people possess a literacy of different lifeworlds and modes of living through exposure to the "rapid circulation of global signs and images," they can be "spatially local but socially cosmopolitan."[8] This understanding of cosmopolitanism as a skill set and a desire for engaging with sociocultural and spatial Others provides an important theoretical tool to account for multiple perspectives in tourism encounters. This body of work has helped me recognize and narrate the multiplicity of gazes surfacing in and through tourism intersections in Langa, a key step in a South African urban context where the hegemony of visual practices and notions of otherness have a long and painful history in the past and present. Enriching approaches to research and writing on tourism and its "gaze" through cosmopolitanism offers two critical elements. It contributes to a recognition of the agency of local actors as visionaries, assets, and allies who, through tourism, ground and locate the globally visible post-apartheid city. Secondly, it makes visible and speaks to encounters with agents like Siya which were vital in reshaping my understanding of the "gaze," its dimensions and possibilities. As a key part of urban practice and theory, work on tourism must be accountable to research practice as well as the rich imaginaries and knowledges formed through its lived everyday realities.

---

[1] Leslie Witz, Ciraj Rassool, and Gary Minkley, "Repackaging the Past for South African Tourism," *Daedalus* 130, no. 1 (2001): 277–296.

[2] John Urry, *The Tourist Gaze: Leisure and Travel in Contemporary Societies* (Thousand Oaks, CA: Sage Publications, 1990).

[3] Every time I write "township" in this piece, I acknowledge the painful history embodied in this term, and the colonial and apartheid regimes that coined it. At the same time, I draw here on the ways in which my informants, most of whom are residents of Langa, employed this term. As one stated: "When I use the notion 'township,' I do so with pride. I want people to know I grew up in a township because it makes me who I am, it makes me strong."

[4] Shelley Ruth Butler, "Curatorial interventions in Township Tours: Two Trajectories," in Fabian Frenzel et al. (eds.), *Slum Tourism: Poverty, Power, Ethics* (New York: Routledge, 2012).

[5] Meghan L. Muldoon, "Gazing Back: A Feminist Postcolonial Lens on Tourism in the Townships of South Africa" (PhD diss., University of Waterloo, 2018), 2.

[6] Ulf Hannerz, "Cosmopolitanism," in David Nugent and Joan Vincent (eds.), *A Companion to the Anthropology of Politics* (Malden: Blackwell Publishing, 2004), 69.

[7] Shameem Black, "Cosmopolitanism at Home: Amitav Ghosh's *The Shadow Lines*," *The Journal of Commonwealth Literature* 41, no. 3 (2006): 46.

[8] Noel B. Salazar, "Becoming Cosmopolitan through Traveling? Some Anthropological Reflections," *English Language and Literature* 61, no. 1 (2015): 54.

Theory and Practice Under Lockdown
By Shourideh C. Molavi

In 2011 Iranian filmmaker Jafar Panahi released a video essay recorded in Tehran titled *This Is Not a Film*. Along with filmmaker and pro-democracy activist Mohammad Rasoulof, Panahi had earlier been sentenced to six years in prison for alleged crimes against the Iranian state and for inciting opposition protests after the 2009 elections. As part of their punishment, the two prominent figures in Iranian cinema were also banned from writing any kind of scripts, making films, traveling abroad, and speaking with local and foreign media for twenty years.

While pursuing his appeal against a sentence designed to cut off oxygen from his livelihood, Panahi was under effective house arrest. In *This Is Not a Film*, Panahi is confined to his apartment and careful to act within the cruel parameters of his injunction, restricting himself to recording with his phone and reflecting on his earlier movies. Speaking in front of a camera held by his friend, an awkward move for a director used to being behind the scenes, Panahi instead reads out the script of the film he wanted to produce. He rearranges the furniture in his living room, using masking tape to transform it into the set he had in mind, for a film he now cannot legally make on the topic of incarceration.

At one point in this creative improvisation, Panahi laments in frustration and exhaustion the impossibility of making a film under these conditions: What does it mean to continue his practice in isolation? How can he capture a human experience without access to the spontaneity that comes with public space? The most precious moments of his earlier works had been improvised, captured unscripted on the street, sourced from the instincts of those around him.

Eventually smuggled out of Iran on a USB stick said to have been hidden inside a cake, the extreme limitations mobilized by Panahi in making *This Is Not a Film* are a source of inspiration for those living in conditions of closure and isolation seeking to continue their intellectual, artistic, and political interventions with real-world urgency.

For practitioners in urban studies, Panahi's inversion of his imposed isolation and provocative use of the elements in his immediate surroundings serve as a useful framework for organizing our work. While Panahi's house arrest is not the lockdown or curfew many of us have been experiencing, it nevertheless points to the need to explore creative modes of urban engagement that work in and between theory and practice—modes that speak to our contemporary context.

The Pandemic as a "Settler-Colonial Moment"
Settler colonialism, the late Patrick Wolfe reminds us, is "a structure, not an event."[1] And while its practices and technologies have transformed over time, the salient features of indigenous and racialized dispossession as an organizing principle of settler-colonial power

structures are ongoing. Today, and particularly in moments of "emergency," these structures function alongside and enhance other forms of intrusion, including imperial, corporate, and extractivist varieties of racialized dispossession.

The incitement of settler-colonial structures to confront the spread of Covid-19 gained increased attention in mid-March 2020, when a non-Indigenous couple from Montreal, apparently fearing the virus, traveled thousands of kilometers across the country to Old Crow, an Indigenous community in northern Yukon. Seeking an "isolated community to hide from Covid-19," the couple expressed that they figured the remote community is "the safest place" to weather through the pandemic.[2]

Emphasizing the particular vulnerability of Indigenous communities such as Old Crow, Chief Dana Tizya-Tramm of the Vuntut Gwitchin First Nation pointed out that, in addition to limited medical services, high respiratory illnesses, and the high number of elderly residents, "we don't even have enough housing for our own members."[3]

As urban elites around the world fled to their second homes and summer cottages in response to the pandemic, non-Indigenous claims for safe accommodation made to remote Indigenous communities such as Old Crow are an extension of Canada's colonial history of extraction. These practices continue to give shape to its contemporary record of Indigenous dispossession. In the context of the pandemic, the logic of extraction and replacement that delimits contemporary settler-colonial structures is activated here with cross-border travel that jeopardizes the lives and livelihoods of Indigenous people. As Chief Tizya-Tramm expressed it: "Our community, albeit remote, is not a life raft for the rest of the world."[4]

The activation of settler-colonial legacies is also reflected in the fact that in places like the United States, the two populations hit hardest by Covid-19 have been Indigenous nations and Black Americans—the same two demographics most impacted by its record of settler colonialism, notably overpolicing and incarceration.[5]

Indeed, whether it is arguments made in April 2020 by Jean-Paul Mira, French doctor and head of intensive care at Cochin Hospital in Paris, to run vaccine trials "in Africa, where there are no masks, no treatments, no resuscitation," or the announcement in late July that Israeli medical researchers will travel to India to try "new rapid coronavirus testing methods on thousands of the country's Covid-19 patients"—structures of whiteness are increasingly being activated during the ongoing pandemic, pointing to the dispensability of colonized and racialized bodies.

In this context, and as explained below, for those engaged in an urbanism that infuses theory with practice, the mobilization of public space, city publics, and home-making in the city for the activation of structures of whiteness calls for new modes of interventionist research.

Rethinking the "End of Public Space"

Although to different extremes, the first months of the spread of Covid-19—and the spread of lockdowns—inverted many of our daily binaries and, to some extent, instigated their temporary collapse. Practices that passed by quickly before lockdown we began to experience as slowing down. Our lived and private indoor spaces were projected outside through online mediums used for work, teaching, and collaboration. And our local contexts became immediately internationalized with increased cross-continental phone calls and meetings becoming a repeated daily norm.

Moreover, as the months passed, the pandemic enabled a rise in racialized policing, militarized silencing of public protests against state violence, economic disenfranchisement, and heightened global border controls and digital surveillance through the activation of "states of emergency." In so doing, the global health crisis significantly altered our engagement with the city—and with public space in general. Together, these struggles brought to the fore the contradictions of exclusion, access, confiscated properties, militarized environments, and legacies of coloniality in public space to which critical urban scholars have been pointing for years.

Farmers near the border in Gaza, 2018 © Photo: Shourideh C. Molavi and Ain Media Gaza

For scholars, community organizers, and practitioners working on public space and the racialized urban present, a rising sense of urgency to continue our engaged work was met with (infra)structural limitations preventing mobility and cutting access. The urban "everyday"—where ordinary people and publics build lives, confront state and corporate violence, occupy land, and creatively claim a right to the city and access to its resources—was transforming, pushing us to interrogate the theoretical and practical nature of our collaborative partnerships around everyday city struggles.

But rather than the "end of public space," the pandemic, as well as the racist and classed violence it has since reactivated, has instead shifted the delimitations of public space. Rather than remaining stationary or centralized around specific infrastructural markers, local practices and political interventions are increasingly assuming mobile, virtual, and hidden forms, thereby pushing our understanding of public space beyond its traditional realizations of squares, parks, and streets. As the pandemic denies the public access to this infrastructure, it also changes the definitions of and engagement with "public space."

Damaged leaves from Israeli spraying of herbicides, Gaza, 2018 © Photo: Shourideh C. Molavi and Ain Media Gaza

Relevant to the pedagogical focus that gives shape to our Critical Urbanisms program, this repositioning of public space begins to surface when we examine how the urban present and racialized inequalities are experienced by communities across the Mediterranean, the Middle East, Africa, and Europe.

Whether it is public protests taking place on rooftops in Palermo, where lockdown orders impose movement and prohibit people from standing still in public, the rise of informal mobile coffee shops to serve the public in secret on the back of private trucks on the policed streets of Cairo, or the subversive use of drones by Palestinians in the besieged Gaza Strip to creatively document their emptied streets under lockdown while also resisting the Israeli occupation of the sky and the surveillance of their communities—the reshaping of public space to moments of exchange and practice points to the proximity that exists, and has always existed, among these imagined regions through their colonial legacies and regional hierarchies of power.

Interlacing Theory and Practice

Subversive techniques of resistance such as these point to the ever greater need to continue to weave together theory and practice in our research. This means approaching conceptual frameworks not as a precursor to engaged work with communities and movements on the ground, but rather as an active result of directed actions.

In my case, the theoretical paradigms that have resulted from my work in Palestine were a product of a multifaceted and interdisciplinary approach to research—one that moves along and across legal, academic, artistic, architectural, activist, and communal discourses, priorities, and spaces.

For instance, my two-year study into *Herbicidal Warfare in Occupied Gaza* started with a question around the disappearing trees in the besieged enclave. The eastern perimeter of Gaza, known for its lush farmlands and citrus orchards, has been transformed from an agriculturally active border zone into parched ground, cleared of vegetation. The borders around Gaza continue to be hardened and heightened into a sophisticated system of under- and over-ground fences, forts, and surveillance technologies. And part of this system has been the production of an enforced and expanding military no-go area—or "buffer zone"—on the Palestinian side of the border.

A project initially fueled by a desire to examine the forced changes in cultivation resulting from Israeli colonial practices—including regular bulldozing, flattening of residential and farm land, and aerial herbicide—took lead from Palestinian farmers and human rights organizations, including the Gaza-based United Arab Workers' Union and the Al Mezan Center for Human Rights, to examine the links between slow and fast processes of violence.

In 2018 and 2019, when this eastern perimeter of Gaza became the site of the Great March of Return, weekly popular marches for the Palestinian Right of Return, allies and colleagues in Gaza pointed to Israel's extreme use of sniper fire as a tool of crowd control. Israeli occupation forces used unprecedented amounts of live ammunition against civilian protesters in this barren and exposed area, which offered no hiding place, killing over a hundred Palestinians and injuring over 30,000, including more than 8,000 children.

What became clear was that long-term Israeli environmental violence resulting in the disappearing of trees in Gaza had also provided the occupation forces with visibility along the eastern "border"—visibility that has also left Palestinian civilians, including farmers, youth, and families, further exposed to Israeli fire from hundreds of meters away. And so, as I was documenting the disappearing trees, the testimony of the land and the slow process of "desertification" quickly revealed vegetation in occupied Gaza as "bio-indicators" or "silent witnesses" to Israeli settler-colonial violence. Together, the slow violence of spatial degradation through the mobilization of environmental elements had accelerated into eruptive violence.

Interventions such as this one—like others I have conducted with friends, colleagues, and allies in Palestine over the years—invited an interlacing of theory and practice. It brought together different types of media, lived experiences, memories, and various forms of data, and placed them in critical conversation with material collected through embedded practices on the ground—involving physical traces and human

Bounding Box, Triple Chaser, project by Forensic Architecture and Praxis Films that combines machine learning with ground truth techniques in collaboration with activists around the world, Mexico, 2019 © Photo: Forensic Architecture

Photorealistic images of Triple Chaser tear gas cannisters, 2019
© Photo: Forensic Architecture

Incendiary kites collective, occupied Gaza, 2018 © Photo: Shourideh C. Molavi and Ain Media Gaza. This form of resistance was made possible with the slow flattening of the eastern perimeter of the besieged Gaza Strip by the Israeli occupation forces. Engaged work with farmers along this perimeter opened other arenas of research, showing how the space is mobilized by Palestinians as part of their resistance.

Kites as a form of resistance from the 2018 Great March of Return in Gaza, 2018 © Photo: Shourideh C. Molavi and Ain Media Gaza

experience gathered through firsthand relations and testimonies. In addition to an invitation to share my research findings, such methodology revealed the assembled techniques and diffused networks of relations that shape my political and intellectual practice.

These assembled techniques also call for various forms of exchange, where the mediums through which findings are disseminated are similarly multiverse. In my case, part of the political depth and communal importance of the interventions to which I contribute is that the work is presented in multiple forums, often simultaneously, and with each having its own grammar protocols and conditions of annunciation. Whether in courts, legal or academic reports, books, or in cultural venues, each space where I present my work mobilizes and activates another kind of presentation, another kind of demand, and gives space to different kinds of visibility and debate. And with this multiplicity, real-world engagement with the project framework and findings also began to take root beyond the traditional confines of discourse and discipline.

Interventionist Research in Times of Covid-19
The interlacing of theory and practice, along with ongoing global transformations that bring to the fore ongoing legacies of colonial practice and racialized hierarchies, invite us as urban researchers to amend and interrogate both our theoretical and practical approaches to studying urban relations and space.

At a conceptual level, this requires probing the relationship between knowledge production and the lived experiences of publics. In a historical moment in which our lives and pedagogies are being increasingly abstracted behind screens, there is a greater need to profoundly shift our own theoretical frameworks, and our programmatic positionality and motivations.

Calls to action to address racialized violence and inequities that demand attention in the present context require a concerted effort toward a decolonized theoretical framework for studying the urban. Research that in the past might have escaped decolonial theory and bypassed questions of representation of and engagement with communities of color can no longer take up space in our programs, classrooms, and syllabi. Furthermore, a theoretical framework that engages with this call to action is one where the design, content, and tone of the knowledge we produce as urbanists go beyond infusing anti-racist and decolonial engagement in our thinking: a framework that also involves deepening these engagements in the context of a pandemic that has aggravated existing forms of state violence and urban exclusion.

Adopting a rigorous and malleable theoretical framework to give shape to our research also delimits the types of interventions and practices we are able to engage as a result. Like other thinkers and community organizers in the early months of the pandemic, I immediately thought of the Palestinian experience as a useful political lens through which we can understand the activation of existing settler-colonial structures during the pandemic. Indeed, examining the ways in which the pandemic has further activated settler-colonial exclusions in Palestine is a helpful framework through which we can understand the mobilization of similar repressive practices and structures elsewhere.

However, while the erasure of space in the Palestinian context is relevant beyond its hyper-militarized borders, the unique ways in which colonial practices play out in the context of Israeli sovereign power compared to practices in, say, Canadian, Australian, or American settler-colonial societies must also be emphasized. And so, as much as it points to how these shared colonial practices are used by states in their health strategies against the pandemic, it also exposes the important dividing lines across movements that set these struggles and lived experiences apart.

Taken together, adopting a decolonial theoretical framework and deepening our engagements in urban research requires us to be aware of the dangers of overemphasizing similarities and differences in collective experiences of exclusion and violence. Despite the temptation to draw lines of continuity during a global health crisis—linking everyday experiences of the urban and anti-oppression movements across geographies—such a conceptual and practical approach can narrow our understanding of the tactics mobilized by resisting communities to claim their right to the city.

The ongoing pandemic—along with the economic and state-sanctioned violence to which it has given rise—has forced universities and societies to reckon with their endemic racism, anti-Blackness, and state-sanctioned violence against people of color. What this has meant for interventionist instructors and researchers in urban studies is a realization that our political and pedagogical practice needs updating. Our communities are more vulnerable, we are more isolated from our spaces of organizing and learning, and the changing nature and texture of state violence have aggravated the impact of the pandemic on our networks. While it is unclear how exactly the current global health crisis and the layered violence that has surfaced in this period will need to inform our thinking and practice, what has become apparent is that our interventionist urban research ought to be situated, engaged, and context-specific. These tenets, responsive to the political and social changes around us, serve as the ethos of our engagement with an urbanism that infuses theory with practice.

---

[1] Patrick Wolfe, "Settler Colonialism and the Elimination of the Native," *Journal of Genocide Research* 8 (December 2006): 388.

[2] "Quebec Couple's COVID-19 Escape to Old Crow, Yukon, Short-Lived, Says Chief," *National Post Online*, March 21, 2020, https://nationalpost.com/pmn/news-pmn/canada-news-pmn/quebec-couples-covid-19-escape-to-old-crow-yukon-short-lived-says-chief.

[3] Ibid.

[4] Sabrina Tremblay-Huet, "COVID-19 Leads to a New Context for the 'Right to Tourism': A Reset of Tourists' Perspectives on Space Appropriation Is Needed," *Tourism Geographies* 22, no. 3 (2020): 720–723.

[5] Kollibri terre Sonnenblume, "COVID-19 Denialism Is Rooted in the Settler Colonial Mindset," *Counter Punch Online*, July 10, 2020, https://www.counterpunch.org/2020/07/10/covid-19-denialism-is-rooted-in-the-settler-colonial-mindset/.

Rooted in the City
By Sophie Oldfield

Introduction

Working with community organizations, social movements, and ordinary residents challenges researchers to pay attention to diverse practices that shape housing access and its city politics. It roots research in the expertise ordinary residents and movements build in their daily struggles to find and secure homes. Collaborative research work is an approach to theory and research practice that, as Edgar Pieterse suggests, "demands immersion into profoundly fraught and contested spaces of power and control."[1] Through it, as Linda Peake argues, we can "disorient" and "reorient" research "by starting with the everyday struggles of urban dwellers."[2]

In immersing myself in community-based housing struggles, in settlements, in their engagements and struggles with the city, in entangling research in these fraught spaces and "wicked problems," in these varied practices, the project of theorizing becomes collaborative and collective. Doing so, as feminist geographer Richa Nagar proposes, processes of knowledge-making shift, turning "theoretical goals from a 'northern' [university] academic project to the struggles of those with whom we collaborate."[3] This is work that, Geraldine Pratt argues, is "open to other geographies and histories. It puts the world together differently, erasing some lines on our taken-for-granted maps and bringing other borders into view."[4] The foundation for an epistemological and political critique, this approach to research opens up the ways in which, and for whom, we build theory.

Experimenting with varied types of partners and forms of collaboration has been central to my own research journey and thinking. In this short piece, I share three Cape Town–based collaborative research projects, part of the City Research Studio, in which I teach students from the Master's in Critical Urbanisms at the University of Basel and the MPhil in Southern Urbanism at the University of Cape Town. Below I introduce the projects, their framing in the course, and in each neighborhood context. I explain the collaborative process, which provides students with an invaluable opportunity to engage everyday struggles and the roles ordinary people, organizations, and movements play in engaging and making policy relevant, I draw on this reflection to explore the ethos and practices, which root the research in concrete lived struggles to build homes and lives, in NGO interventions to support these initiatives, and in the city and the practices that constitute it.

Projects, Partners, Processes

Since 2017 I have worked in partnership with People's Environmental Planning (PEP), a Cape Town–based nongovernmental organization that draws on participatory approaches to support residents in housing projects stalled for technical and political reasons. PEP was established in 1998 to provide sociotechnical housing support to people-driven housing processes across South Africa. Subsequently, it has trained community building teams and assisted in the construction of thousands of People's Housing Process (PHP) homes across South Africa. Since 2010 PEP has supported the unblocking of stalled projects through the provision of titles and housing, and through the negotiation of complicated land use management regulations.

The projects have been planned to align with existing project trajectories and community priorities. The first project in 2018 in Ruo Emoh in Mitchells Plain, Cape Town, documented the experiences of residents who had recently moved into their formal new homes, secure for the first time. This housing scheme was the product of over twenty years of housing struggles and organizing, and the long-term collaborative work between PEP and its residents. The collaborative research focused on the meaning of finally moving into formal and permanent homes. The second project in 2019 in Hazeldean-Ekuphumleni in Philippi, Cape Town, engaged with residents' fight for city-supplied services and their ongoing struggle to access legal titles to their homes, twenty years after their building. The collaborative research tracked the practices of meanings of home building in this context, despite the lack of legal title. The third project, located in the Napier Informal Settlement, in the Overberg two hours outside of Cape Town, documented settlement residents' histories of migration and housing access, and access to essential water and sanitation services. The research aimed to inform the planned upgrading of the settlement.

With PEP and community-partners, I undertake initial preparatory work, discussing the project, meeting in the community partners, planning the details of the focus for the research work to ensure it aligns with ongoing neighborhood organizing. The research work unfolds over the university semester, setting a rhythm to each project. In each project, teams of students and community-based researchers work together, interviewing residents and conducting research on the ways in which families find, build, and secure homes, and encounter the state and its settlement policies. The collaborative work is built within this practice, where students join community partners to conduct the research. For research teams, projects prove an opportunity to figure out and develop interview questions, talk to families, record their stories, and engage nuances of each context. Working with residents to interview families in each project opens up ways in which families navigate insecurity, and the ongoing struggle to find shelter, build homes, improve them, and access title deeds, the legal markers of security.

In interviewing in the homes of residents, one student explained, "We learned about the lives of people living in this space; their struggles and quiet triumphs"[5]—a context described by another as spaces in which "stories were easily shared and there was an intimacy of conversation in these domestic worlds."[6] Guidance and engagement with partners was essential. As a student reflected: "Interviews represented a steep learning curve for many of us, and we were guided by the knowledge, intuition, and life experiences of our local partners."[7] Built carefully and respectfully, this approach made possible what was described by one participant as "knowledge exchange as opposed to one-way streaming of resources of story, knowledge, and experience": something that was, she articulated, "viscerally felt and seen, a mixing of students and community members, laughter and story."[8] Alongside interviewing, students worked in class to develop layers of initial reflection and analysis; one student reflected that this allowed herself and others "to recalibrate, reflect, and sense our way forward."[9]

Learning moments in the research came with layered opportunities to engage with the complex realities of neighborhood contexts, the intricacies of housing struggles. Some came with the confidence of conducting interviews, the inspiration found in the hardships and possibilities of families' lives. Others linked to writing, from narration of interviews to the thread of a story, a key to an argument, what a student explained cogently as "the tension of telling the struggles of others through collaborative research."[10] This carefully curated method and pedagogy built the collaborative research process.

Forms of Accounting and Debating

Ways to account for and debate our work together were central to the collaboration.

Two-thirds of the way through the process, for instance, students presented to our partners on campus an event and methodology to debate and share findings, at an early stage, what shapes analytical papers. Narratives from interviews were shared with residents to check and to approve the work, which was drawn together to produce the three powerfully nuanced and beautifully presented books that share the work across the collaboration and its partners. The first project book, *Ruo Emoh, Our Home, Our Story: From Housing Struggles to Hope in New Homes* (2018) tracked family housing struggles, their meanings, and hardships, which led to mobilizing for this neighborhood and its new homes. The second project book, *Building Homes Bit-by-Bit: The Stories of Hazeldean-Ekuphumleni* (2019), shared the ways in which families saved for and self-built homes, what these struggles and investments meant, and how they continue, shaped by a lack of legal titles and shifting (in)securities. The third book, *Present and Visible: The Napier Settlement and its Stories* (2020), documented settlement family stories of homemaking and their struggles to belong, self-build, garden, navigate challenges such as insufficient access to toilets and a lack of waste infrastructure, and the ways families secured livelihoods in small businesses and farm work.

As publications, the books were a crucial element of the collaboration. My partner in Ruo Emoh, Melanie Manuel, explained two years after the book's publication: "I keep the book very dear to my heart. Because it tells a story of my own life, of where I come from, what I have done in my life as a mother and as a community leader. It shows that I could be part of change, that change is possible." The books were important because they accurately and intimately shared the preciseness of struggles, as described by Melanie: "We had to fight for our homes.

Building Houses Bit-by-Bit: Stories of Hazeldean-Ekupumleni, 2019 © Sophie Oldfield and Alma Viviers (eds.), African Centre for Cities, Cape Town

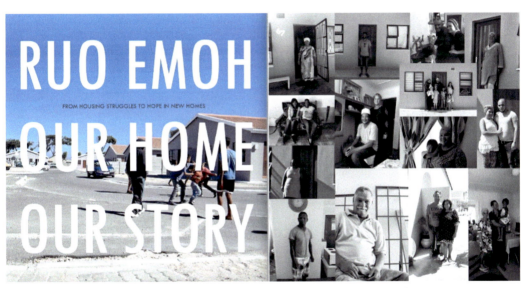

Ruo Emoh, Our Home, Our Story, 2018 © Sophie Oldfield (ed.), African Centre for Cities, Cape Town

Present and Visible: Napier Settlement and Its Stories, 2020 © Sophie Oldfield, Geetika Anand, and Alma Viviers (eds.), African Centre for Cities, Cape Town

It's not a house, it became a home for us. It's our future. This is where we can build. We can teach our children different things. That's what the book does for me, it tells this story. My children reading it can really be proud, know this story, be proud of what their mother has achieved and what the community has achieved over the years."[11] Her feelings resonated with Charlotte Adams, my partner in Hazeldean Ekupumleni. A year after the completion of our project and the publishing of the book, she explained: "We have something that we can show generations to come, and our children, our grandchildren, and their children's children. [...] It shows them it wasn't easy for us to just occupy this land or to buy land. [...] The book helps us remember. The story that the book tells is that you might be poor, but you are not helpless. You are able to do things for yourself. You can achieve working with a community and pulling through as one voice. The book actually meant a lot and it still means a lot to us."[12] When asked about *Present and Visible* and what its most important messages are Lindile Mhlaba, a community leader and participant researcher, commented: "The book is very important because it carries the good and the bad stories about *iKasi* [settlement] life, the poor conditions we are living under, how we are helping each other and how we help ourselves. The book is important because now we understand what each individual is going through. It is really telling the truth."[13]

In each project, books were distributed to partners and to everybody interviewed, as well as to local institutions and interested individuals. The book form, its stories, its rootedness in practice make it resonant. In an interview Melanie Manuels, for instance, recounted her surprise when she received the book: "Nobody really comes back to you and says here's your story, here's your information, here's your data. But the students came back with a hard bang, they actually threw me off my feet when they came back with that book." She elaborated further on why the book's form and its content really matter: "[I]t is not just taking your story, it is taking it, changing it, and bringing it back to us in a manner in which we understood it. Sometimes you get people that give you back data or information or a book or something in their own language that we don't understand. But this book is user-friendly, we can understand, we can share it with people, we can show them the book. They can read it and understand it immediately. It's not full of big high words or words that we don't understand, or words that we can't pronounce. We can actually read our own book."[14] Readable, visually rich, the books are resonant for neighborhood partners, who shared practices critical to accessing homes, to the hard struggles that shape their lives, to meaningful ways of building community and organizing.

Why Collaborative Research Matters

The collaborative research work resonated across our partnerships, built on relationships and trust, a commitment to make things work and to communicate throughout the process. We cultivated a research practice and ethos: ways to engage and produce knowledge, embedded in expertise across the city. This approach translated into research that was grounded, rigorous, and relevant.

For PEP, the process, engagement, and feedback delivered new insights and affirmations of their work. It offered, as Noah Schermbrucker reflected, "a template for conducting fair and reciprocal research with academic institutions. Research that is not merely the 'extraction' of academic knowledge but a more equal and fair process with transfer in both directions."[16] Beyond documenting struggles to which they have dedicated their work, Dolly Mdzanga from PEP suggested that the research has provided a more detailed understanding of community dynamics, which PEP drew on to deepen relationships and understanding with neighborhood leadership.[17]

For community leaders who participated there are many benefits. Lele Kakana in Napier explained in relation to our 2020 work that "as a leader, the book helps me understand better the struggles that people are facing in their day-to-day lives. It gives me a fuller understanding, which will help me have much stronger relationships with people so I can help as much as I can. I also hope we can use the research to make sure that leaders do not try and divide us as they did. They must treat us equally as residents, despite the party politics we have [in the settlement and area]." All three books are a record, as Melanie Manuels explained: "We share the book with people that come to the community. We share the book with other families. This is our story; this is our history. And nobody can take that away from us because now it is in black-and-white; people really understand. They can read. They can see it and read it."

For university partners, collaborative research approaches have allowed me to reimagine research as a process of experimenting, of building conversations and relationships in the ordinary work of everyday city-building and living. At the heart of this work were relationships built on respect and trust, nurtured with care, in city struggle. In this work, I built a practice, an ethos to produce theory embedded in publics and complex practices which shape the city.

[1] Edgar Pieterse, "Epistemological Practices of Southern Urbanism," African Centre for Cities Seminar series, University of Cape Town (2014): 23.
[2] Linda Peake, "The Twenty-First Century Quest for Feminism and the Global Urban," *International Journal of Urban and Regional Research* 40, no. 1 (2016): 219–227.
[3] Richa Nagar, "Footloose Researchers, 'Traveling' Theories, and the Politics of Transnational Feminist Praxis," *Gender, Place and Culture: A Journal of Feminist Geography* 9, no. 2 (2002): 179–186.
[4] Geraldine Pratt, *Families Apart: Migrant Mothers and the Conflicts of Labor and Love* (Minneapolis: University of Minnesota Press, 2012).
[5] Jinty Jackson, 2020 student participant, project evaluation, October 2020.
[6] Deirdre Prins-Solani, 2019 student participant, project evaluation, October 2020.
[7] Jackson (see note 5).
[8] Prins-Solani (see note 6).
[9] Jackson (see note 5).
[10] Romeo Dipura, 2020 student participant, project evaluation, October 2020.
[11] Melanie Manuels, personal interview, October 28, 2020.
[12] Charlotte Adams, personal interview, October 27, 2020.
[13] Lindile Mhlaba, personal interview, October 30, 2020.
[14] Manuels (see note 11).
[15] Ibid.
[16] Noah Schermbrucker, PEP partner, project evaluation, October 2020.
[17] Dolly Mdzanga, personal interview, July 20, 2019.
[18] Manuels (see note 11).

An Ethos of Critical Urbanism

Conclusion

"Critical Urbanisms" is a program situated at extremes,
connecting a Swiss university with a long humanities tradition in the quaint and wealthy city of Basel to one of the leading research centers of African urbanism, located in Cape Town, one of the most unequal cities in the world. It is a program of critical urban studies from which alternative modes of learning, practices of knowledge translation, and an ethos of engagement have emerged. It is an experiment in simultaneously inhabiting the academy and the city across continents, working with rigor and joy in and between both theory and practice to address a world undergoing constant and often radical changes.

Critical urbanism challenges cultures of expertise and decompartmentalizes urban knowledge.
Extending from the university as a dominant site of knowledge production, we embrace the different, unexpected, everyday, minor, major, forgotten, banal, and neglected ways of knowing and experiencing the city. If urban life contradicts the separation, compartmentalization, and specialization of knowledge produced in and around the university, we aim to take these contradictions as a starting point to develop new ways of thinking. If the city prompts us to question dominant cultures of expertise, critical urbanism opens up disciplinary containers to rewire urban studies with reflexivity and precision.

Critical urbanism is built on reciprocal and relational learning through an ethos of engagement.
Placing oneself into the picture is not an act of solipsism; it is a way to move out of the center to make space for others. Critical urbanism means building horizontal relationships with urban actors and thinkers in a way that leaves space for incommensurability and disagreement. Beyond tired oppositions between objective fact and subjective understanding, between pure knowledge and mere technical application, we start from an engagement with partial perspectives to develop new insights and practices.

Critical urbanism fosters new narratives and publics through creative experiments.

Disentangling urbanism from the purview of planning and policy opens up a range of positions between the university, the urban professions, and the multiple publics that make up the city. Critical urbanism means experimenting with urban publics to build new political spaces of expression and transformation. It means communicating with the senses in space, marshaling the aesthetics to build collective transformation. Critical urbanism is creative as it moves in the tension between the urgency to intervene and the merit of reflection, between the impetus to resolve and the privilege to problematize.

Critical urbanism is propelled by the search for justice, the power of critique, and an openness to the unexpected.

Our cities and other earthly environments are radically transforming in a world of increasing inequality and deepening crisis. At the same time, struggles for justice are reconfiguring with renewed intensity. Critical urbanism aims to contribute to ongoing movements by holding a terrain of inquiry and intervention. Neither bothered with the myths of free thought nor circumscribed by instrumental rationality, we aim to address urgent questions without having preconceived answers.

Critical urbanism reimagines the past to build an alternative future.

Because the past is never settled, it can be reread to make a difference in how we experience the present. And since our experience of the present shapes how we orient ourselves to the future, any future is always shaped by the past. Starting from the openness of the past rather than master-planning the future, we mobilize history as a verb. Against forgetting and erasing, critical urbanism nurtures past struggles to imagine alternative futures.

Reflecting on our journey of translation, collaboration, and experimentation, this volume has articulated rigorous and creative ways to pursue critical urbanism. Rooted in cities across the North and South, confronted with challenges and blessed with creative opportunities, we celebrate the work of our students in particular—a next generation of urbanists, practitioners, and thinkers whose ethos of openness, intellectual generosity, and engaged agility we are confident will carry our cities forward. We hope you found inspiration in tracing these pathways across different geographies, in this eclectic mix of the narrative and the visual, and in our pedagogical journey and in the research it has inspired.

Acknowledgements

This book is the outcome of a fortunate and felicitous collaboration between friends, colleagues, and interlocutors. The idea of establishing the field of Urban Studies at the University of Basel first emerged in conversations between the then rector Antonio Loprieno and the architects Jacques Herzog and Pierre de Meuron. We thank them for their vision and their courage to go beyond the existing scope of disciplines of the university. Their initiative laid the foundation for establishing our Urban Studies program, which was, from the very beginning, conceived as a collaboration with the African Centre for Cities at the University of Cape Town. We are also immensely grateful for the generous support of the Lucius and Annemarie Burkhardt Foundation. Their loyal backing allowed for a diversity of voices to flourish within our program.

Within both universities we are very much indebted to wonderful conversations with and critical feedback from Ralph Ubl, Till Förster, Julia Tischler, Bilgin Ayata, Elisio Macamo, Max Bergmann, Edgar Pieterse, Vanessa Watson, Susan Parnell and Tanja Winkler in shaping our curriculum, highlighting potential subjects and topics, and influencing our methods of teaching and research. Their input has proven to be invaluable. We could not have completed this book without our colleagues over these years, including Anna Selmeczi, Geetika Anand, Ademola Omoegun, Alicia Fortuin, Rosca van Rooyen, Abdullahi Ali Hassan, Alma Viviers, Marie-Laure Allain Bonilla, Ginger Nolan, Solange Mbanefo, Maren Larsen, and Shourideh Molavi, all of whom have tirelessly contributed to a learning environment that excites and motivates us every day. We are fortunate to have you as our colleagues. We are also very grateful to visiting faculty members, academic staff, and personal friends who were incredibly generous in offering critique and, with their seminars and lectures, providing inspiring new thoughts and ways of thinking about cities and landscapes: Prita Meyer, Bradley Rink, Mercy Brown-Luthango, Alan Mabin, Ananya Roy, Faranak Miraftab, Mona Fawaz, Charles Heller, Aylin Tschoepe, Jana Häberlein, Xenia Vytuleva, Remo Reginold, Bárbara Maçães Costa, Jana Magdalena Keuchel, and Katharina Knust.

Much of the research presented in this book relates to investigations in and beyond our two bases of Basel and Cape Town. We are hence much indebted to the many people who guided us, enabling us to discover places through their eyes and expertise. These encounters opened up new universes of knowledge and urban life to us in Brazil, the Democratic Republic of Congo, Ethiopia, Ghana, Kenya, Mexico, Mozambique, Palestine, the Western Sahara, and Zambia. In Ghana, we would particularly like to thank former Mayor of the City of Accra Nat Nunoo-Amarteifio, Chair of the ArchiAfrika Foundation Joe Osae-Addo, Director of the ArchiAfrika Foundation Berend van der Lans, Dele Adenyemo, Irene A. Addo, KNUST Chair of Planning Department Michael Poku Boansi, and Sam Amoah for their magnanimous exchange of ideas in Accra. In Cape Town, we would particularly like to thank the ACC-based Southern Urbanism MPhil students who engaged Critical Urbanisms students as colleagues, co-conspirators, partners, and friends. We also thank Adnaan Hendricks and Melanie Johnson in Ruo Emoh, Charlotte Adams in Hazeldean-Ekupumleni, Lele Kakana and Professor aka Lindile Mhlaba in Napier, and Noah Schermbrucker, Dolly Mdzanga, and Shawn Cuff at People's Environmental Planning for the commitment and inspiration at the heart of the City Research Studio; to Lucy Campbell, Brent Thomas, Nadjwa Damon, Keanon Pohlman aka Urban Khoi Soldier, Stacy-Anne Michaels, Luzann Isaacs and their team at the Edith Stephens Nature Reserve, Joy Warries and the WOWMovement, Brenda Skelenge, Ncumisa Mkabile, Mercia Malan at Solms Delta, and the Somali Association of South Africa for sharing their lived experiences and expert guidance during our Contemporary South African debates course. For the innovation and creativity to sense and run the city, we thank Barry Christianson, Fatima Van de Rheede, Zarina Brewer-Meyer, Caroline Peters, and the Itheko, Nantes, and Central Athletic Clubs. Lastly, for providing a nourishing and nurturing environment for our annual research design workshops, we would also like to thank Johan and Diana Simons and their dedicated team at Fynbos Estate in Malmesbury.

We are immensely grateful for the critical intelligence of the doctoral and master students in our research studios, seminars, lecture courses, fieldwork trips and collaborative research projects, many of whom have contributed to this volume: Adesola Adelowo, James Clacherty, Janine Eberle, Evan Escamilla, Florence Siegenthaler, Sebastian Steiner, Basil Studer, Oliva Andereggen, Anna Buser, Swann Cherpillod, Leandra Choffat, Alexander Crawford, Carla Cruz, Shahin Haghinavand, Vishruti Shastri, Aline Suter, Diana Vazquez, Linda Wermuth, Lee Wolf, Rachel Malana Rogers Bursen, Naomi Samake, Alessandro Rearte, Linus Suter, Isabella Baranyk, Elena Antoni, Ana Lea Morgan, Hanna Baumann, Giulia Scotto, Ernest Sewordor, Saad Amira, Thomas Betschart, Jacob Geuder, Alaa Dia, and Lea Nienhoff. They have been wonderful companions on this trajectory and have challenged us at every step with their insights, their questions, and their creativity.

All the work would have been impossible without the fantastic administrative and organizational support from Michelle Killenberger, Gernot Biersack, Shandré Petersen, Khaya Salman, Shakira Jeppie, Marlene Joubert, Maryam Waglay, Ithra Najaar and Shirley-Ann Jennifer Felsenberg. With their diligence and precision, combined with sincerity and personal warmth, they proved to be anchors of our team, even in times of turmoil and insecurity.

We are particularly indebted to Thomas Kramer, chief editor of Park Books, for his immediate excitement when we proposed the book to him and his constant support, to Chris Reding from Park Books for the realization of this book, to Camille Sauthier for his graphic design work, to Maayan Sharon for her scrupulous copyediting work, to Sarah Quigley for her tactful copyediting and revision of the manuscript, and to Keonaona Peterson for her thorough proofreading.

Finally, one person who was a key figure in the founding of our program and in shaping its spirit, its concepts, and its ethics was Dominique Malaquais. She taught with us as a visiting lecturer, inspiring our students and our faculty alike to think about African arts and urban cultures as sites of decolonial struggle and transformation. A free spirit, she disliked labels and narrowness of any kind, and was always thinking outside the box. She cherished collaborative work above all, which is reflected in everything she did with us. She tirelessly and passionately wrote, taught, curated, published, collaborated, and promoted outstanding artists. Her critical mind mixed with an intelligent sense of humor, her boundless generosity, her elegant gentleness and her true kindness will be greatly missed. This book could never have existed without her.

Editors' Biographies

Kenny Cupers is Professor of Architectural History and Urban Studies at the University of Basel. His research focuses on the role of housing in urban and state transformation, the epistemology and geopolitics of modernism, and the power and aesthetics of infrastructure. His publications include *The Social Project: Housing Postwar France, Use Matters: An Alternative History of Architecture, Spaces of Uncertainty: Berlin Revisited, and Neoliberalism on the Ground: Architecture and Transformation from the 1960s to the Present.*

Sophie Oldfield held the Professorship of Urban Studies at the University of Cape Town and the University of Basel until 2021. She is internationally recognized as an urban and human geographer for research on cities in the Global South through her theoretical and primary research. She has a track record of excellence in collaborative research practice, challenging how academics work in and between university and community. Commitment to this collaborative approach lies at the heart of her research and writing on cities of the global south. She is presently Chair of and Professor in the Department of City and Regional Planning at Cornell University.

Manuel Herz was Assistant Professor of Architectural, Urban, and Territorial Design at the University of Basel. He is an architect whose research focuses on the relationship between the discipline of planning and (state) power. He has worked extensively on the architecture and urbanism of refugee camps, with a regional focus on Saharan and sub-Saharan Africa. His books include *From Camp to City—Refugee Camps of the Western Sahara* (Lars Müller Publishers, 2013) and the award-winning book *African Modernism—Architecture of Independence* (Park Books, 2015).

Laura Nkula-Wenz is a lecturer and coordinator for the MA in Critical Urbanisms. Based at the African Centre for Cities and in Urban Studies at the University of Basel, Laura is an urban geographer with a keen interest in postcolonial urban theory, African urbanism, and public culture. Her research focuses on the transformation of urban governance and the construction of local political agency, on questions of urban experimentation and knowledge networks, as well as the nexus of cultural production and urban change.

Emilio Distretti is a researcher and an educator. He studied Philosophy at the University of Bologna (Italy) and holds a PhD in Aesthetics and the Politics of Representation from the School of Art and Design at Portsmouth University (UK). Emilio's research takes on interrelated avenues on the politics of space, architectural heritage, Italian Fascist colonialism, postcolonial and decolonial politics in the Mediterranean (Italy, North Africa and the Levant) and in the Horn of Africa.

Myriam Perret is an architect and urbanist currently working for the NGO Swiss Heritage Society.
She has held research positions in Urban Studies at the University of Basel, at the Future Cities Laboratory Singapore (FCL), the Swiss Federal Institute of Technology in Zurich (ETH) and Swiss Federal Institute of Technology in Lausanne (EPFL). She has taught architecture, urban planning and urban studies and co-edited *City as Resource* and the forthcoming *African Modernism 2*.

Imprint

Editors: Kenny Cupers, Sophie Oldfield, Manuel Herz, Laura Nkula-Wenz, Emilio Distretti, and Myriam Perret
Design concept: Myriam Perret and Camille Sauthier
Project coordination publishing house: Chris Reding
Copyediting: Maayan Sharon and Sarah Quigley
Proofreading: Keonaona Peterson
Design: Camille Sauthier, Lausanne
Lithography, printing, and binding: DZA Druckerei zu Altenburg, Thuringia

Fonts in use: Suisse BP Int'l and Swiss BP Serif by www.swisstypefaces.com
Paper: ProfiBulk 1.1 Vol., 135 g/m^2

© 2022 the editors and Park Books AG, Zurich

© for the texts: the authors
© for the images: the artists / see image captions

Park Books
Niederdorfstrasse 54
8001 Zurich
Switzerland
www.park-books.com

Park Books is being supported by the Federal Office of Culture with a general subsidy for the years 2021–2024.

All rights reserved; no part of this publication may be reproduced, stored in a retrieval system or transmitted in any form or by any means, electronic, mechanical, photocopying, recording, or otherwise, without the prior written consent of the publisher.

ISBN 978-3-03860-282-8